365 Favorite Pasta Salad Recipes

(365 Favorite Pasta Salad Recipes - Volume 1)

Lisa Ford

Content

365 Awesome Pasta Salad Recipes

***

1. 3 Cheese Pasta Salad Recipe

Serving: 4 | Prep: | Cook: | Ready in:

Ingredients

- 1 pkg. cheese tortellini (255g)
- 1/4 c grated parmesin cheese
- 2 green onions (sliced finely)
- 1 celery stalk (chopped)
- 1 c cubed cheddar cheese
- 1 c broccoli florets (blanched)
- 1/3c ceasar dressing
- 1 tbsp milk
- 1c red peppers (chopped)

Direction

- Cook pasta and drain
- Combine in a large bowl) all ingredients together (except Caesar dressing and milk)
- Combine in a separate bowl dressing and milk
- Pour over pasta mixture and mix well.
- Chill

2. 30 MINUTE SHRIMP AND PASTA SALAD WITH FENNEL AND FETA Recipe

Serving: 6 | Prep: | Cook: 12mins | Ready in:

Ingredients

- We like to use medium-sized shrimp in this dish; however, extra-large shrimp (21/25) can be substituted.
- INGREDIENTS
- 6 tablespoons extra-virgin olive oil
- 1/2 cup feta cheese , finely crumbled
- 1/4 cup red wine vinegar
- 1 shallot , minced
- 1 garlic clove , minced
- 1 1/2 teaspoons minced fresh oregano
- salt and ground black pepper
- 1 pound farfalle pasta
- 1 fennel bulb , trimmed, cored, and sliced thin
- 1 1/2 pounds medium pre-cooked shrimp (31/40), peeled
- 1 1/2 ounces baby arugula (2 cups)
- 1/2 cup pitted kalamata olives , sliced

Direction

- 1. BOIL WATER FOR PASTA: Bring 4 quarts water to boil in large pot.
- 2. MAKE DRESSING: Meanwhile, whisk olive oil, feta, vinegar, shallot, garlic, oregano, 1/2 teaspoon salt, and 1/2 teaspoon pepper together in bowl large enough to hold entire pasta salad.
- 3. COOK FARFALLE: Add farfalle and 1 tablespoon salt to boiling water, and cook, stirring often, until tender. Drain, shaking off excess water.
- 4. MARINATE PASTA: Add hot, drained farfalle, fennel, and shrimp to bowl with dressing and toss. Cover and refrigerate until cooled, about 15 minutes.
- 5. FINISH: Just before serving, stir in arugula and olives and season with salt and pepper to taste.

3. Aarons Vegetable Pasta Salad Recipe

Serving: 10 | Prep: | Cook: 10mins | Ready in:

Ingredients

- 3 small tomatoes diced
- 2 small cucumbers peeled and diced
- 1 med. onion diced
- 1 package ranch dressing mix
- 1 1/2 cup mayo
- 1/2 cup milk
- 3 cups rotini or elbow pasta cooked and drained

Direction

- Mix Ranch dressing, mayo, and milk together.
- Add first three ingredients.
- Mix well.
- Add cooked and drained pasta. Fold in.
- Chill overnight.

4. Alaska Salmon And Avocado Pasta Salad Recipe

Serving: 4 | Prep: | Cook: 10mins | Ready in:

Ingredients

- 6 ounces dry bow tie pasta
- 14-3/4 ounce Alaskan salmon
- 2 tablespoons French dressing
- 1 red bell pepper thinly sliced
- 3 tablespoons cilantro chopped
- 1 lime juiced and rind grated
- 1 tablespoon tomato paste
- 1/2 cup sour cream
- 1/8 teaspoon paprika
- 1 bunch green onions thinly sliced
- 2 tablespoons mayonnaise
- 3 ripe avocados diced
- lettuce leaves

Direction

- Cook pasta according to package directions then drain and toss with dressing then allow to cool.
- Drain and flake the salmon then add to pasta with onions, bell pepper and cilantro.
- Whisk together lime juice, rind, mayonnaise, sour cream and tomato paste until combined.
- Toss pasta salad with dressing then season with salt and pepper then cover and chill.
- Before serving gently toss avocados into the salad and spoon onto a bed of lettuce leaves.
- Sprinkle with paprika for garnish then serve immediately.

5. Alaskan Salmon And Avocado Pasta Salad Recipe

Serving: 4 | Prep: | Cook: 20mins | Ready in:

Ingredients

- 6 ounces dry pasta
- 14-3/4 ounce Alaskan salmon
- 2 tablespoons French dressing
- 1 red bell pepper thinly sliced
- 3 tablespoons cilantro chopped
- 1 lime juice and rind grated
- 1 tablespoon tomato paste
- 1/2 cup sour cream
- 1/2 teaspoon paprika
- 1 bunch green onion thinly sliced
- 2 tablespoons mayonnaise
- 3 ripe avocados diced

Direction

- Lettuce leaves to serve on
- Cook pasta according to package directions then drain well and toss with French dressing.
- Allow to cool then drain and flake salmon.
- Add to pasta with green onions, sliced bell pepper and cilantro.

- Whisk together lime juice and grated rind, mayonnaise, sour cream and tomato paste.
- Mix until thoroughly combined then toss pasta with dressing and season with salt and pepper.
- Cover and chill then right before serving gently toss avocados into salad.
- Spoon salad onto a bed of lettuce leaves then sprinkle with paprika for garnish.

6. Albacore Pasta Salad Recipe

Serving: 4 | Prep: | Cook: 15mins |Ready in:

Ingredients

- 4 cups cooked spiral pasta
- 1 cup Italian salad dressing
- 1 cup tomatoes diced
- 1 cup cucumbers diced
- 1 cup black olives diced
- 1 cup red bell pepper diced
- 1 cup carrots shredded
- 2 cups lettuce
- 1 can albacore tuna

Direction

- Cook pasta according to directions.
- Drain and mix with salad dressing.
- Refrigerate for 1 hour.
- Tear lettuce into bite size pieces and refrigerate.
- Mix vegetables with pasta then gently stir in tuna and arrange lettuce in bowl.
- Place pasta mixture on lettuce and serve.

7. Alfredos Pasta Salad Recipe

Serving: 20 | Prep: | Cook: 10mins |Ready in:

Ingredients

- 1 lb. box of pasta (I like the tri-color fusilli or spirals, but mom always made it with small shells or choo-choo wheels)
- This is also awesome with spinach pasta, or better yet, tortellini!
- 1 bell pepper (medium)
- 1 onion (medium)
- 2 radishes
- 15 oz can of baby peas
- 2 carrots
- 2 stalks of celery
- 1/2 c. milk
- 1/2 c. honey dijon salad dressing
- 1 c. Miracle Whip

Direction

- Prepare pasta according to box (al dente), then chill pasta
- Dice celery, onion and pepper
- Thin-slice carrots and radishes (almost paper thin!)
- Combine pasta, honey Dijon salad dressing, diced/sliced veggies and can of peas.
- Mix well
- Combine milk and Miracle Whip.
- Add to mixture and fold in.
- For best results, cover tightly with cellophane wrap and chill in GLASS bowl(s) [this recipe makes a lot!] for 4 hours. It's even better overnight!
- Optional add-ins: 1/2 c. walnuts; or pepperoni (quarter cut each slice).

8. Amped Up Pasta Salad Recipe

Serving: 8 | Prep: | Cook: 15mins |Ready in:

Ingredients

- 1 box Betty Crocker Suddenly pasta Salad- bacon Ranch
- 1/2 cup Miracle Whip light
- 2 cups chopped fresh spinach (may substitute lettuce)

- 1 large tomato- diced
- 1/4 cup diced cilantro
- 3/4 cup diced mushrooms (fresh- not canned)
- 1 8oz package diced, cooked ham
- 1 4 oz can diced black olives, drained
- salt/pepper to taste

Direction

- Prepare boxed pasta salad according to directions on the box
- Meanwhile chop spinach, tomatoes, cilantro, and mushrooms
- Drain pasta
- In a large bowl mix pasta with Miracle Whip according to box directions and stir in remaining ingredients
- Chill in refrigerator for at least 2 hours
- Eat up!!!

9. Antipasta Salad Recipe

Serving: 0 | Prep: | Cook: 90mins | Ready in:

Ingredients

- 1lb rotini or similar pasta, dry
- 2-3 bell peppers, diced(should equal about 1 cup)
- 1 medium onion, diced(about 3/4-1cup)
- 1/2 cup sliced mixed Greek or Italian olives
- 4-5 peppadews, diced(or sub about 1/3 cup chopped sun dried tomatoes, if desired)
- 1/2 cup fresh basil leaves, chopped
- 4oz goat cheese, crumbled
- For red wine Vinaigrette
- 1/4 cup red wine vinegar(with garlic, if possible)
- juice from about 1/2 lemon
- 1 cup salad quality olive oil
- 1-2t honey
- 1T Dijon
- 1t dried oregano(or sub 2t fresh, minced, but add it to the salad, not the dressing)
- 1/4-1t red pepper flakes

- 1 clove garlic, crushed(omit if using garlic vinegar)
- kosher or sea salt and fresh ground pepper

Direction

- Cook pasta per package directions until JUST al dente. At about the halfway point of the pasta being done, add the onions and bell peppers to the pasta in the boiling water.
- Drain pasta and veggies when done.
- Add to large serving bowl and add olives, peppadews and basil and toss to combine.
- Add vinaigrette (you may not use it all, just use to taste) from below and goat cheese and fold or toss together. The cheese will melt into the dressing and create a great additional flavor to the salad.
- Refrigerate at least 1 hour and toss again prior to serving.
- For Red Wine Vinaigrette
- Combine all ingredients other than oil in medium bowl and slowly drizzle in oil, whisking constantly, until well combined and emulsified, OR do as above but use a blender, OR combine all ingredients in a glass jar with a tight fitting lid and shake the bejesus out of it for a couple of minutes :)

10. Antipasto Mushroom Pasta Salad Recipe

Serving: 8 | Prep: | Cook: | Ready in:

Ingredients

- 4 cups pasta cooked and cooled
- 2 cups white mushrooms sliced
- 1 cup roasted red peppers chopped
- 1 cup salami cut into bite size pieces
- 1 cup provolone cheese cut into bite size pieces
- 6 ounce jar marinated artichoke hearts with liquid
- 1/4 cup Italian dressing
- 1/4 teaspoon salt

- 1 teaspoon freshly ground black pepper
- 1/2 cup chopped fresh basil

Direction

- To the pasta add mushrooms, peppers, salami, cheese and artichoke hearts with liquid.
- Mix in Italian dressing then season with salt and pepper.
- Top with chopped basil.
- Allow flavors to blend for at least 30 minutes before serving.

11. Antipasto Not Pasta Picnic Salad Recipe

Serving: 12 | Prep: | Cook: | Ready in:

Ingredients

- 1lb mozzarella cheese,1/2 inch cubes
- 2(6oz) cans whole black olives
- 2 jars quartered marinated artichoke hearts(including liquid)
- 2 bell peppers(any color),cubed (I used yellow &orange)
- 1 (8oz) chub italian dry salami,cut into 1/2 inch cubes
- 1/4 cup sliced fresh basil
- *** you could also add green olives,or mushrooms
- **Most of the time I drain the artichokes and use a bottled Italian dressing

Direction

- Toss together all ingredients in a large bowl.
- Cover and refrigerate for several hours to let marinate, stirring occasionally

12. Antipasto Pasta Salad Recipe

Serving: 12 | Prep: | Cook: | Ready in:

Ingredients

- 1 pound pasta, seashell variety
- 1/4 pound pepperoni sausage, diced
- 1/4 pound genoa salami, diced
- 1/2 pound asiago cheese, finely chopped
- 1 (6 oz) can black olives, liquid removed and chopped
- 1 green bell pepper, chopped
- 1 red bell pepper, finely chopped
- 3 tomatoes, diced
- 3/4 cup extra virgin olive oil
- 1/4 cup balsamic vinegar
- 1 tbsp parmesan cheese, grated
- 1 (.7 oz) packet dry Italian-style salad dressing mix
- 2 tbsp dried oregano
- 1 tbsp dried parsley
- salt and ground black pepper, to taste

Direction

- In a large pot of salted water, boil the pasta until al dente. Drain, and run under cold water to cool.
- Mix together the cooled pasta, pepperoni sausage, salami, Asiago cheese, black olives, peppers and tomatoes. Add in the dressing mix then cover, and place in the refrigerator for at least 1 hour.
- To make the dressing, whisk together the olive oil, balsamic vinegar, Parmesan cheese, oregano, parsley, salt and pepper. Right before serving, add the dressing onto the salad, and mix thoroughly.

13. Apricot Macaroni Salad Recipe

Serving: 8 | Prep: | Cook: 10mins | Ready in:

Ingredients

- 8 ounce package macaroni
- 20 ounce can pineapple chunks drained
- 1/2 cup chopped red pepper

- 1/2 cup shredded cheddar cheese
- 2/3 cup mayonnaise
- 1/2 cup apricot preserves

Direction

- Cook macaroni according to package directions then drain and cool.
- Combine macaroni, pineapple, pepper and cheese in medium bowl.
- Mix mayonnaise and preserves then mix into salad.
- Refrigerate one hour before serving.

14. Artichoke And Olive Pasta Salad Recipe

Serving: 10 | Prep: | Cook: 10mins | Ready in:

Ingredients

- balsamic vinaigrette
- 2/3 cup olive oil
- ½ cup balsamic vinegar
- 4-5 cloves garlic
- 2 T. italian seasoning
- fresh ground pepper
- salt to taste
- place all the ingredients in a screw-top jar and shake to combine. Taste and adjust the seasonings.
- 1 lb tri-color rotini
- 10-12 canned or frozen artichoke hearts
- 2 C. frozen baby carrots
- ¾ C. green olives
- 1 can black olives
- 1 C. marinated mushrooms, halved or fresh sliced mushrooms
- 1 large red onion, cut in strips
- 1 pint cherry tomatoes, halved
- ½ C. parmesan cheese, grated

Direction

- Make dressing the night before and store in refrigerator. Cook pasta according to box instructions. Turn off heat and put frozen veggies in pan with pasta. Immediately pour in colander to drain. Place in a large bowl. Add olives, mushrooms, onions, and cherry tomatoes. Toss all ingredients in the bowl. Add the dressing to the salad and mix thoroughly. Taste and adjust salt and pepper. Lastly, toss in parmesan cheese and mix.

15. Asian Noodle Salad Recipe

Serving: 5 | Prep: | Cook: 40mins | Ready in:

Ingredients

- thx to foodtv and pioneer wwoman
- Asian Noodle Salad
- Recipe courtesy of Ree Drummond
- Total Time:
- 40 min
- Prep:
- 30 min
- Cook:
- 10 min
- Yield:
- 6 servings
- Level:
- Easy
- Ingredients
- Salad:
- 8 ounces thin spaghetti
- One 8-ounce bag julienne/fine-cut carrots (about 1 1/2 cups)
- One 6-ounce bag baby sweet peppers, seeded and sliced thinly into rings (about 1 cup)
- One 4-ounce bag bean sprouts (about 1 cup)
- 3 English cucumbers, peeled and sliced
- 3 scallions, sliced
- Up to 1 bunch fresh cilantro, chopped
- 1/2 head or more napa cabbage, sliced
- 1/2 head or more purple cabbage, sliced

- 1/2 bunch kale, leaves torn off the stalks and shredded
- 2 cups peanuts, chopped
- Dressing:
- 1/2 cup olive oil
- 1/3 cup low-sodium soy sauce
- 1/4 cup oyster sauce
- 1/4 cup rice wine vinegar
- 1/4 cup brown sugar
- 3 tablespoons chopped fresh ginger
- 2 tablespoons sesame oil
- 2 to 3 cloves garlic, chopped

Direction

- Directions
- For the salad: Bring a pot of water to a boil. Cook the spaghetti to al dente according to the package directions. Drain, rinse and let cool.
- Mix together the cooked spaghetti, carrots, peppers, bean sprouts, cucumbers, scallions, cilantro, napa cabbage, purple cabbage and kale. Add the peanuts and toss together.
- For the dressing: Whisk together the olive oil, soy sauce, oyster sauce, rice wine vinegar, brown sugar, ginger, sesame oil and garlic in a medium bowl.
- Pour the dressing over the salad and mix together with tongs or your hands. If the salad seems a little dry, just mix up a little more of the wet ingredients of the dressing and throw it in. It's a very organic process.
- Transfer to a large platter and serve.

16. Asian Pasta Salad With Fried Tempeh Bits Recipe

Serving: 68 | Prep: | Cook: 15mins | Ready in:

Ingredients

- peanut pasta Salad with Fried tempeh Bits
- 8 oz block of organic tempeh, crumbled
- 2 tablespoons sesame oil for frying
- 1 8 oz. package of pasta spirals

- 3 cups organic broccoli florets, cut into bite-size pieces
- 1 large organic carrot, julienne
- 1 organic red pepper, cut into thin strips
- peanut sauce
- 3 tablespoons creamy organic peanut butter
- Filtered water for large pot
- 1-2 tablespoons shoyu, to taste
- 1 Tablespoon each sesame oil, agave nectar, apple cider vinegar
- nnbsp;2 Tablespoons fresh ginger, minced

Direction

- 1. Heat skillet and oil, then fry tempeh until slightly crispy (about 10 minutes) stirring occasionally.
- 2. Bring water to a boil in large pot. Blanch the carrots and broccoli separately until they turn bright in color (about 30 seconds). Don't overcook. Drain and set aside.
- 3. Cooked pasta according to directions on the package in the blanching water, drain, rinse in cold water and set aside.
- 4. Wisk together all the sauce ingredients. Toss veggies, pasta, and sauce together

17. Aunt Bonnies Ring Macaroni Tuna Salad Recipe

Serving: 8 | Prep: | Cook: 15mins | Ready in:

Ingredients

- 1 (7 ounce) box ring macaroni, prepared as directed on box
- 1 (8 1/2 ounce) can Le Sueur early june peas, drained (or 1 cup Green Giant Select Le Sueur frozen baby peas, thawed)
- 1 cup celery, finely diced
- 2 (6 ounce) cans tuna, drained
- 1/4 cup onions, finely diced
- 1 cup Miracle Whip
- 1 teaspoon salt (or less, use to taste)

Direction

- Gently mix all ingredients together and refrigerate 2 to 3 hours.

18. Avocado Pasta Salad Recipe

Serving: 6 | Prep: | Cook: 20mins | Ready in:

Ingredients

- 1 lb bag dry pasta
- 1/2 cup crumbled feta cheese
- 1/2 pint cherry tomatoes cut in eighths
- 1 bunch green onions, ends removed, thinly sliced
- 1 to 2 ripe avocados, peeled and chopped
- Dressing:
- 2 to 3 Tbsp Country French vinaigrette (Penzy's)
- 2 to 3 Tbsp water
- 3 to 4 Tbsp balsamic or red wine vinegar
- 1 cup light mayonnaise
- 1/4 cup olive oil
- 1 Tbsp honey

Direction

- Boil the pasta according to the package directions. While it is cooking, clean and chop the vegetables and crumble the cheese. In a large serving bowl, mix the Country French Dressing Base with water, let stand a few minutes, then whisk in the rest of the dressing ingredients. Drain and rinse the pasta, toss with dressing, add onions, tomatoes, avocado and cheese, then toss again and serve.

19. Awesome Italian Pasta Salad Recipe

Serving: 12 | Prep: | Cook: 8mins | Ready in:

Ingredients

- 1 lb. cooked rotini pasta (mulit-colored or plain), drained and cooled
- 2 cups raw broccoli florets, chopped
- 2 large tomatoes, seeded and diced
- 6 oz. sliced pepperoni, chopped
- 1 14oz. can medium black olives, sliced or chopped
- 6 oz. block colby-jack cheese, cubed small
- 1 1/2 cups Italian dressing
- 1/4 cup finely grated parmesan cheese

Direction

- Add all ingredients except parmesan cheese to cooked pasta and mix well. If too dry add more dressing.
- Sprinkle parmesan cheese on top and refrigerate.
- The longer it chills, the better it tastes.
- For a lighter version, use low-cal / low-fat Italian dressing.

20. Awesome Shrimp Pasta Salad Recipe

Serving: 8 | Prep: | Cook: | Ready in:

Ingredients

- 1 pound spinach linguine, cooked
- 8 oz.Italian salad dressing
- 1 1/4 c. mayo
- 2 T parsley flakes
- 1/4 t. basil
- 2 T chives
- 1/4 t. oregano
- 2 T red wine vinegar
- 1 T. garlic salt
- 1 c. shredded parmesan
- 1 can tiny shirmp
- 1 can black olives, sliced

Direction

- Make dressing: Combine Italian salad dressing, mayo, parsley flakes, basil, chives, oregano, red wine vinegar and garlic salt.
- Toss pasta with parmesan, shrimp, and black olives.
- Add dressing.
- Toss to coat.
- Chill 4 hours or overnight.

21. BBQ Macaroni Salad Recipe

Serving: 10 | Prep: | Cook: 12mins | Ready in:

Ingredients

- Most recipes for barbecue-flavored macaroni salad drown the pasta in ketchupy barbecue sauce, creating a salad that is much too sweet and sticky. Here's what we discovered about how to produce a well-balanced smoky and spicy side dish.
- Test Kitchen Discoveries
- A combination of mayonnaise and barbecue sauce is more effective than barbecue sauce alone, as the tang of the barbecue sauce is balanced by the neutral creaminess of the mayonnaise.
- This salad works best with a sweet, smoky-flavored barbecue sauce.
- If the salad sits and becomes dry, adding a little warm water will make it creamy again.
- table salt
- 1 pound elbow macaroni
- 1 red bell pepper , seeded and chopped fine
- 1 rib celery , chopped fine
- 4 scallions , sliced thin
- 2 tablespoons cider vinegar
- 1 teaspoon hot sauce
- 1 teaspoon chili powder
- 1/8 teaspoon garlic powder
- Pinch cayenne pepper
- 1 cup mayonnaise
- 1/2 cup barbecue sauce (see note above)
- ground black pepper

Direction

- 1. Bring 4 quarts water to boil in large pot. Add 1 tablespoon salt and macaroni and cook until nearly tender, about 5 minutes. Drain in colander and rinse with cold water until cool, then drain once more, briefly, so that pasta is still moist; transfer to large bowl.
- 2. Stir in bell pepper, celery, scallions, vinegar, hot sauce, chili powder, garlic powder, and cayenne pepper, and let sit until flavors are absorbed, about 2 minutes. Stir in mayonnaise and barbecue sauce and let sit until salad is no longer watery, about 5 minutes. Season with salt and pepper and serve. (The salad can be covered and refrigerated for up to 2 days. Check seasonings before serving.)

22. BLT MACARONI SALAD Recipe

Serving: 6 | Prep: | Cook: | Ready in:

Ingredients

- 1 box elbow macaroni (8oz)
- 2/3 cup mayonaise
- 1/3 cup plain yogurt
- 1 tbsp vinegar
- 1/4 tsp each salt & pepper
- 8 slices bacon; cooked & crumbled
- 3 green onions finely chopped
- 1 large tomato chopped
- Chopped romaine lettuce (bitesize pieces)

Direction

- Cook pasta according to package directions.
- Drain and rinse.
- Set aside.
- Meanwhile in a large bowl, combine mayo, yogurt, vinegar, salt and pepper.
- Add pasta and remaining ingredients to mayo mixture.
- Cover and refrigerate until ready to serve.

- Up to 24 hours. (After the 24 hour mark the lettuce sogs)

23. BLT Pasta Salad Recipe

Serving: 8 | Prep: | Cook: 10mins | Ready in:

Ingredients

- 1- 8 oz box of penne pasta (you can use any pasta you have in cupboard)
- 1 cup of mayo
- 1/2 cup sour cream
- 1 cup crumbled cooked bacon
- 1/2 bunch green onion
- 1-2 fresh diced tomatoes
- 1 cup of fresh spinach
- salt & pepper to taste
- 1 tsp granulated garlic

Direction

- Boil pasta according to directions on box. Drain and chill.
- To chilled pasta combine remaining ingredients and mix thoroughly chill and serve. (You may need to add more mayo and sour cream before serving).

24. Bacon And Corn Pasta Salad With Mustard Dressing Recipe

Serving: 10 | Prep: | Cook: 20mins | Ready in:

Ingredients

- 500g large pasta crests
- 1 tbs olive oil
- 250g button mushrooms, halved
- 4 rashers rindless bacon (250g), chopped coarsely
- 230g baby corn
- 1 medium red onion (170h), chopped coarsely

- 1 large avocado (320g), chopped coarsely
- 1 cup fresh flat-leaf parsley leaves
- mustard Dressing:
- 1 cup (250ml) bottle caesar salad dressing
- 1 tbs wholegrain mustard

Direction

- Cook pasta in large saucepan of boiling water, uncovered, until just tender, drain. Rinse under cold water, drain.
- Meanwhile, heat oil in large frying pan, add mushroom and bacon and cook stirring, until beginning to brown. Remove mixture from pan then add corn and cook, stirring, until browned all over.
- Combine dressing ingredients for the mustard dressing in a small bowl or jug.
- Place pasta, mushroom mixture and corn in large bowl with onion, avocado, parsley and dressing; toss gently to combine

25. Bacon Feta Greek Pasta Salad Recipe

Serving: 6 | Prep: | Cook: 20mins | Ready in:

Ingredients

- 1 (12 oz) package of whole wheat penne pasta
- 3 slices turkey bacon, cooked and crumbled
- 1 green bell pepper, chopped
- 1 red bell pepper, chopped
- 1 cup baby spinach, chopped
- 1/2 cucumber, chopped
- 1/4 cup black olives, sliced
- 8 pepperoncini peppers, chopped
- 1 tomato, chopped
- 1 red onion, sliced
- 1/2 cup Absolutely Fabulous Greek/House Dressing (from this AllRecipes)
- 1/2 cup feta, crumbled

Direction

- Bring a large saucepan full of water to a boil. Once boiling, add the pasta and let it cook for about 8 minutes or until it is al dente.
- Meanwhile, in a skillet sprayed with cooking spray, add the bacon and cook per package directions.
- Once the pasta is done, drain it well.
- Add the drained pasta to a large bowl. Add the bacon, red and green bell pepper and vegetables. Pour the dressing on top and toss until thoroughly distributed. Top with crumbled feta cheese.

26. Bacon Ranch Pasta Salad Recipe

Serving: 810 | Prep: | Cook: 10mins | Ready in:

Ingredients

- 1 box pasta (I use tri-color rotini for color)
- 1 bottle ranch dressing
- 1 pkg bacon crumbles (Please don't use immitation bacon bits! Big chunks of bacon are best. If you make your own, blot it really well.)
- 1 pkg cheese crumbles (or chop your own into small bits - not shredded)
- 1 each red and green bell pepper, chopped
- 1 red onion, chopped
- Options:
- chopped marinated artichoke hearts
- chopped green or black olives
- corn
- sun-dried tomatoes, chopped
- fresh or dried dill
- garlic
- black pepper
- use your imagination!

Direction

- Cook pasta al dente - not mushy! Remember that it soaks up a bit of dressing too. Drain, rinse, cool.

- Chop veggies while pasta cooks.
- Mix all ingredients together to taste and appearance, except dressing.
- Add dressing a little at a time, then mix. Add more until desired creaminess.
- Chill until flavors are "well-acquainted".
- Add more dressing as needed - pasta will soak some up.

27. Bacon Tomato Pasta Salad Recipe

Serving: 8 | Prep: | Cook: |Ready in:

Ingredients

- 2 cups uncooked elbow macaroni
- 5 green onions finely chopped
- 2 large tomatoes diced
- 1-1/4 cup celery diced
- 1-1/4 cup mayonnaise
- 5 teaspoons white vinegar
- 1/4 teaspoon salt
- 1/4 teaspoon pepper
- 1 pound cooked bacon crumbled

Direction

- Cook macaroni according to package directions.
- Drain and rinse in cold water.
- In large bowl combine macaroni, green onions, tomatoes and celery.
- In a small bowl combine mayonnaise, vinegar, salt and pepper then pour over macaroni mixture then stir to coat and put in rectangular baking pan.
- Cover and chill for 2 hours.
- Just before serving add bacon.

28. Baja Chicken Pasta Salad Recipe

Serving: 8 | Prep: | Cook: |Ready in:

Ingredients

- 3/4 pound chicken breast cooked
- 6 ounces dried mixed fruit
- 1 cup ring macaroni cooked
- 1 cup jicama cubed
- 2 green onion tops sliced
- 1/2 cup mayonnaise
- 2 tablespoons sour cream
- 1 teaspoon ground red chilies
- 1/4 teaspoon salt

Direction

- Combine all ingredients and mix well then chill several hours before serving.

29. Basil Pesto Pasta Salad Recipe

Serving: 810 | Prep: | Cook: 20mins |Ready in:

Ingredients

- 3/4 cup pine nuts
- 2 medium cloves garlic , unpeeled
- table salt
- 1 pound farfalle (bow ties) pasta
- 1/4 cup extra virgin olive oil plus 1 additional tablespoon
- 3 cups packed fresh basil leaves (about 4 ounces)
- 1 cup baby spinach (packed), about 1 ounce
- 1/2 teaspoon ground black pepper
- 2 tablespoons fresh lemon juice from 1 lemon
- 1 1/2 ounces finely grated parmesan cheese (about 3/4 cup), plus extra for serving
- 6 tablespoons mayonnaise
- 1 pint cherry tomatoes , quartered, or grape tomatoes, halved (optional)

Direction

- 1. Bring 4 quarts water to rolling boil in large pot. Toast pine nuts in small dry skillet over medium heat, shaking pan occasionally, until just golden and fragrant, 4 to 5 minutes.
- 2. When water is boiling, add garlic and let cook 1 minute. Remove garlic with slotted spoon and rinse under cold water to stop cooking; set aside to cool. Add 1 tablespoon salt and pasta to water, stir to separate, and cook until tender (just past al dente). Reserve 1/4 cup cooking water, drain pasta, toss with 1 tablespoon oil, spread in single layer on rimmed baking sheet, and cool to room temperature, about 30 minutes.
- 3. When garlic is cool, peel and mince or press through garlic press. Place 1/4 cup nuts, garlic, basil, spinach, pepper, lemon juice, remaining 1/4 cup oil, and 1 teaspoon salt in bowl of food processor and process until smooth, scraping sides of bowl as necessary. Add cheese and mayonnaise and process until thoroughly combined. Transfer mixture to large serving bowl. Cover and refrigerate until ready to assemble salad.
- 4. When pasta is cool, toss with pesto, adding reserved pasta water, 1 tablespoon at a time, until pesto evenly coats pasta. Fold in remaining 1/2 cup nuts and tomatoes (if using); serve.

30. Bbq Pasta Salad Recipe

Serving: 6 | Prep: | Cook: 45mins |Ready in:

Ingredients

- 1/4 cup red onion, minced
- 3/4 cup celery, thinly sliced
- 1/2 cup sweet pickle relish (or dill)
- 1/4 cup black olives, chopped or sliced
- 3/4 cup mayonnaise or Miracle Whip (or a combination)
- 1/2 cup roasted peppr salsa

- 1/4 tsp chili powder
- 8 oz salad macaroni
- Salt & pepper

Direction

- In a large bowl combine the onion, celery, pickle relish, and olives; set aside.
- Whisk together the mayonnaise, salsa, and chili powder; pour over the onion/celery mixture.
- Cook the pasta according to pkg. directions; drain and run cool water for a few seconds over the pasta to cool a little.
- Add to the salad and gently toss together. Taste and season with salt and pepper. Chill for 3-4 hours before serving.

31. Best Antipasta Salad With Anchovy Vinaigrette Recipe

Serving: 12 | Prep: | Cook: 45mins | Ready in:

Ingredients

- For the vinaigrette:
- 1 Tablespoons capers, drained
- 2 teaspoons anchovy paste (I couldn't find paste, so I had to use 4 anchovy filets)
- 6 roasted garlic cloves (or mince about 3 medium garlic cloves)
- 6 Tablespoons red wine vinegar
- 2 Tablespoons aged balsamic vinegar
- ¼ teaspoon ground oregano
- 8 Tablespoons extra virgin olive oil
- For the salad:
- 8 ounces dry, tri-color rotini pasta, cooked as directed
- 1 medium cucumber, seeded and cut into small chunks
- 1 cup halved grape or cherub tomatoes
- 10 asparagus spears, roasted with a little olive oil and garlic salt, chopped
- 1 cup cubed good quality Fontina or Fontinella cheese

- ½ cup cubed aged white cheddar
- ½ cup fresh shaved Parmesan cheese
- 3 or 4 ounces cubed Italian Genoa salami
- 3 or 4 ounces cubed Sopressata
- 3 or 4 ounces cubed Pepperoni ring
- 1 cup thinly sliced red onion
- 1 cup pitted kalamata olives, chopped
- 1/2 cup "deli sliced" jarred peperoncini
- 1/2 cup chopped roasted red peppers
- 1/2 cup marinated artichoke hearts, chopped
- 2 Tablespoons capers, drained

Direction

- Cook pasta in a large pot of boiling salted water, according to package directions. Drain pasta, rinse with cold water and set aside.
- For vinaigrette, puree capers, anchovies or paste and garlic in a blender or food processor. Add red wine vinegar, balsamic vinegar and oregano; pulse to puree completely. Slowly drizzle in oil and blend until emulsified.
- Mix together cooked pasta and all of the salad ingredients in a large bowl. Toss with vinaigrette to coat.
- Refrigerate several hours or overnight.

32. Bills Simple Macaroni Salad But Simply Delicious Recipe

Serving: 16 | Prep: | Cook: 10mins | Ready in:

Ingredients

- 1 (16 ounce) package macaroni
- 8 ea hard boiled eggs, chopped; or more or none
- 2 red bell peppers, chopped
- 1 green bell pepper, chopped; optional
- 1 bunch chopped green onions
- 1 ea onion, medium; diced
- 5 stalk celery, diced (optional); or more
- 1 ea parsley, 1/4 bunch; cut finely
- 1 tablespoon olive oil

- 1 cup mayonnaise
- 1 cup buttermilk
- 4 tbsp vinegar
- 1 packet dry vegetable soup mix or more; onion soup optional
- shrimp for decoration with paprika
- 1/4 cup relish
- 4 ea parsley stems with leaves
- 1/2 cup pickle juice
- 1 tbsp. mustard djion type wet
- 1 tablespoon celery salt
- 1 tablespoon poatato salad seasoning salt

Direction

- Bring a large pot of lightly salted water to a boil with uncooked eggs in it. Add pasta and cook for 8 to 10 minutes, or until al dente. Drain, and rinse with cold water until no longer hot. Transfer noodles to a large bowl.
- Cool, peel and chop eggs and mix in chopped eggs with noodles.
- Stir in red bell peppers, green bell peppers, green onions, onion, celery and olive oil. Mix in mayonnaise, vinegar and soup mix and rest of ingredients except shrimp and eggs. Refrigerate at least a few hours before serving. I wait overnight and add more buttermilk if dry.
- Before decorating, check to see if pasta has absorbed all the liquid and add more buttermilk, if necessary. Decorate with shrimp and paprika or Old Bay before serving.

33. Birthday Pasta Salad Recipe

Serving: 0 | Prep: | Cook: 30mins | Ready in:

Ingredients

- 1 lb. salad macaroni (ditalini)
- 1 cup Vegenaise or regular mayonnaise
- 2 tsp yellow mustard
- 1 tbls white vinegar
- 1 tbls parsley

- 2 tsp granulated onion
- 2 cloves of garlic, minced
- 1 medium red onion, diced
- 3-4 stalks of celery, diced
- 2 cucumbers, diced
- 2 cups small cherry tomatoes
- 1 cup black olives, sliced
- 1 cans of garbanzo beans, well rinsed
- salt and pepper to taste

Direction

- Put water on to boil. Clean and chop veggies. Rinse beans. Boil pasta until al dente. Drain and rinse with cold water until pasta is cool to the touch. Mix in mayo, mustard, spices, veggies, and beans. Salt and pepper to taste. Place in fridge for at least 4 hours; overnight is best. Taste again before serving and if necessary add additional salt, pepper, mustard, granulated onion or granulated garlic.

34. Black Bean And Couscous Salad

Serving: 6 | Prep: | Cook: 15mins | Ready in:

Ingredients

- 1 cup uncooked couscous
- 1 ¼ cups chicken broth
- 3 tablespoons extra virgin olive oil
- 2 tablespoons fresh lime juice
- 1 teaspoon red wine vinegar
- ½ teaspoon ground cumin
- 8 medium (4-1/8" long)s green onions, chopped
- 1 red bell pepper, seeded and chopped
- ¼ cup chopped fresh cilantro
- 1 cup frozen corn kernels, thawed
- 2 (15 ounce) cans black beans, drained
- salt and pepper to taste

Direction

- Bring chicken broth to a boil in a 2 quart or larger sauce pan and stir in the couscous. Cover the pot and remove from heat. Let stand for 5 minutes.
- In a large bowl, whisk together the olive oil, lime juice, vinegar and cumin. Add green onions, red pepper, cilantro, corn and beans and toss to coat.
- Fluff the couscous well, breaking up any chunks. Add to the bowl with the vegetables and mix well. Season with salt and pepper to taste and serve at once or refrigerate until ready to serve.
- Nutrition Facts
- Per Serving:
- 253 calories; protein 10.3g 21% DV; carbohydrates 41.1g 13% DV; fat 5.8g 9% DV; cholesterol mg; sodium 414.7mg 17% DV.

35. Black Eyed Pea And Macaroni Salad Recipe

Serving: 4 | Prep: | Cook: |Ready in:

Ingredients

- 1/2 cup cold black-eyed peas
- 1 pound package elbow macaroni cooked and cooled
- 2 tablespoons sweet pickle relish
- 1/4 cup mayonnaise
- 1/4 cup chopped green bell peppers
- 1/4 cup chopped celery

Direction

- Mix and serve on lettuce leaves.

36. Blackberry Chicken Pasta Salad Recipe

Serving: 4 | Prep: | Cook: 5mins |Ready in:

Ingredients

- 3 cups spiral pasta
- 1 cup pea pods cut in half and trimmed
- 2 cups cooked chicken pieces
- 1 cup sliced celery
- 2 cups fresh blackberries
- 1/2 cup finely chopped red pepper
- 1/4 cup finely chopped red onion
- 1/4 cup red wine vinegar
- 2/3 tablespoon chopped fresh basil
- 1 cup red wine vinegar dressing
- 1/2 cup freshly grated parmesan cheese

Direction

- Cook pasta according to package directions.
- Just before pasta is ready add all remaining ingredients except parmesan cheese and dressing.
- Take off heat when pasta is cooked and drain then add parmesan and dressing and mix well.
- Serve immediately or place in refrigerator and eat cold.

37. Blt Pasta Salad Recipe

Serving: 6 | Prep: | Cook: 10mins |Ready in:

Ingredients

- 2c dried pasta like macaroni, rotini or mini bow tie
- 1 large tomato, seeded and diced
- 2 green onions, finely chopped
- 2 stalks of celery, diced
- 1 1/4c mayonnaise
- 4 tsp champagne vinegar
- 1/4 tsp sugar
- 1/4 tsp salt
- 1/4tsp pepper
- 6 slices of bacon, well cooked and crumbled

Direction

- Cook pasta in salted boiling water to al dente.
- Drain and rinse in cold water.
- Whisk mayonnaise, vinegar, sugar, salt and pepper.
- Pour over pasta, tomatoes, onion and celery and toss.
- Cover and refrigerate for at least 2 hrs.
- Top with bacon before serving.

38. Blue Cheese Macaroni Salad Recipe

Serving: 8 | Prep: | Cook: 10mins | Ready in:

Ingredients

- blue cheese macaroni Salad
- 4 ounces elbow macaroni
- 1/2 cup coarsely chopped walnuts
- 1/2 cup reduced-fat mayonnaise
- 1 1/2 teaspoon dijon-style mustard
- 1-2 ounces blue cheese, crumbled
- 1/2 cup halved seedless grapes

Direction

- Cook macaroni according to package directions; drain and set aside to cool.
- Mix together walnuts, mayonnaise, mustard, blue cheese and grape halves. Combine with cooled pasta and refrigerate until ready to serve.

39. Blueberry Chicken Pasta Salad Recipe

Serving: 4 | Prep: | Cook: 10mins | Ready in:

Ingredients

- 3 cups spiral pasta
- 1 cup pea pods cut in half and trimmed

- 2 cups cooked chicken pieces
- 1 cup sliced celery
- 1 brimming cup fresh blueberries
- 1/2 cup finely chopped red pepper
- 1/4 cup finely chopped red onion
- 1/4 cup red wine vinegar
- 2/3 tablespoon chopped fresh basil
- 1 cup red wine vinegar dressing
- 1/2 cup freshly grated parmesan cheese

Direction

- Cook pasta according to package directions.
- Just before pasta is ready add all remaining ingredients except parmesan cheese and dressing.
- Take off heat when pasta is cooked and drain then add parmesan and dressing and mix well.
- Serve immediately or place in refrigerator and eat cold.

40. Blueberry Pasta Fruit Salad Recipe

Serving: 4 | Prep: | Cook: | Ready in:

Ingredients

- 1 packet three cheese tortellini pasta
- 1 cup fresh blueberries
- 1 cup sliced fresh strawberries
- 3/4 cup green grapes
- 1/4 cup almonds sliced
- 1 can mandarin orange segments drained
- 1/2 cup poppy seed dressing

Direction

- Cook pasta then empty into a large bowl.
- Add all salad ingredients and pour salad dressing over and toss lightly.
- Store in refrigerator until ready to serve.

41. Blushing Pasta Salad Recipe

Serving: 8 | Prep: | Cook: 8mins | Ready in:

Ingredients

- Salad:
- 1 pound bow tie pasta
- 1 small bag baby carrots
- 1 pound fresh or frozen peas
- 1 red bell pepper, chopped
- 1 yellow bell pepper, chopped
- 1/2 cup grated Parmesan Reggiano
- 1/2 cup fresh minced flat leaf parsley
- Dressing
- 1 cup mayonnaise
- 1/4 cup heavy cream
- 1/4 cup chili sauce
- 1 teaspoon worcestershire sauce
- 1/4 cup chopped green onion
- 2 tablespoons lemon juice
- Salt and pepper, to taste

Direction

- Cook bow ties for a total of 8 minutes. After bow ties have cooked for 3 minutes, add carrots, and bell peppers. Add frozen peas 1 minute later or fresh peas 3 minutes later.
- Drain pasta and vegetables and rinse with ice cold water until well cooled.
- Place pasta and vegetables in a large bowl and stir in cheese and parsley. Fold in as much Louis sauce as needed to lightly dress salad.
- Chill for several hours to allow flavors to mellow.

42. Boiled Shrimp Pasta Salad Recipe

Serving: 4 | Prep: | Cook: 30mins | Ready in:

Ingredients

- 1 lb. dry egg and spinach fusilli pasta
- 2 lbs. medium-size shrimp, boiled, peeled and deveined
- 2 tbls. pine nuts
- 3 to 4 tbls. olive oil
- 1/4 lb. chevre (goat cheese), cut into one-fourth-inch pieces
- 2 tbls. snipped fresh chives
- 2 tsp. chopped fresh basil
- 8 sundried tomatoes marinated in olive oil, coarsely chopped
- 8 to 10 kalamata olives, pitted and quartered
- 2 garlic cloves
- balsamic vinegar

Direction

- Cook the fusilli pasta in boiling water until al dente, rinse in cold water, and drain. Transfer to a serving bowl or platter and toss with olive oil. Mix the garlic and basil with the pasta. Then fold in the tomatoes, olives, pine nuts, and shrimp. Sprinkle the salad with the balsamic vinegar to taste (about 1 to 2 tablespoons). Add the cheese and toss lightly. Garnish with chives and serve.

43. Bow Tie Pasta Salad With Ham And Peas Recipe

Serving: 8 | Prep: | Cook: 25mins | Ready in:

Ingredients

- 1 pound Bow Tie Pasta (or pasta of your choice)
- 1/2 cup olive or canola oil
- 1/3 cup of vinegar (I use half lemon juice and vinegar) Use any vinegar you like, red wine, apple cider etc...
- 2 tsp's dried basil
- 1 tsp dried oregano
- 2 tsp's parsley flakes
- 1 clove of garlic, minced
- 1/4 tsp pepper
- 1/2 cup chopped green onions

- 1/2 cup finely diced red pepper
- 1/3 cup grated parmesan or romano cheese
- 2 cups of diced cooked ham
- 1/2 cup Fresh Shelled Peas or frozen and thawed peas
- 1/2 cup diced cheddar cheese (optional)
- * salt n pepper to taste, keeping in mind the ham and cheeses will be salty*
- ~Makes about 5-6 cups of pasta salad.

Direction

- Cook the pasta according to the box instructions, making sure it's tender but firm. Drain and rinse with cold water; set aside to finish draining.
- While the pasta is cooking, mix the oil, vinegar (and/or lemon juice) with dried herbs, garlic and black pepper. Chop the green onions and add the whites to the dressing.
- Once the pasta has cooled and drained, mix in the dressing and add the remaining green onions, red pepper, ham, peas and cheddar cheese. Refrigerate for at least 4 hours, stirring thoroughly before serving. Check for seasonings and add more herbs, dressing etc. to suit your tastes.
- All measurements are guidelines, you can add as little or as much ham, peas, veggies, cheese etc. as you like! (You can always make more dressing if the pasta becomes dry, it really depends on humidity of the vegetables and type of pasta you use)

44. Broccoli Cheese Pasta Salad Recipe

Serving: 6 | Prep: | Cook: 20mins | Ready in:

Ingredients

- 8 oz. Rigatoni, uncooked
- 4. C. fresh broccoli, flowerets
- 4 oz. mozzarella cheese, cubed
- 1/3 C. chopped fresh parsley

- 2 Tbsp. chopped fresh basil
- mustard vinaigrette
- lettuce leaves
- Cherry tomato halves for Garnish

Direction

- Cook pasta according to package directions; drain. Rinse with cold water, and drain. Cook broccoli in a small amount of boiling water 2 to 3 minutes or until slightly tender; drain. Rinse with cold water, and rain. Combine pasta, broccoli, mozzarella cheese, and herbs in a large bowl, toss with Mustard Vinaigrette, and serve on a lettuce-lined platter.
- Mustard Vinaigrette
- 1/2 C. Vegetable Oil
- 1/3 C. Lemon Juice
- 2 tsp. Dijon Mustard
- 3 cloves Garlic, minced
- 1/2 tsp. Salt
- 1/2 tsp. Pepper
- Combine all ingredients in a jar, cover tightly, and shake vigorously. Cover and chill.

45. Buffalo Chicken Pasta Salad Recipe

Serving: 12 | Prep: | Cook: 20mins | Ready in:

Ingredients

- 1 box pasta (any vaviety)
- I package chicken nuggets
- 1 Jar blue cheese dressing
- 1small bottle of red hot sauce
- carrots
- celery

Direction

- Cook Pasta and chicken nuggets according to directions.
- Mix whole jar of Blue Cheese and desired amount of hot sauce in a large bowl. Add

Pasta, desired amount of sliced carrots and Celery and mix. Cut up Chicken nuggets and combine with Pasta.

46. Buttery Artichoke Tapenade Pasta Recipe

Serving: 10 | Prep: | Cook: 20mins | Ready in:

Ingredients

- 2 Heaping Cups of Farfalle (Bowtie) pasta
- 1/3 Cup Gertie's Artichoke Tapenade
- 3-4 long green onions chopped
- 2 Tbs Pesto Sauce
- Parmesan Cheese shredded(To Taste) I use 1/4 Cup
- 4 Tbs Butter Melted

Direction

- Boil Farfalle Pasta for 12-14 minutes and drain
- Reserve a few Tbsp. of the pasta liquid to reincorporate into the pasta.
- Melt your butter in a saucepan then add the Artichoke Tapenade and the chopped long green onions and blend.
- Next add 2 Tbsp. Pesto Sauce and Blend.
- Add your Pasta and Blend.
- Top with Parmesan Cheese and serve.
- Add salt or lemon pepper to taste.

47. CHICKEN BLUEBERRY PASTA SALAD Recipe

Serving: 6 | Prep: | Cook: 20mins | Ready in:

Ingredients

- 1 pound boneless, skinless chicken breast, trimmed of fat
- 1 - 8 ounce pkg fusilli

- 3 tbsp extra-virgin olive oil
- 1 large shallot, thinly sliced
- 1/3 cup reduced-sodium chicken broth
- 1/3 cup crumbled feta cheese
- 3 tbsp lime juice
- 1 cup fresh blueberries
- 1 tbsp dill
- 1 tsp freshly grated lime zest
- 1/4 tsp salt

Direction

- Place chicken in a skillet or saucepan and add enough water to cover; bring to a boil. Cover, reduce heat to low and simmer gently until cooked through and no longer pink in the middle, 12 to 15 minutes.
- Transfer the chicken to a cutting board to cool.
- Shred into bite-size strips. Bring a large pot of water to a boil.
- Cook pasta until just tender, about 9 minutes or according to package directions. Drain. Place in a large bowl.
- Meanwhile, place oil and shallot in a small skillet and cook over medium-low heat, stirring occasionally, until softened and just beginning to brown, 2 to 5 minutes.
- Add broth, feta and lime juice and cook, stirring occasionally, until the feta begins to melt, 1 to 2 minutes.
- Add the chicken to the bowl with the pasta. Add the dressing, blueberries, dill, lime zest and salt and toss until combined.
- Make Ahead Tip: Add everything except the blueberries and dressing to the pasta salad. Cover and refrigerate pasta salad, blueberries and dressing separately for up to 1 day. Toss together just before serving.

48. CHICKEN MACARONI SALAD Recipe

Serving: 10 | Prep: | Cook: 30mins | Ready in:

Ingredients

- 1/2 KG OF macaroni pasta
- 1/2 KG OF chicken MEAT
- 1 MEDIUM SIZE CAN OF pineapple tidbits (450 grms)
- 50 grms of raisins
- 500 grms to 1 kg of mayonaise (ITS UP TO YOU)
- 100 grms of kraft cheese
- 1 piece of carrots
- 1 onion
- salt AND pepper TO TASTE
- 1/4 can of condense milk (about 125 grms)
- a spoonfull of sweet pickle relish

Direction

- Bring to a boil with salt the macaroni pasta, drain and set aside
- Bring to a boil the chicken meat with salt, drain and set aside
- Drain pineapple tidbits
- Cut into cubes the cheese, carrot and onion
- Cut into small cubes or thinly the chicken meat
- Get a big bowl and begin to mix all the ingredients carefully one by one. First put in the bowl the pasta then the chicken, pineapple tidbits, raisins, cheese, carrots, onion, sweet pickle relish, condense milk and mayonnaise. Salt and pepper to taste. Mix well but carefully. Adding more mayonnaise is depends of your taste. Put on the salad rack and chill for at least an hour before you eat. So try and enjoy this simple CHICKEN MACARONI SALAD. IT'S SO DELICIOUS.

49. Caesar Chicken Pasta Salad Recipe

Serving: 12 | Prep: | Cook: 12mins |Ready in:

Ingredients

- 1 pound penne pasta, cooked and drained

- 3 eggs, hard-boiled
- 1/2 red pepper, cut into thin slivers
- 1/2 yellow bell pepper, cut into thin slivers
- 1/4 cup red onion, diced
- 1/2 cup parmesan cheese, freshly grated
- 1/4 cup fresh parsley, finely minced
- 2 chicken breasts, pre-roasted from the store, shredded (save rest of chicken for another use)
- 1 cup caesar salad dressing, Cardini's - use more or less depending on how moist you want the salad

Direction

- Toss all ingredients together, refrigerate until 1/2 hour before serving time.
- NOTE: Use gluten-free penne pasta to make this gluten-free.

50. Caesar Chicken Pasta Salad Recipe

Serving: 6 | Prep: | Cook: 15mins |Ready in:

Ingredients

- 1 pkg. (10 oz.) Perdue Shortcuts Original roast chicken or 3 cups grilled, shredded chicken
- prepared penne (about 6 ounces uncooked pasta), run under cold water to chill
- 2 cups thinly sliced romaine lettuce
- 1-1/2 cups grape tomatoes
- 1/2 cup thinly sliced fresh basil
- 1/2 cup chopped green onions
- 1/3 cup fat-free caesar salad dressing
- 1/4 cup chopped fresh parsley
- 1 pkg. (4 oz.) crumbled feta cheese
- 1 clove garlic, minced

Direction

- Combine all ingredients in a large bowl; toss well to coat.

51. Cajun Macaroni Salad Recipe

Serving: 10 | Prep: | Cook: 40mins | Ready in:

Ingredients

- 2 lbs shrimp, unpeeled with heads on
- 1 quart water
- 2 tbs liquid crab boil
- 1 medium onion, quartered
- 3 tbs salt
- 1 1/2 cups uncooked elbow macaroni
- 1 large onion, chopped
- 1 cup chopped celery
- 1/2 lb bacon, cooked, drained and crushed. Reserve bacon fat.
- 1 tbs garlic, minced
- 1 cup fresh parsley chopped
- 5 boiled egges
- 1 tsp cayenne pepper
- 1 tsp salt
- 1 tsp crab boil
- 1 cup mayonnaise
- reserved bacon fat
- 1 tbs paprika

Direction

- Cook shrimp with heads on and unpeeled in 1 quart of water. Add 2 tbsp. of crab boil and medium quartered onion to water and boil for 20 minutes.
- Remove from heat and add 3 tbsp. of salt, stir and let stand for 5 minutes. Drain and peel shrimp. Reserve liquid and cook the elbow macaroni in it until al dente.
- In a large bowl, combine drained macaroni, chopped onion, celery, bacon, garlic, chopped egg whites and parsley.
- In a separate bowl, combine mashed egg yellows with 1 tsp. salt, 1 tsp. cayenne, 1 tsp. crab boil, mayonnaise and bacon fat until well blended.
- Add to macaroni and mix well. Sprinkle paprika on top.

52. California Pasta Salad Recipe

Serving: 8 | Prep: | Cook: 20mins | Ready in:

Ingredients

- 1 (12 ounce) jar marinated artichoke hearts
- 1/8 teaspoon ground black pepper
- 8 ounces medium shell pasta, cooked and drained
- 1/4 cup white wine vinegar
- 1 tablespoon Dijon mustard
- 1/4 cup shelled sunflower seeds
- 1 small cucumber, halved and sliced
- juice of 1 lime
- 1 clove garlic, minced
- 2 tomatoes, seeded and diced
- 1/2 teaspoon salt
- 1/2 teaspoon dried marjoram

Direction

- Drain artichokes, reserving marinade.
- Whisk reserved marinade with vinegar, mustard, lime juice, garlic, salt, marjoram and pepper.
- Toss together pasta, artichokes, sunflower seeds, cucumber and tomato.
- Pour dressing over. Toss to coat.

53. Cannelloni And Macaroni Salad With Tomatoes Basil And Olives Recipe

Serving: 6 | Prep: | Cook: 10mins | Ready in:

Ingredients

- 1-1/2 tablespoons extra virgin olive oil
- 1 pound plum tomatoes halved lengthwise
- 1-1/2 cups small elbow macaroni
- 3 tablespoons red wine vinegar
- 6 tablespoons chopped fresh basil

- 1 garlic clove minced
- 15 ounce can cannelloni beans rinsed and drained
- 1/2 cup chopped red onion
- 1/4 cup chopped pitted kalamata olives
- 1/3 cup chopped fresh Italian parsley

Direction

- Prepare barbecue to medium high heat.
- Drizzle 1/2 tablespoon oil over cut side of tomatoes then sprinkle with salt and pepper.
- Grill tomatoes cut side up until skin begins to char about 2 minutes then turn and grill 1 minute.
- Cool completely then cut tomatoes into 1" pieces.
- Cook macaroni in large saucepan of boiling salted water until tender but still firm to bite.
- Stir occasionally then drain well and transfer macaroni to large bowl and cool.
- Mix in grilled tomatoes and any accumulated juices, 2 tablespoons vinegar, basil, and garlic.
- Season with salt and pepper then transfer salad to large platter.
- Mix beans, onion, olives, parsley, remaining oil and 1 tablespoon vinegar in medium bowl.
- Season with salt and pepper then spoon bean salad over center of macaroni salad and serve.

54. Caprese Pasta Salad Recipe

Serving: 6 | Prep: | Cook: 12mins | Ready in:

Ingredients

- 1 pound penne pasta (this can be increased if you have many guests, or decreased if you want more intense flavour.
- 6 ripe roma tomatoes, insides removed (cherry tomatoes will work, but it is more labour intensive to remove the insides.)
- 3/4 pound fresh mozarella
- 3/4 hard salami
- 1 bunch basil, chopped roughly

- salt and pepper to taste

Direction

- Boil pasta per instructions on package.
- While pasta is boiling, cut tomato, salami, and mozzarella into bite-sized pieces.
- When pasta is cooked, drain and coat lightly with extra virgin olive oil or butter.
- Add all ingredients to pasta, toss, and serve warm.

55. Ceasar Salmon Salad With Pasta Recipe

Serving: 6 | Prep: | Cook: 12mins | Ready in:

Ingredients

- 1 tablespoon olive oil
- kosher salt
- 8 ounces medium pasta shells
- 1 head romaine lettuce
- 3 ounces smoked salmon, sliced or flaked
- 1/2 teaspoon fresh ground black pepper
- 1/2 cup creamy caeser salad dressing, (bottled or home-made)
- 2 tablespoons capers, drained
- 1/2 medium red onion, thinly sliced
- 1 med ripe red tomato, thinly sliced
- 1 cup parmesan cheese, grated
- 1 cup croutons

Direction

- Fill a large pot with water.
- Add oil and 2 pinches kosher salt. Bring to a boil over high heat.
- Add pasta shells and cook according to package instructions.
- Drain, rinse with cold water, and refrigerate for 10 minutes.
- Meanwhile, wash, dry, and tear lettuce into medium size pieces. Combine in a large serving bowl with cooked pasta, smoked

salmon, black pepper, salad dressing, capers, tomatoes and onions; mix well.

- Before serving, top with Parmesan cheese and croutons.

56. Cheddar Macaroni Salad Recipe

Serving: 4 | Prep: | Cook: 10mins | Ready in:

Ingredients

- 1 cup elbow or medium shell macaroni
- 3/4 cup cubed cheddar cheese
- 1 stalk celery sliced
- 1/2 small green bell pepper chopped
- 1/2 cup frozen peas thawed
- 1/3 cup chopped onion
- 1/4 cup mayonnaise
- 1/4 cup sour cream
- 2 tablespoons milk
- 2 tablespoons sweet pickle relish

Direction

- Cook macaroni according to package directions then drain and rinse with cold water.
- Drain again.
- Combine macaroni, cheese, celery, bell pepper, peas and onion then stir gently to combine.
- Mix mayonnaise, sour cream, milk, pickle relish, and 1/4 teaspoon salt then toss with macaroni.
- Cover and chill several hours or overnight then stir in additional milk if necessary.

57. Cheese And Pasta Salad Recipe

Serving: 6 | Prep: | Cook: 10mins | Ready in:

Ingredients

- 8 ounces rotelle pasta cooked and drained

- 1 cup cooked black beans drained and cooled
- 1/2 cup finely chopped red onion
- 1/4 cup chopped green bell pepper
- 1/2 cup sliced radishes
- Dressing:
- 2/3 cup cider vinegar
- 1/4 cup fresh lime juice
- 2 tablespoons extra virgin olive oil
- 2 tablespoons chopped marinated jalapeno chilies
- 1 tablespoon chopped fresh cilantro leaves
- 2 teaspoons dried oregano leaves crushed
- 1/2 teaspoon freshly ground black pepper
- 2 cups finely shredded monterey jack cheese
- 3/4 cup crumbled feta cheese (reserve 1/4 cup)

Direction

- In large bowl combine pasta, beans, onion, bell pepper and radishes then set aside.
- In a small bowl combine vinegar, lime juice, olive oil, jalapeno chilies, cilantro, oregano and black pepper.
- Toss salad with half of the dressing then cover and refrigerate.
- Add cheeses to remaining dressing and cover and refrigerate for one hour.
- Toss remaining dressing with pasta salad just before serving.
- Garnish with reserved cheese and serve.

58. Cheesy Peas Pasta Salad Recipe

Serving: 6 | Prep: | Cook: 10mins | Ready in:

Ingredients

- 1 lb frozen peas
- 3 cups dry pasta (rotini, bowties, or macaroni)
- 1/2 lb. colby or cheddar cheese, 1/4" cubed
- 1/2 lb. ham, 1/4" cubed
- 1 to 1 1/2 cups Miracle Whip
- 1/2 cup ranch dressing
- A pinch or two of dill weed

- salt and pepper, to taste

Direction

- Place peas in a colander and rinse with cold water. Allow to thaw, but do not cook.
- In a pot of boiling, salted water, cook pasta according to package directions. Drain and cool, but do not rinse. Add the peas and pasta to the cheese and ham in a large mixing bowl.
- In a smaller bowl, whisk together the two salad dressings, dill weed, and salt and pepper.
- Pour the dressing over the other ingredients in large bowl, and toss to mix.
- Cover the bowl and chill in the refrigerator for a couple of hours before serving, for the flavors to blend.

59. Cheesy Tortellin Pasta Salad Recipe

Serving: 10 | Prep: | Cook: 40mins | Ready in:

Ingredients

- Ingredients
- 1 (14 oz) can of drained and quartered artichoke hearts
- 1 (10 oz) cont. of halved grape tomatoes
- 1 (6 oz) can of drained and sliced medium black olives
- 1 diced green bell pepper
- 1 (20 oz) package of cheese-filled egg tortellini, cooked al dente,
- 1/3 c.of olive oil,
- 1/4 c of parmesan cheese, the kind in the can
- 1 (8 oz) jar of basil pesto
- 1/2 tsp of salt
- 2 tsp of minced garlic
- 12 oz of cubed mozzarella cheese
- 8 oz of half of a 1 lb. box rotini pasta, cooked al dente, drained

Direction

- First you want to cook pastas, then set aside to drain.
- Cool.
- Now take a large bowl or punch bowl, add the rest of the ingredients, folding gently till well mixed.
- Then add in the pastas.
- Next you want to adjust seasoning to taste, meaning, add more salt, parmesan, etc., till you like it.
- Cool.
- Serve.

60. Cherylanns Pasta Salad Recipe

Serving: 16 | Prep: | Cook: 240mins | Ready in:

Ingredients

- 1 12 oz. package white rotelli
- 1 16 oz. package colored rotelli, or Whacky Mac
- 1 16 oz. package crab meat, or lobster meat, shredded
- 4 hard-boiled eggs, chopped
- 6 green onions, thinly sliced
- 1 green bell pepper, chopped
- 2 stalks celery, thinly sliced
- 1/2 pound grape tomatoes, halved
- 1 6 oz. (drained weight) large ripe olives, quartered
- 1 small jar green olives with pimento, halved
- 1 cup mozzarella cheese, cut into 1/4" cubes
- 1 large bottle of Kraft Deluxe Caesar/Parmesan salad dressing, or
- (if you can't find it - Newman's Own Caesar)

Direction

- Cook the pasta according to package directions. Drain and rinse with cold water to cool the pasta; drain.
- Pour pasta into a large bowl. Add the remaining ingredients, except for the dressing. Toss to combine.

- Pour salad dressing over pasta mixture in the bowl. Toss until pasta mixture is completely coated with the dressing.
- Cover and refrigerate for at least 4 hours.

61. Chicken And Pasta Salad With Creamy Chamomile Dressing Recipe

Serving: 4 | Prep: | Cook: 15mins | Ready in:

Ingredients

- 3 chamomile tea bags
- 1/4 cup white vinegar
- 3/4 cup light mayonnaise
- 1-1/2 tsp fresh tarragon
- 1 lb pasta (any variety)
- 2 Tbs olive oil
- 4 boneless, skinless chicken breasts
- 1/2 cup diced red peppers (approximately 1 small pepper, or 1/2
- medium)
- 1/2 cup diced green peppers (1 small pepper, or 1/2 medium)

Direction

- Steep the tea bags in the vinegar for 15 minutes.
- Squeeze out the excess liquid before discarding the bags.
- Mix in the mayonnaise and tarragon, and chill.
- Meanwhile, cook the pasta according to the package directions until al dente.
- Drain pasta and reserve.
- Heat the oil in a skillet and sauté the chicken until it is cooked through, 10 to 15 minutes.
- Remove the chicken to a plate to cool.
- Shred the chicken.
- Combine the chicken, pasta, peppers and dressing in a large bowl.
- Toss and chill.
- Serve with an arugula and frisee salad.

62. Chicken Club Pasta Salad Recipe

Serving: 6 | Prep: | Cook: 8mins | Ready in:

Ingredients

- 8 oz corkscrew or spiral pasta
- ¾ c Italian dressing
- ¼ c mayonnaise
- 2 c chopped, cooked rotisserie chicken
- 1 c Muenster or monterey jack cheese, cubed
- 12 strips crisp-cooked bacon, crumbled
- 1 avocado, chopped
- 1 c each chopped celery and green pepper
- 8 oz cherry or grape tomatoes, halved

Direction

- Cook and drain the pasta according to the package directions and rinse it with cold water.
- Whisk the dressing with the mayonnaise in a large bowl, then stir in the pasta and remaining ingredients.
- Chill.

63. Chicken Dijon Pasta Salad Recipe

Serving: 2 | Prep: | Cook: 10mins | Ready in:

Ingredients

- 4 ounces pasta swirls uncooked
- 8 ounces plain yogurt
- 1/3 cup wheat germ
- 3 tablespoons white wine vinegar
- 1 tablespoon Dijon mustard
- 1/8 teaspoon freshly ground black pepper

- 1 cup boneless skinless chicken breasts cooked and diced
- 3/4 cup broccoli florets diced
- 1/2 cup tomato chopped and seeded
- 1/3 cup red onion chopped

Direction

- Cook pasta according to package directions.
- In medium bowl combine yogurt, wheat germ, vinegar, mustard and pepper then mix well.
- Add pasta and remaining ingredients then toss to coat.
- Serve immediately or chill before serving.

64. Chicken Macaroni Salad Filipino Style Recipe

Serving: 8 | Prep: | Cook: 30mins | Ready in:

Ingredients

- 1 box macaroni noodles
- 2-3 big chicken breast
- mayonnaise
- 1 can pineapple chunks or tidbits
- 1 onion
- 1/2 cup sweet pickle relish
- 1 cup shredded cheddar cheese
- 1/2 cup raisins
- 2 to 3 medium sized carrots(optional)
- salt
- pepper

Direction

- Boil chicken breast in water with salt and pepper until it's tender. Drain chicken and shred it in 1 inch length.
- Peal skin and boil carrots in water for 15-20 minutes or until cooked. Drain carrots and let it cool. (OPTIONAL)
- Cook macaroni noodles according to package cooking instructions. Make sure it's el dente. Drain and cool.

- Drain pineapple chunks or tidbits.
- Finely chop onions
- Combine the macaroni, shredded chicken, pineapple, sweet pickle relish, raisins, shredded cheese, carrots, and slowly add the mayonnaise while mixing all ingredients. (You can put more or less mayo in your salad, all up to you)
- Add salt and pepper to taste.
- Refrigerate, then serve.

65. Chicken Macaroni Salad Recipe

Serving: 8 | Prep: | Cook: 60mins | Ready in:

Ingredients

- 500 grams elbow macaroni
- 1 large chicken breast, boiled and shredded
- 1 cup boiled, diced carrots
- 1 cup raisins
- 1 cup diced sweet ham
- 1 cup frozen peas
- 1 cup pineapple chunks
- 1/2 cup diced red capsicum
- 3 cups mayonnaise or any low-cal equivalent (adjust to suit taste)
- dash of salt and pepper

Direction

- Boil macaroni according to package instructions. Drain and set aside.
- In a large bowl, mix all the ingredients then season to taste.
- Chill for at least 1 hour before serving.

66. Chicken Parmesan Pasta Salad Recipe

Serving: 6 | Prep: | Cook: 25mins | Ready in:

Ingredients

- 8 oz. penne pasta
- 1 green pepper, cut in 2x1/2" strips
- 1 tsp dried oregano
- 1 pkg (12 oz.) fully cooked Italian-style breaded chicken cutlets
- 1/2 c bottled olive oil and vinegar dressing
- 1/4 c pizza sauce from a jar
- 1/4 tsp salt
- 1-1/2 c grape tomatoes,7 oz.,halved
- 8 0z. bocconcini (mini mozzarella balls),halved
- 1/2 c fresh basil leaves
- 1/3 c pitted kalamata olives,halved
- 2 Tbs shredded parmesan cheese

Direction

- Cook pasta according to directions, adding pepper last 2 mins of cooking. Drain
- Preheat oven to 425. Coat baking sheet with cooking spray. Press oregano onto both sides of chicken. Place on sheet. Bake, turning once, 5 -6 mins per side. Cool; cut into 1/2" wide slices
- In serving bowl, combine dressing, sauce and salt. Add pasta mixture, chicken, tomatoes, bocconcini, basil and olives; toss to combine. Sprinkle with parmesan.

67. Chicken Pasta Salad Recipe

Serving: 6 | Prep: | Cook: 45mins | Ready in:

Ingredients

- 3 Large cooked chicken breasts, cubed
- 1 bag of multicolored twisty pasta (any 12 to 16 oz bag of pasta works).
- 3 large stalks of celery
- 1/2 to 1 red onion (depending on strength of flavor)
- 1 medium can of sliced black olives
- 1 c mayonnaise (Approx)
- salt & pepper to taste

Direction

- If you haven't cooked the chicken yet, I recommend thyme, salt, pepper and chicken flavor in water to boil until done. Then cut them up in desired sized bites.
- Cook the pasta
- While the pasta cooks, dice the onion and celery and put in a large bowl along with the olives.
- Add the chicken after it has cooled a bit
- Drain the pasta (rinse in cold water if desired) and add to contents of bowl. Mix up well.
- Add Mayonnaise, salt and pepper to taste.
- Best is to let it refrigerate for a few hours for the flavor to really develop, however, it never seems to last that long in my house. Also, for a family of 5, there are leftovers for several of us the next day.

68. Chicken Pasta Salad With Cucumber Recipe

Serving: 8 | Prep: | Cook: 2mins | Ready in:

Ingredients

- 1 cup uncooked macaroni
- 3/4 cup mayonnaise
- 1 tablespoon onion.finely chopped
- 1/2 teaspoon salt
- 1/4 teaspoon pepper
- 1/1/2 cups cooked chicken(Rotisserie grocery-store bought works great.)
- 1 cup chopped cucumber(FarmersMarket in season.)
- 1 rib celery,chopped(FarmersMarket in season.)

Direction

- Cook macaroni to your taste.
- Combine mayonnaise, onion, salt and pepper in bowl; mix.

- Add warm macaroni, chicken, celery, and cucumber, mix.
- Chill, covered 2 hours.

69. Chicken Portobello Pasta Salad Recipe

Serving: 4 | Prep: | Cook: 10mins | Ready in:

Ingredients

- 8 0z rigatoni pasta
- 2 chicken breasts, grilled (I got Trader Joe's)
- 1 garlic clove, minced
- 5 green onions, sliced
- 2 portobello mushroom caps, trimmed, cleaned and sliced
- 10-15 cherry tomatoes, halved
- Balsamic vinaigrette dressing (Trader Joes's is good)
- grated parmesan cheese

Direction

- Cook pasta according to package, about 10 minutes
- Drain and put into a large bowl
- Slice grilled chicken into thin strips
- Put all ingredients except dressing and cheese into the bowl with the pasta and toss
- Add the amount of dressing you want and sprinkle with Parm
- Chill well before serving
- Pasta soaks up the dressing pretty well, so you may have to add more before serving

70. Chicken Ranch Pasta Salad Recipe

Serving: 8 | Prep: | Cook: | Ready in:

Ingredients

- 1 box rotini noodles
- chicken chunks, cooked. (as much as you want)
- 1 head of broccoli cut into bite size pieces
- grape tomatoes cut in half (as much as you want)
- 1/2 onion chopped
- 4 cups ranch dressing
- 3 -4 tablespoons grated parmesan cheese
- 1 16 oz package shredded cheddar cheese (can use less if desired)
- parsley

Direction

- Cook noodles per directions
- Prepare broccoli, onion, and tomatoes.
- Mix everything together in a bowl and refrigerate or serve

71. Chicken Spaghetti Salad Recipe

Serving: 8 | Prep: | Cook: 20mins | Ready in:

Ingredients

- 1 (1 lb) box spaghetti (break in three's)
- 1 (8 oz) bottle Zesty Italian dressing
- 2 bunches scallions, diced (tops & bottoms)
- 1 pint grape tomatoes
- 1 big heads broccoli chopped small
- 1 large cucumber diced
- 1 carrot shredded
- 3 cups shredded cooked chicken
- 1 (2 5/8 ounce) bottle Salad Supreme dry seasoning mix (found in spices)

Direction

- Cook spaghetti (remember to break into three's) and drain, rinsing with cold water to stop cooking process.
- Add all ingredients except Salad Supreme and chicken, mixing well.
- Add enough Salad Supreme to personal taste.

- Sprinkle chicken on top.
- Put in refrigerator to chill, serve with homemade bread, and voila! Great summer dinner for keeping the heat out of the kitchen. (Great made the night before too!)

72. Chicken And Pasta Salad Recipe

Serving: 4 | Prep: | Cook: 30mins | Ready in:

Ingredients

- 4 chicken breast halves, skinless and boneless
- 8 oz pasta, rotini style
- 1 head romaine lettuce, diced
- 6 cherry tomatoes, diced
- 8 oz mozzarella cheese, cut into cubes
- 1 red onion, diced
- steak seasoning, to taste

Direction

- Preheat the grill at high heat. Season both sides of chicken with the steak seasoning.
- Oil the grill grate, lightly, and grill chicken 6-8 minutes per side, (until juices run clear.) Remove from the heat, and cut into strips when cooled.
- In the meantime, add the pasta to a large pot of lightly salted boiling water. Cook 8-10 minutes, until 'al dente'. Drain, and run under cold water to cool.
- Combine the lettuce, tomatoes, cheese, and onion in a large bowl. Mix together with the cooled chicken and pasta then serve.

73. Chicken And Peanut Pasta Salad Recipe

Serving: 6 | Prep: | Cook: 20mins | Ready in:

Ingredients

- 1 lb spiral pasta cooked
- 1 cup frozen green peas
- 1/2 cup chunky peanut buttter
- 1/3 cup sour cream
- 1 to 2 tsp hot sauce (may be optional)
- 1 Tbs vinegar
- 2 Tbs fresh grated ginger
- 1/3 cup orange juice
- salt and pepper to taste
- 3 cups cooked chopped chicken
- 2 large carrots diced
- 3 scallions chopped

Direction

- Cook pasta, drain and cool.
- In blender add peanut butter, sour cream, ginger, hot sauce, vinegar, orange juice, and blend smooth
- Season to taste.
- If mixture is too thick, add more orange juice.
- In large bowl, combine chicken, carrots and peas and pasta.
- Slowly mix in the peanut dressing and toss lightly to coat well.
- Garnish with scallions

74. Chicken And Vegetable Pasta Salad Recipe

Serving: 8 | Prep: | Cook: 10mins | Ready in:

Ingredients

- 16 ounces tri-colored spiral pasta, cooked and cooled
- 1 cup carrot, peeled and thinly sliced
- 1/2 cup green bell pepper, diced
- 1/2 cup red bell pepper, diced
- 1 cup broccoli florets, cut in bite size pieces (I steam this just a little and cool to give a milder flavor. But just personal preference)
- 1/2 sweet onion, finely chopped (optional)
- 1 pound boneless chicken, diced

- 1 tablespoon vegetable oil
- 1/2 teaspoon garlic powder
- 1/2 teaspoon ground black pepper
- 1/2 cup ranch salad dressing
- 8 to 10 ounces Italian salad dressing
- salt to taste

Direction

- Sauté chicken in oil until fully cooked. Season with garlic powder and pepper. Drain and cool.
- In large bowl, combine pasta, vegetables and chicken.
- Add salad dressings and stir to coat.
- Add 1 to 2 teaspoons water if salad appears dry.
- Season to taste with salt.
- Cover and chill.

75. Chili And Corn Pasta Salad Recipe

Serving: 4 | Prep: | Cook: 5mins | Ready in:

Ingredients

- 2 ounces (1/2 cup) uncooked medium dried pasta shells
- 1 (15-ounce) can vegetarian or turkey chili with beans
- 1 (11-ounce) can whole kernel corn with red and greenpeppers, drained
- 4 cups shredded romaine lettuce
- 1 ounce (1/4 cup) cheddar cheese, shredded
- 1/4 cup sliced green onions
- sour cream, if desired
- corn chips, if desired

Direction

- Cook pasta according to package directions. Drain. Return to pan.

- Add chili and corn to cooked pasta. Cook over medium heat until heated through (2 to 3 minutes).
- To serve, place 1 cup lettuce on each salad plate; top with 1 cup chili mixture, 1 tablespoon cheese and 1 tablespoon green onion. Repeat with remaining ingredients. Serve with sour cream and corn chips.

76. Chilled Shrimp Pasta Salad

Serving: 6 | Prep: | Cook: | Ready in:

Ingredients

- 3 cups uncooked small pasta shells
- 1/2 cup sour cream
- 1/2 cup mayonnaise
- 1/4 cup horseradish sauce
- 2 tablespoons grated onion
- 1-1/2 teaspoons seasoned salt
- 3/4 teaspoon pepper
- 1 pound peeled and deveined cooked small shrimp
- 1 large cucumber, seeded and chopped
- 3 celery ribs, thinly sliced
- Red lettuce leaves, optional

Direction

- Cook pasta according to package directions. Drain; rinse with cold water.
- In a large bowl, mix sour cream, mayonnaise, horseradish sauce, onion, seasoned salt and pepper. Stir in shrimp, cucumber, celery and pasta. Refrigerate until serving. If desired, serve on lettuce.
- Nutrition Facts
- 3/4 cup (calculated without lettuce): 239 calories, 12g fat (2g saturated fat), 72mg cholesterol, 344mg sodium, 20g carbohydrate (3g sugars, 1g fiber), and 11g protein. Diabetic Exchanges: 2 fat, 1 starch, 1 lean meat.

77. Chinese Chicken & Noodle Salad Recipe

Serving: 8 | Prep: | Cook: 30mins | Ready in:

Ingredients

- 2 3-ounce packages low-fat ramen-noodle soup mix
- 1/2 cup slivered almonds
- 2 T sesame seeds
- 1 T canola oil
- 2 lbs boneless, skinless chicken breasts, trimmed
- 6 1/4 inch thick slices fresh ginger
- 1 t salt
- 6 T orange juice
- 6 T cider vinegar
- 3 T reduced-sodium soy sauce
- 3 T sugar
- 1 1/2 t toasted sesame oil
- 4 cups shredded green cabbage
- 2 medium carrots, shredded
- 1 bunch scallions, chopped

Direction

- Preheat oven to 350 degrees F
- Crumble ramen noodles onto a large rimmed baking sheet (discard seasoning packets). Add almonds, sesame seeds and canola oil; toss to coat. Bake for 10 minutes. Stir, then bake until the noodles are golden brown, about 5 minutes more. Let cool on the pan on wire rack.
- Place chicken in a medium skillet or saucepan with water to cover. Add ginger and salt; bring to a boil. Cover, reduce heat to low, and simmer gently until cooked through and no longer pink in the middle, 10 to 15 minutes. Transfer the chicken to a cutting board to cool. Shred into bite-size pieces. (Discard poaching liquid.)
- Meanwhile, combine orange juice, vinegar, soy sauce, sugar and sesame oil in a small bowl or

jar with a tight-fitting lid. Whisk or shake until the sugar has dissolved.
- Just before serving, combine the shredded chicken, cabbage, carrots and scallions in a large bowl. Add the toasted noodle mixture and the dressing; mix well.

78. Chinese Style Chicken Pasta Salad Recipe

Serving: 8 | Prep: | Cook: 240mins | Ready in:

Ingredients

- 1 16-ounce packages dried fettuccine or linguine
- 4 cups chopped cooked chicken*
- 1-1/2 cups thinly bias-sliced celery
- 1/2 cup sliced green onions
- 1/4 cup snipped fresh cilantro or parsley
- 1 8-ounce bottle Asian vinaigrette salad dressing
- 2 teaspoons sesame seeds, toasted

Direction

- Cook fettuccine according to package directions; drain. Rinse with cold water; drain again. Transfer fettuccine to a very large bowl. Stir in chicken, celery, green onions, and cilantro. Pour dressing over all; toss to coat well. Cover and chill for 4 to 24 hours. Just before serving, sprinkle with sesame seeds.

79. Citrus Walnut Pasta Salad For Those Walnut Pasta Lovers Recipe

Serving: 6 | Prep: | Cook: 15mins | Ready in:

Ingredients

- 3/4 cup chopped walnuts
- 3 cups bow tie pasta
- 1 cup smoked cheese such as Gouda
- 1 cup celery and cut thin in diagonal slices
- 1/3 cup finely chopped red onion
- 3 tablespoons fresh chives
- 2 tablespoons chopped fresh parseley
- Dressing:
- 1/3 cup fresh orange juice
- 1/4 cup fresh lemon
- 4 tablespoons evoo extra virgin olive oil
- 1 tablespoon stone ground mustard
- ground pepper to taste
- 2 teaspoons rice vinegar

Direction

- Here we go
- Place walnuts on a cookie sheet and bake for about eight to ten minutes. This makes salad terrific...
- Cook pasta according to directions
- Put dressing ingredients in a large bowl and use whisk to blend
- Add pasta, cheese, celery, red onion, walnuts, chives and parsley to the dressing mix and serve.
- If you want to you can add chicken if you are not a vegetarian....
- I eat it without chicken but it goes with chicken, too....
- Enjoy this light and yummy salad loaded with good stuff.

80. Classic Macaroni Salad

Serving: 12 | Prep: | Cook: 10mins |Ready in:

Ingredients

- 1 cup mayonnaise
- ¼ cup white vinegar
- 2 tablespoons Dijon mustard
- 2 teaspoons kosher salt, or more to taste
- ½ teaspoon ground black pepper

- ⅛ teaspoon cayenne pepper
- 1 tablespoon white sugar, or more to taste
- 1 cup finely diced celery
- ¾ cup diced red bell pepper
- ½ cup grated carrot
- ½ cup chopped green onions, white and light parts
- ¼ cup diced jalapeno pepper
- ¼ cup diced poblano pepper
- 1 (16 ounce) package uncooked elbow macaroni
- 1 tablespoon mayonnaise
- 1 tablespoon water

Direction

- Whisk 1 cup mayonnaise, vinegar, Dijon mustard, salt, black pepper, and cayenne pepper together in a bowl until well blended; whisk in sugar. Stir in celery, red bell pepper, carrot, onions, and jalapeno and poblano peppers. Refrigerate until macaroni is ready to dress.
- Bring a large pot of well salted water to a boil. Cook elbow macaroni in the boiling water, stirring occasionally until cooked through, 8 to 10 minutes. Drain but do not rinse. Allow macaroni to drain in a colander about 5 minutes, shaking out moisture from time to time. Pour macaroni into large bowl; toss to separate and cool to room temperature. Macaroni should be sticky.
- Pour dressing over macaroni and stir until dressing is evenly distributed. Cover with plastic wrap. Refrigerate at least 4 hours or, ideally, overnight to allow dressing to absorb into the macaroni.
- Stir salad before serving. Mix 1 tablespoon mayonnaise and 1 tablespoon water into salad for fresher look.
- Nutrition Facts
- Per Serving:
- 294.5 calories; protein 5.4g 11% DV; carbohydrates 32g 10% DV; fat 16.1g 25% DV; cholesterol 7.4mg 3% DV; sodium 508.1mg 20% DV.

81. Classic Macaroni Salad Recipe

Serving: 8 | Prep: | Cook: 10mins | Ready in:

Ingredients

- 2 cups cooked macaroni
- 2 eggs hard boiled and chopped
- 1/4 cup chopped celery
- 1/4 cup chopped onion
- 1/2 cup mayonnaise or salad dressing
- 2 teaspoons sugar
- 2 teaspoons vinegar
- 1/2 teaspoon salt
- 1/2 teaspoon prepared mustard
- 1 teaspoon freshly ground black pepper

Direction

- Combine all ingredients and stir well.
- Cover and chill for several hours before serving.

82. Club Pasta Salad Recipe

Serving: 8 | Prep: | Cook: 10mins | Ready in:

Ingredients

- 1 8oz.. package of rotini (tri-colored looks nice) cooked and cooled
- 1 Med. onion diced
- 2 tomatoes diced
- 1 cup of fresh cleaned spinach
- 1 cup of dice turkey (can use leftover deli meat)
- 1 cup of dice ham (can use leftover deli meat)
- 1/2 cup crumbled bacon
- 1 cup of shredded cheddar cheese
- 1 cup of ranch dressing
- 1/2 cup of mayo
- 2 tsp of salt
- 1 tsp of black pepper

- 1 tsp. of dill

Direction

- Mix together all ingredients chill and serve.

83. Cold Italian Pasta Salad Recipe

Serving: 15 | Prep: | Cook: 10mins | Ready in:

Ingredients

- 1 Box spiral noodles
- 2-3 Med. tomatoes
- 1-2 Med. green peppers
- 1 Med. onion
- 1 Sm. jar green olives
- 1 Sm. jar black olives
- 1/4 Lb. Each:
- hard salami
- Capacola (can substitute ham)
- pepperoni
- provolone cheese
- sharp cheddar cheese
- Dressing:
- 1 C olive oil (vegetable oil is ok too!)
- 3/4 C cider vinegar
- 1 Tbs sugar
- 1 tsp oregano

Direction

- Boil noodles according to box instructions. Drain well.
- Chop tomato, onion, pepper, olives, salami, capicola, pepperoni, provolone and cheddar into bite sized pieces and put into the bowl.
- Add the noodles.
- Dressing:
- Add oil, vinegar, sugar and oregano into a blender and mix well.
- Pour over all ingredients and toss gently.
- See if you can actually wait for it to chill for several hours! :)

- Enjoy the amazing blend of colors, smells and best of all, flavors!

84. Cold Salmon Pasta Salad Recipe

Serving: 6 | Prep: | Cook: 60mins | Ready in:

Ingredients

- 1 box of shaped pasta (angel hair, linguine and spaghetti won't work)
- 1 can of salmon or left over cooked salmon
- 1 small can of chopped or sliced black olives
- 1 small onion chopped
- 1 tomato chopped
- Mayo
- salt & pepper to taste
- tarragon
- dill

Direction

- Cook pasta al dente and let cool.
- In a mixing bowl mix the salmon, black olives, onion and tomatoes together.
- Add the cooled pasta to the bowl and mix with above ingredients.
- Take about 2 spoonfuls of mayo and mix into the mixture, it should be coated but not creamy.
- Add salt, pepper, dill and tarragon to taste.
- Put the mixture in the refrigerator for at least one hour to cool. Be sure to cover it.
- When you take it out of the fridge, it may need a little mayo that's ok, just add to the mixture and serve.

85. Cold Spaghetti Salad Recipe

Serving: 0 | Prep: | Cook: 25mins | Ready in:

Ingredients

- ~ 16 oz. box angel hair spaghetti
- ~ 1 Large bottle Kraft Zesty Italian Dressing
- ~ 1 bottle McCormick Salad Supreme (found in the spice section of grocery store, Secret ingredient!)
- ~ 2 Med. - Lg tomatos
- ~ 1 cucumber
- ~ 1 Green or red pepper
- ~ 1 small onion (I like to use sweet onion like Vidalia)

Direction

- ~ Cook spaghetti according to box, rinse and set aside
- ~ dice all veggies in small pieces
- ~ put all ingredients into large bowl (spaghetti, Italian dressing, McCormick Salad Supreme, tomatoes, cucumber, green pepper and onion.
- ~ Mix well and refrigerate overnight.
- ~ YUM!

86. Colorful And Fruity Pasta Salad Recipe

Serving: 25 | Prep: | Cook: 15mins | Ready in:

Ingredients

- 1 1-pound package campanelle (bellflower) pasta or bow-tie pasta
- 8 ounces fresh sugar snap or snow pea pods, trimmed (2-1/2 cups)
- 3 cups cubed honeydew melon
- 1 cup purchased poppyseed dressing
- 1-1/2 teaspoons finely shredded orange peel
- 4 cups strawberries, hulled and quartered lengthwise
- 1-1/2 cups honey-roasted cashews (optional)
- Additional purchased poppyseed dressing

Direction

- In a Dutch oven or large pot cook pasta in salted water according to the package directions, adding the pea pods to the pasta the last 1 minute of cooking. Drain pasta and pea pods. Rinse with cold water and drain again. Transfer to a very large mixing bowl. Add melon and toss to combine.
- In a small bowl stir together the dressing and orange peel. Add to pasta mixture and toss to coat. Cover and chill up to 24 hours.
- To serve, gently stir in the strawberries and, if desired, nuts. If necessary, stir in up to 1/2 cup additional poppy seed dressing to moisten. Transfer to a serving bowl

87. Cool Pasta Salad With Fresh Basil Vinaigrette Recipe

Serving: 8 | Prep: | Cook: 15mins | Ready in:

Ingredients

- 6 boneless chicken breasts, grilled or roasted and diced
- 1 box (1 lb.) curly-que shaped noodles (I like gemelli)
- 2 jars marinated artichoke hearts
- 2 avocado, pitted
- 1 jar capers, drained
- 4 roma tomatoes
- 4 scallions
- fresh basil DRESSING:
- 1 cup fresh basil
- 2/3 cup good olive oil
- 1/4 cup red wine vinegar
- juice of one lemon
- garlic clove, crushed
- 1 tablespoon Dijon mustard
- 1/4 tsp cayenne pepper (optional)
- 1/2 tsp black pepper
- salt to taste

Direction

- Cook the noodles in a large pot of lightly salted water for 8 minutes. I like to add a bit of olive oil to the water for boiling.
- Rinse noodles in cool water immediately to stop cooking process. You're going for an al dente' texture with the noodles.
- Chop the avocado, artichokes (drained), tomatoes and scallions.
- Toss into the bowl with above ingredients.
- For the dressing: Blend everything in a small-bowl food processor until uniform consistency is achieved. Toss with salad ingredients.
- Best when chilled for a few hours before eating.
- Enjoy!!
- NOTE: If you're making this ahead of time, wait until last minute to add the avocado. Just chop it up before you leave, toss it in some lemon juice, keep it cool in a Tupperware container and add it to the salad at the venue. Avocado likes to go bad pretty quickly!! --Kn0x--

88. Corn And Tomato Pasta Salad Recipe

Serving: 8 | Prep: | Cook: 120mins | Ready in:

Ingredients

- 1-1/2 cups bow-tie pasta
- 2 fresh ears of corn or 1 cup whole kernel frozen corn
- 1 cup shredded, cooked chicken
- 1 large tomato, seeded and chopped (about 3/4 cup)
- 1/4 cup olive oil
- 3 tablespoons vinegar
- 2 to 3 tablespoons pesto
- 1 tablespoon chicken broth or water
- 1/4 teaspoon salt
- 1/8 teaspoon pepper
- Romaine leaves

- 2 tablespoons finely shredded parmesan cheese
- Snipped fresh basil

Direction

- Cook pasta according to package directions. Drain pasta, rinse in cold water, and drain again. Meanwhile, if using fresh corn, cut the kernels off the cobs. Cook corn, covered, in boiling water for 10 minutes or until corn is tender; drain. (If using frozen corn, cook according to package directions; drain.) Let cool slightly.
- In a large bowl combine pasta, corn, chicken, and tomato. In a screw-top jar combine the olive oil, vinegar, pesto, chicken broth or water, salt, and pepper. Cover and shake well. Pour over pasta mixture; toss gently to coat. Cover and chill for at least 2 hours or up to 24 hours.
- To serve, line a serving platter with romaine leaves. Arrange salad on romaine leaves. Sprinkle Parmesan cheese and basil over top.

89. Couscous Salad Recipe

Serving: 6 | Prep: | Cook: 10mins | Ready in:

Ingredients

- For the dressing
- 2 T . Olive oil
- 2 T . Fresh lemon juice
- 1/4 t.. Salt
- Ground black pepper to taste
- For the salad
- 1 1/2 cups of water , or chicken broth
- 1 t. olive oil
- 1 cup couscous
- 1 cup quartered cherry or grape tomatoes
- 5 T. pitted , sliced Kalamata olives
- 5 T. fresh parsley , chopped
- 4 o.z. feta cheese , crumbled

Direction

- Whisk dressing ingredients in a small bowl, and set aside.
- In medium sauce pan, heat water, (or chicken broth), and olive oil to a boil.
- Stir in couscous, cover and remove from heat.
- Let stand 3 mins. Uncover, and fluff with a fork.
- Place couscous in a medium serving bowl.
- Pour dressing ingredients over couscous, and toss with a fork.
- Add tomatoes, olives, parsley, and feta cheese. Toss to combine.
- Serve hot, or at room temp.

90. Crab And Pasta Salad Recipe

Serving: 6 | Prep: | Cook: | Ready in:

Ingredients

- 1 (12 ounce) package tri-colored spiral pasta
- 1 small head broccoli, cut into bite-size pieces
- 1 small head cauliflower, cut into bite-size pieces
- 2 chopped tomatoes
- 1/2 cup chopped chives or onion
- 12 ounces crabmeat, or imitation crabmeat
- 1 (16 ounce) bottle creamy Italian salad dressing

Direction

- Cook pasta in boiling salted water until al dente.
- Drain and rinse.
- In a large bowl combine the broccoli, cauliflower, tomatoes, chives, crabmeat and pasta.
- Pour entire bottle of oil and vinegar salad dressing over all and toss to coat.

91. Crab Cake Pasta Salad Recipe

Serving: 0 | Prep: | Cook: | Ready in:

Ingredients

- 8-12 oz Louisiana Lump crab meat
- 1 Box of elbow macaroni
- 1 Tablespoon Liquid crab Boil   1 Tablespoon of garlic
- 1 shallot finely diced
- 1 red bell pepper cut into matchsticks
- ¼ Cup finely chopped celery
- ¼ Cup chopped fresh parsley
- Remoulade Sauce
- ½ Cup Mayo
- salt and pepper
- cajun seasoning of your choice
- lemon   1 Cup panko bread Crumbs
- 1 Bunch of chives

Direction

- Bring water to a boil according to instructions. Add 1 tablespoon of salt and 1 tablespoon of crab boil and pasta. Cook as directed. Drain, reserving 1 cup of pasta water, and set aside in a large bowl to cool.
- Sauté garlic and shallot in a small pan with about a teaspoon of oil or butter for 3 minutes on low heat. *Deglaze with a splash of white wine. Add to cooling pasta.
- To the pasta add peppers, celery and parsley and stir to combine.
- Whisk together equal parts Remoulade sauce and mayo. Add a bit of pasta water to loosen if necessary. Season with Cajun seasoning to taste. Stir into pasta mixture.
- Gently fold crab into pasta salad and chill for 10-15 minutes in the fridge. At this point you could add more seasoning if you want it spicier.
- When ready to serve, place in a bowl and sprinkle toasted bread crumbs and chopped chives.
- * White wine can be left out entirely based on preference.

92. Crab Pasta Salad Recipe

Serving: 4 | Prep: | Cook: 20mins | Ready in:

Ingredients

- 12 ounce package tri colored swirl pasta
- 1 small head broccoli cut into bite size pieces
- 1 small head cauliflower cut into bite size pieces
- 2 chopped tomatoes
- 1/2 cup chopped chives
- 12 ounces crabmeat
- 16 ounce bottle oil and vinegar salad dressing

Direction

- Cook pasta in boiling salted water until al dente then drain well and rinse.
- In large bowl combine broccoli, cauliflower, tomatoes, chives, crabmeat and pasta.
- Pour entire bottle of oil and vinegar salad dressing over all and toss to coat.

93. Crab Seafood Pasta Salad Recipe

Serving: 6 | Prep: | Cook: 12mins | Ready in:

Ingredients

- 12 ounces medium pasta shells
- salt
- 1/2 pound imitation crab meat, broken into pieces
- 1 cup mayonnaise
- 1/2 cup buttermilk
- 4 green onions, thinly sliced
- 1/4 cup EACH red and green pepper
- 2 stalks celery chopped
- 1 lemon, juiced

- 1 teaspoon chopped scallion
- 1/2 teaspoon chopped garlic
- 1/2 teaspoon seasoned salt
- 2 tablespoons chopped parsley
- salt and pepper to taste

Direction

- Cook the pasta in a large pot of boiling, salted water until al dente, 10 to 12 minutes. Rinse, drain and set aside.
- Meanwhile, in a large bowl, combine the crab, mayonnaise, buttermilk, onions, peppers, celery, lemon juice, scallion, garlic, seasoned salt, parsley and pepper to taste. Add the pasta shells and mix again. Cover and chill overnight.
- Enjoy

94. Crab Pasta Salad Recipe

Serving: 4 | Prep: | Cook: 30mins | Ready in:

Ingredients

- 8 oz. uncooked medium pasta shells
- 1 pound creamy coleslaw
- 1/2 cup mayoniase
- 1 Tbs. chopped onion
- 1 tsp. dill weed
- dash salt
- 2 cups chopped imatation crab

Direction

- Cook pasta according to package. Meanwhile in large serving bowl combine coleslaw mayonnaise onion dill salt Stir in crab
- Drain pasta rinse in cold water
- Add coleslaw to mixture toss to coat. Chill until ready to serve
- Yields 4 servings
- To all the seafood lovers

95. Crazy Spirals Pasta Salad Recipe

Serving: 5 | Prep: | Cook: 10mins | Ready in:

Ingredients

- 1 Bag of spiral pasta
- 2 Bunches of green onion
- 1 green pepper
- 2 red peppers
- 1 red onion
- 1 Brick of feta
- Lg pinch of opal basil and sweet basil, or just plain basil if thats all you have
- 1 cucumber
- 1/2 cup of cider vinager
- 2T of lime juice
- Lg pinch of garlic powder
- Lg pinch of salt and pepper
- 1 cup of olive oil
- 1T of margrine

Direction

- Cook pasta till edible, coat lightly with margarine and set aside to cool
- Chop 1 bunch of green onions coarsely
- Julienne the green pepper, one and half of the red pepper, and the cucumber
- Dice the red onion
- Crumble the feta
- Chop the basil
- Combine the newly chopped peppers, onions, cucumber, basil and feta with the cooled down pasta
- Finely chop the rest of the green onions
- Finely dice the rest of the red peppers
- Combine the newly chopped green onions and red peppers to the cider vinegar, lime juice, garlic powder, and salt and pepper. Mix.
- While whisking, slowly add the olive oil
- Pour the newly made dressing over top of the pasta salad and toss.

96. Creamy Caesar Pasta Salad Recipe

Serving: 10 | Prep: | Cook: 8mins | Ready in:

Ingredients

- 1 bag Tri color pasta
- Head of broccoli, cut into florets
- cheese cubes
- about 1/2 cup fresh parmesan cheese
- pepper to taste
- a few shakes of garlic powder (opt...gives it a slightly stronger garlic flavor))
- 1 bottle Cardini caesar salad dressing (or your own, homemade)
- _____

- **I don't really use measurements on this one...it's a matter of personal taste

Direction

- Boil pasta until cooked, but still slightly firm
- Allow to cool completely
- Lightly steam broccoli (about 1 minute)...do not overcook!
- Mix all ingredients together
- Refrigerate for an hour, or overnight.
- Serve cold
- **I usually use 2/3 of the bottled dressing, and reserve the remaining 1/3 to mix in right before serving.
- ***you can add cut up chicken for a complete meal
- ****Great at bridal and baby showers and pot luck, tailgate or block parties

97. Creamy Chicken Pasta Salad Recipe

Serving: 6 | Prep: | Cook: 10mins | Ready in:

Ingredients

- CHILL TIME 3 HOURS
- 1 can (10 3/4 ounces) Campbell's® Healthy Request® condensed cream of celery soup
- 1/2 cup plain low-fat yogurt
- 1/4 cup water
- 2 tbsp. dijon-style mustard
- 1 tbsp. vinegar
- 1/8 tsp. ground black pepper
- 4 cups corkscrew-shaped pasta, cooked without salt
- 2 stalks celery, sliced (about 1 cup)
- 1 cup diced tomato
- 2 cups cubed cooked chicken

Direction

- Stir the soup, yogurt, water, mustard, vinegar and pepper with a whisk or fork in a large bowl. Add the pasta, celery, tomato and chicken, tossing until well coated.
- Cover and refrigerate the salad for at least 3 hours. Stir

98. Creamy Chipotle Salad Recipe

Serving: 10 | Prep: | Cook: 45mins | Ready in:

Ingredients

- CREAMY CHIPOTLE SALAD
- Sweet Tomatoes Restaurant Copycat Recipe
- Serves 10
- 10 cups water
- 1 tablespoon salt
- 1 pound whole wheat penne pasta
- 1 tablespoon canola oil
- 1 1/3 cups mayonnaise
- 3 tablespoons soy sauce
- 3 tablespoons fresh lemon juice
- 1 1/2 tablespoons brown sugar
- 1 tablespoon vegetable base powder
- 2 teaspoons chipotle pepper in adobo sauce (puree)

- 2 teaspoons finely minced garlic
- 1 3/4 cups canned kidney beans (drained and rinsed)
- 1 1/2 cups frozen corn
- 1 1/2 cups 1/4 inch julienne red bell pepper
- 1 cup sliced black olives
- 3/4 cup canned diced green chilies
- 1/2 cup chopped cilantro

Direction

- Pasta: In a large pot bring water and salt to a boil. Add pasta and cook until al dente (soft, but still firm). Immediately drain pasta and flash cool in cold water. Drain water. Coast pasta with oil to prevent sticking.
- Dressing: Combine mayonnaise, soy sauce, fresh lemon juice, brown sugar, vegetable base powder, chipotle pepper in adobo sauce, and minced garlic. Blend all ingredients with either a stick blender or a blender until emulsified.
- To assemble: in a large bowl combine pasta, kidney beans, corn, red bell pepper, black olive, red onion, green chilies, and cilantro. Stir to combine. Pour dressing over all and mix until well blended. Store in an air tight container for at least 30 minutes before serving for best flavor.

99. Creamy Pasta And Corn Salad Recipe

Serving: 4 | Prep: | Cook: | Ready in:

Ingredients

- 1 english cucumber chopped
- 1 green pepper, chopped
- 1 red pepper, chopped
- 1 medium onion, chopped
- ½ bunch parsley, finely chopped (or as desired)
- 1 tin corn kernels, drained
- 500 spiral noodles or shells salt and pepper to taste

- 1 Tsp mixed herbs
- 250 ml mayonnaise

Direction

- Toss all ingredients together and mix with mayonnaise.
- Serve on the side of your favorite meat at your next bbq

100. Creamy Tuna Pasta Salad Recipe

Serving: 8 | Prep: | Cook: 20mins | Ready in:

Ingredients

- 1 POUND pasta(I USED THE MINI SHELLS)
- 1 CUP MAYO
- 2/3 CUP SOUR CRAM
- 1/3 CUP ranch dressing
- DASH OF MINCED dried onions
- DASH OF garlic powder
- 1 POUND BAG OF frozen peas
- 2 6 OZ.CANS OF tuna(DRAINED)
- 1 SMALL JAR stuffed green olives(DRAINED)

Direction

- BOIL PASTA ACCORDING TO DIRECTIONS
- WHILE PASTA COOKS
- THAW PEAS IN COLLINDER RUN WARM WATER OVER UNTIL
- THAWED (ABOUT 30 SECONDS SHOULD DO IT)
- IN LARGE BOWL COMBINE MAYO, SOUR CREAM, RANCH DRESSING, MINCED DRIED ONIONS AND GARLIC POWDER
- WHEN PASTA IS DONE - TAKE PEAS OUT OF COLLIDER - PLACE IN LARGE BOWL - ADD DRAINED TUNA - MIX GENTLY
- DRAIN PASTA AND RUN COLD WATER OVER TO COOL
- DRAIN WELL ADD TO BOWL WITH PEAS AND TUNA

- ADD DRAINED STUFFED GREEN OLIVES
- PLACE MAYO/SOUR CREAM DRESSING AND MIX ALL TOGETHER
- COVER AND PLACE IN FRIDGE TO LET THE FLAVORS ABSORB TOGETHER!

101. Creole Macaroni Salad Recipe

Serving: 6 | Prep: | Cook: 15mins | Ready in:

Ingredients

- 4 cups cooked macaroni (6 or 7 ounces or 2 cups uncooked)
- 2 cups diced tomatoes
- 1 cup grated sharp cheddar cheese, or your favorite!
- 1 cup mayonnaise
- 1/4 cup sliced pimiento stuffed olives
- 1/2 small onion, grated
- 1 - 2 cloves garlic, more or less, depending on your taste
- 1/8 teaspoon cayenne pepper, or more if you like

Direction

- If macaroni is uncooked, prepare according to package directions, boiling until tender, but not mushy, blanch (rinse well in cold water), drain until thoroughly dry.
- Mix all together.
- Refrigerate several hours (at least 4), or overnight.
- Can be served on lettuce leaves or just as it is.
- Enjoy!

102. Crunchy Shrimp Pasta Salad Recipe

Serving: 7 | Prep: | Cook: 10mins | Ready in:

Ingredients

- 1/2 C fat-free cottage cheese
- 1 Tbl. fresh lemon juice
- 1 Tbl. olive oil
- 1 Tbl. light mayonnaise
- 1/2 tsp. salt
- 1/4 to 1/2 tsp. black pepper
- 1/8 tsp. hot sauce
- 1 1/2 C chopped cooked shrimp
- 3 C cooked elbow macaroni (about 1 1/2 C uncooked)
- 1 C chopped cauliflower florets
- 1/3 C sliced pimiento-stuffed olives
- 1/3 C finely chopped red bell pepper
- 1/3 C finely chopped green bell pepper
- 1/3 C chopped onion
- 1 Tbl. chopped fresh cilantro (I omit this)

Direction

- Place the cottage cheese in a food processor; process until smooth.
- Combine cheese, juice, and next 5 ingredients (juice through hot sauce), stirring well with a whisk.
- Add shrimp; toss well.
- Add pasta and remaining ingredients; toss well.
- Cover and chill completely.

103. Cucumber Pasta Salad Recipe

Serving: 8 | Prep: | Cook: 10mins | Ready in:

Ingredients

- 1 box Mostaccioli noodles
- 2 Large cucumbers
- 1 bunch green onions
- 1 C sugar
- 1 C apple cider vinegar
- 1/2 C vegetable oil
- 2 T dry mustard

- 1 tsp garlic powder
- 1 T parsley flakes

Direction

- Cook pasta according to directions on box, use cold rinse
- Peel cucumbers and cut into bite size pieces
- Chop green onion into pieces, greens and all
- Take large plastic bowl with lid that seals tight
- Mix together the remaining ingredients in the large bowl
- Add cucumber pieces, chopped onion, and cooked pasta
- Toss all ingredients together
- Seal lid onto bowl and shake it up to mix all ingredients together
- Refrigerate Before Serving
- The trick to this salad is storing it upside down in the refrigerator
- The flavor stays at the top and mixes back through the pasta when served instead of settling to the bottom of the bowl

104.   DARLAS PASTA SALAD Recipe

Serving: 6 | Prep: | Cook: 15mins | Ready in:

Ingredients

- 1 lb. Tricolor pasta; cooked & drained
- 1 lg. Onion; chopped
- 5 stalks Celery; chopped
- 1 Whole green pepper; seeded & chopped
- 1 can Pitted black olives; coarsely chopped
- (4-oz.) can mushroom (may use fresh)
- 1 Whole plum tomato; peeled and chopped
- (8-oz.) Feta Cheese; crumbled
- 1/2 c. pine nuts (optional)
- 1/2 c. balsamic vinegar
- 1/2 c. olive oil

Direction

- Mix all ingredients and chill.

105.   Dad's Pasta Salad Recipe

Serving: 10 | Prep: | Cook: 45mins | Ready in:

Ingredients

- 1 box of tri colored rotini
- 2 cans of drained black olives - sliced
- 2 roma tomatoes
- 1 avacado (optional)
- 2 carrots
- 5 radishes
- 1 cucumber
- 1 bottle of Italian dressing (any brand)
- salt and pepper

Direction

- Cook rotini until firm - do not overcook.
- Drain and run cold water over noodles while straining until noodles are no longer hot.
- Put noodles in a covered bowl in refrigerator.
- Cut up carrots, cucumber, radishes, avocado (optional), and tomatoes in small pieces.
- Add vegies and drained sliced black olives to noodles, stir and add 1 bottle (give or take) of Italian dressing.
- Add salt and pepper to taste.
- Refrigerate another 15-20 minutes then serve.

106.   Deep Dish Mexican Salad Recipe

Serving: 8 | Prep: | Cook: 20mins | Ready in:

Ingredients

- 8 ox corkscrew pasta
- 3 limes,zested and juiced
- 1/4 c vegetable oil

- 1/4 c fresh cilantro
- 1 Tb chopped garlic
- 2 c tortilla chips
- 2 tsp ea.Dijon mustard and honey
- 1/2 tsp ground cumin
- 6 c chopped romaine
- 2 lg. tomatoes,chopped
- 1 c each canned black beans and corn kernals
- 1/2 c ea. chopped red onions,sliced black olives,and shredded Mexican blend cheese
- 1 small fresh jalapeno pepper,sliced

Direction

- Cook pasta according to directions. Drain, rinse in cold water.
- In bowl, whisk together 1/4 c lime juice, 1 tsp. lime zest, oil, cilantro garlic, Dijon, mustard, honey and cumin. Season with salt and ground black pepper, if desired. In separate bowl, gently toss pasta with 1/2 dressing mixture.
- In large serving bowl, layer lettuce, tomatoes, pasta, beans, corn, red onions, olives, cheese and jalapeno pepper as desired. Drizzle with remaining dressing.
- Arrange tortilla chips around top of bowl. Garnish with fresh cilantro, if desired...

107.   Deli Style Pasta Salad Recipe

Serving: 4 | Prep: | Cook: 15mins | Ready in:

Ingredients

- 1/2 of a 16-ounce package (about 2 cups) frozen cheese-filled tortellini or one 9-ounce package refrigerated cheese-filled tortellini
- 1 1/2 cups broccoli flowerets
- 1 large carrot, thinly sliced
- 1/4 cup white wine vinegar
- 2 tablespoons olive oil
- 1 teaspoon dried Italian seasoning, crushed
- 1 teaspoon dijon-style mustard

- 1/4 teaspoon black pepper
- 1/8 teaspoon garlic powder
- 1 medium red or yellow sweet pepper, cut into thin strips

Direction

- In a large saucepan cook pasta according to package directions, except omit any salt and oil. Add broccoli and carrot the last 3 minutes of cooking; drain. Rinse with cold water; drain again.
- Meanwhile, for dressing, in a screw-top jar combine the vinegar, oil, Italian seasoning, mustard, black pepper, and garlic powder. Cover and shake well. Set aside.
- In a large bowl combine the pasta mixture and sweet pepper. Shake dressing. Pour the dressing over pasta mixture; toss gently to coat.

108.   Dill Orzo Pasta Salad With Cucumber And Feta Recipe

Serving: 8 | Prep: | Cook: 10mins | Ready in:

Ingredients

- orzo pasta Salad with Tomato, cucumber, red onions and feta Ingredients
- 1 lb orzo pasta
- 1 sm English cucumber; peeled,
- 1/4 c olive oil
- 1/2 c Coarsely chopped fresh dill (or more, to taste)
- 1 cup champagne vinegar
- 1/2 c rice wine vinegar
- 1 sm Red onion; minced
- 1/2 lb Feta cheese; crumbled (FRENCH FETA is creamier and works best)
- 1 lg clove garlic; minced
- salt and pepper
- 1 pt Yellow cherry tomatoes

Direction

- Instructions for Orzo Pasta Salad with Tomato, Cucumber, Red Onions and Feta
- Boil orzo until just tender, about 8 minutes.
- Drain and transfer to a bowl.
- Add vinegar immediately and let cool a bit.
- Add oil, onion, dill and garlic and stir well.
- When pasta is cooled to room temp, add cherry tomatoes, cucumber, dill and vinegar. Add feta, salt and pepper and stir gently.
- Chill for several hours to allow flavors to meld.

109.   EASY SUMMER PASTA SALAD Recipe

Serving: 4 | Prep: | Cook: | Ready in:

Ingredients

- 1 C. uncooked small shell shaped pasta
- 2 C. frozen peas (do not thaw)
- 1 C. thinly sliced celery
- 1/2 C. chopped sweet red pepper
- 1/4 C. shredded carrots
- scant 1/4 C. chopped green onion
- 1 C. cooked cubed ham
- 1/4 tsp. salt
- Dash of ground black pepper
- 3/4 C. mayonnaise

Direction

- Cook pasta according to package directions. Drain well and put in a large bowl. Add all of the remaining ingredients and stir gently to combine. Cover tightly and refrigerate until ready to serve. Stir again just before serving.
- Note: You can easily make as much or as little as you want by adjusting the amounts of the ingredients. To save time on the prep, get the small amounts of vegetables needed from the salad bar at your local grocery store.

110.   Easty Pasta Salad Recipe

Serving: 8 | Prep: | Cook: 2mins | Ready in:

Ingredients

- Any kind of pasta (even spaghetti probably. I like elbow mac)
- Bottle of Italian dressing
- Container of italian seasonings (like the 50 cent kind at W-Mart)
- Red and green sweet bell peppers
- A roma tomato or two
- Anything else you like in pasta salad :)

Direction

- Cook pasta till done
- Drain pasta and rinse in cool water
- Put pasta in a bowl
- Put Italian dressing on (to taste)
- Cut up the bell peppers and tomato and throw 'em in :)
- Finish with seasonings, crab meat, pepperoni, and olives, whatever
- Toss and add more dressing till evenly coated and tastes good :)

111.   Easy Italian Pasta Salad Recipe

Serving: 12 | Prep: | Cook: 15mins | Ready in:

Ingredients

- Salad:
- 1 bag (16 oz.) Tri-color radiatore or rotini pasta
- 1 ½ c. fresh broccoli florets, cut into about ½" – ¾" florets
- 1 c. bell pepper (red, orange, or yellow are prettiest, but green's okay) chopped
- ½ c. scallions (green onions), sliced

- 1 c. (8 oz.) mozzarella cheese, cut into small ½" cubes
- ¾ c. Fresh shredded parmesan cheese
- 1 small pk. Sliced pepperoni, sliced into thin strips
- 1 small pk. Sliced Italian dried salami, sliced into thin strips
- 1 small jar Marinated button mushrooms, drained and sliced in half
- 1 small jar marinated artichoke hearts, drained and cut into bite size pieces
- 1 can Large black olives, drained and cut in half
- ½ c. oil-packed, sun dried tomatoes drained and sliced into thin strips
- Dressing:
- 1 bottle (8 oz.) Kraft Zesty Italian salad dressing (try Kraft roasted red pepper Italian, too)
- 1 c. mayonnaise

Direction

- Boil pasta according to package directions, adding the broccoli during the last 1 - 2 minutes of cooking time. To get the best result, test a noodle; if it's almost done, add the broccoli. Drain the pasta and broccoli in a colander and rinse with cold water until cool.
- Prepare other ingredients as directed. At least 4 hours before serving, put everything into a large bowl except for the dressing ingredients and set aside.
- Mix the salad dressing and mayonnaise in a small bowl, whisk to combine well. Pour half of the dressing over salad ingredients and stir to combine. Cover and refrigerate at least 4 hours. Refrigerate remaining dressing. The salad will absorb a lot of the dressing while it is chilling. Before serving, check the salad; it may need to be re-dressed. If so, just add enough of the remaining dressing until the salad is coated to your liking. Chill until ready to serve.

112.   Easy Macaroni Salad Recipe

Serving: 10 | Prep: | Cook: 10mins | Ready in:

Ingredients

- 3 cups elbow macaroni
- 1/2 cup mayonaise
- 1/2 cup lemon poppyseed salad dressing
- 1 carrot
- 1 red pepper
- 2 green onions
- 1/2 green olive slices
- 1 can corn
- 1 can chicken

Direction

- Cook the macaroni in a large pot of boiling salted water, drain and rinse with cold water until it is cool
- Peel and dice the carrot
- Seed and dice the red pepper
- Finely slice the onion
- Drain the corn, chicken, and olives
- Combine all ingredients in a large bowl
- It tastes better if it has a couple hours in the fridge for the flavours to mix.

113.   Easy Pasta Salad Recipe

Serving: 4 | Prep: | Cook: 20mins | Ready in:

Ingredients

- 1 pound pasta - shape of your choice
- 1 or 2 carrots, peeled and diced
- 1 small cucumber, cut into bite-sized pieces
- 1 red pepper, cut into dice
- 1 - 2 cups cut up meat, poultry, or fish (salmon has body and works well)
- 1 large tomato, cut up OR a cup of split cherry tomatoes
- Any additional vegetables you like

- 1 cup frozen peas
- 1 envelope Good Seasons Italian dressing, mixed with vinegar and good olive oil
- Grated parmesan cheese to add on top

Direction

- Bring water to a boil and toss in the pasta to cook for the directed time. While you're boiling the water and the pasta cut up all of your vegetables and the protein and mix the dressing. When the pasta is done cooking pour the frozen peas into your colander and then pour the pasta and its water over the peas. The boiling water will defrost them but leave the peas with body. Mix this in with the other vegetables and cut up protein. Pour the prepared dressing over this to taste, some like it wetter than others. Pass the parmesan to top.

114. Easy Ranch Pasta Salad Recipe

Serving: 6 | Prep: | Cook: 60mins | Ready in:

Ingredients

- 1lb small, shaped pasta(shells, rotini, bow ties, etc)
- 16oz sour cream
- 1 packet dry Ranch seasoning mix
- 1/4 cup mayo
- 2 bell peppers, chopped
- 4 green onions, chopped
- 1 bag frozen baby peas. Thawed, but not cooked
- 1 carrot, shredded
- 2 cups colby cheese, shredded

Direction

- Prepare pasta per box directions and immediately rinse with cold water. Let drain.
- Combine sour cream, ranch mix and mayo in large bowl.

- Add pasta and all other remaining ingredients and toss to coat.
- Refrigerate at least 1 hour.
- Stir well before serving and dust with paprika, if desired

115. Easy Seafood Pasta Salad Recipe

Serving: 12 | Prep: | Cook: | Ready in:

Ingredients

- 2 boxes Ranch and bacon pasta Salad mix
- 1 pound cooked salad shrimp
- 1 pound imitation crabmeat-broken into pieces
- 1 tablespoon paprika

Direction

- Prepare pasta salad according to package instructions.
- Gently stir in shrimp and crabmeat.
- Top with paprika.
- Chill at least 1 hour and serve.

116. Easy Tuna Pasta Salad For One Recipe

Serving: 1 | Prep: | Cook: 15mins | Ready in:

Ingredients

- 1/2 cup elbow macaroni
- 1 (3 ounce) can tuna in olive oil, undrained (I use Genova)
- 1 small tomato, chopped
- 1/2 teaspoon dried basil
- 1 teaspoon lemon juice (or less to preference)
- 1 tablespoon grated parmesan cheese (or more to taste)
- salt and pepper (to taste)

Direction

- Cook macaroni according to package directions. Drain and rinse with cold water to cool.
- In a mixing bowl, combine macaroni and tuna (undrained - the olive oil is key to the recipe). Gently break up tuna while mixing.
- Add tomato, basil and lemon juice. Combine well.
- Mix in Parmesan cheese.
- Add salt and pepper to taste. Combine well.
- Chill to allow flavors to blend at least one hour or overnight.

117.   Easy Tuscan Pasta Salad Recipe

Serving: 4 | Prep: | Cook: 10mins | Ready in:

Ingredients

- 2 cups hot cooked penne pasta
- 1 cup quartered cherry tomatoes
- 1 pkg. (4 oz.) ATHENOS Traditional Crumbled feta cheese
- 1/3 cup GOOD seasonS Sun Dried Tomato vinaigrette with roasted red pepper Dressing
- 1/3 cup loosely packed fresh basil leaves, cut into strips
- 1/4 cup chopped red onions

Direction

- COMBINE all ingredients.
- SERVE immediately. Or cover and refrigerate until ready to serve.
- This is so fresh and good. Try it and check out their site!

118.   Easy Whole Wheat Pasta Salad Recipe

Serving: 8 | Prep: | Cook: 30mins | Ready in:

Ingredients

- 1 Lb whole wheat pasta, such as fusilli rotini or penne. (I like Barilla)
- 2 Tbs olive oil
- 2 carrots
- 1 small head broccoli
- 1 cup fresh or frozen peas
- 1 Red or yellow bell pepper, halved and seeded
- 2 celery stalks
- 4 spring onions
- 1 Large tomato
- 1/2 cup pitted black olives
- 1 Cup diced white cheese, feta, mozzarella whatever you like!
- Dressing:
- 3 Tsp balsamic or wine vinegar
- 4 Tbs olive oil
- 1 Tbs Dijon mustard
- 1 tsp sesame seeds
- 2 tsp finely chopped fresh herbs-your choice of parsley, thyme or basil
- salt and fresh ground pepper

Direction

- Bring a large pan of salted water to boil, add the pasta and cook according to the package directions, until al dente'. Drain and rinse under cold water to stop the cooking process. Drain well and add to large mixing bowl. Toss with the olive oil and allow to cool.
- Lightly blanch the carrots, broccoli and peas in large pan of boiling water.
- Drain and rinse with cold water. Drain well.
- Chop the cooled carrots and broccoli, then add to the pasta with the peas.
- Slice the celery, pepper, spring onions and tomato in small pieces. Add to the salad mix with the olives.

- Prepare the dressing, buy whisking the vinegar with the oil and the mustard in a small bowl. Stir in the sesame seeds and the mixed herbs and season with salt and pepper. Whisk all to combine then pour over the salad mixture. Toss all together, then stir in the cheese.
- Chill for about 30 minutes.
- Add Salt and pepper to taste and serve!

119.   Easy Pasta Salad Recipe

Serving: 1520 | Prep: | Cook: 15mins | Ready in:

Ingredients

- 2 boxes of colored rotini pasta
- 1 crown of broccoli
- 1 crown of cauliflower
- 1 lg purple onion
- 1 lg green pepper
- 1 lg red pepper
- 1 lg yellow pepper
- 1 bag of cheddar cheese crumbles
- 1 lg bottle of robusto Italian dressing

Direction

- Boil water and add pasta
- Make sure pasta is not too over done (pasta tends to get soft from sitting with the veggies and you don't want the pasta to be mush!)
- While pasta is boiling, break up and chop veggies.
- Combine in a large bowl and toss!
- Cool pasta in cold water when done boiling. Drain. Add to veggies.
- Add dressing to your liking.
- Place in fridge for about an hour before serving
- Re toss salad and serve!!!

120.   EuroPasta Salad Recipe

Serving: 6 | Prep: | Cook: 180mins | Ready in:

Ingredients

- 6 artichoke hearts, quartered
- ½ cup pitted and sliced black olives
- ¾ cup roasted red peppers, chopped
- ½ stalk celery, diced
- 2 tsp Dijon mustard
- ¼ cup mayonnaise
- 2 tbsp sweet chili sauce
- 1 tsp black pepper
- ¼ tsp crushed red pepper flakes
- ¼ tsp garlic powder
- 2 cups cooked whole-wheat bow-tie pasta, warm

Direction

- Mix all ingredients but pasta in a small bowl.
- Place pasta in serving dish, pour dressing over and toss well.
- Place in refrigerator for a minimum of 3 hours.
- Toss well before serving.

121.   Fajita Pasta Salad Recipe

Serving: 8 | Prep: | Cook: 12mins | Ready in:

Ingredients

- Dressing
- 1/4 cup lime juice
- 3 teaspoons cumin
- 1/2 teaspoon chili powder
- 1/2 cup packed fresh cilantro
- 1/2 cup olive oil
- Salad
- 8 ounces bowtie pasta, cooked and drained
- 1 (15 ounce) can black beans, drained
- 1 (10 ounce) can shoe peg corn
- 2 medium tomatoes, chopped
- 1 cup favorite salsa

- 2 cups crushed tortilla chips
- 1 cup shredded Mexican or cheddar cheese

Direction

- DRESSING
- Combine first 5 ingredients in food processor or blender.
- Process until almost smooth.
- With machine running, drizzle olive oil in a steady stream.
- SALAD
- Combine pasta with beans, corn, salsa, tomatoes and dressing. Toss to combine.
- Mix in cheese and tortilla chips.

122.   Fantabulous Semi Homemade Mediterranean Pasta Salad Recipe

Serving: 6 | Prep: | Cook: 15mins | Ready in:

Ingredients

- 1 box Betty Crocker Suddenly Salad basil pesto pasta salad mix
- 1/3 cup cold water
- 3 TBS olive oil
- 2 cups grilled chicken, cut into cubes
- 1 cup grape tomatoes, halved
- 1. Large cucumber , peeled and coarsely chopped
- 4 oz (1 cup) crumbled feta cheese
- 1 can (2 1/4 oz) sliced ripe olives, drained. (I used black olives)
- 1 can sliced mushrooms, drained and chopped

Direction

- Cook and drain pasta as directed on box.
- In large bowl, stir together seasoning mix, water olive oil; stir in chicken.
- Add drained pasta and remaining ingredients to chicken mixture. Refrigerate at least 1 hour.
- Cover; refrigerate any remaining salad.

123.   Feta And Tomato Pasta Salad Recipe

Serving: 6 | Prep: | Cook: 15mins | Ready in:

Ingredients

- 1 lb bowtie pasta
- about 1/4 c pesto
- pint of cherry tomatoes cut in half
- about 6 oz feta cheese crumbled

Direction

- Cook bowties
- Drain pasta and mix in pesto
- Once pasta is cooled stir in tomatoes and goat cheese.
- Makes a great side dish for grilled chicken or as a meal itself.
- See the alterations for second salad.

124.   Feta And Vegetable Rotini Salad Recipe

Serving: 8 | Prep: | Cook: 20mins | Ready in:

Ingredients

- 3 c tricolor rotini pasta,cooked,drained and cooled
- 1 c traditional crumbled feta cheese
- 1 c halved cherry tomatoes
- 1 c chopped cucumbers
- 1/2 c sliced black olives
- 1/2 c zesty Italian dressing
- 1/4 c finely chopped red onions

Direction

- Combine all ingredients
- Refrigerate 1 hour. Serve

125.   Firecracker Pasta Salad Recipe

Serving: 0 | Prep: | Cook: 18mins | Ready in:

Ingredients

- 13.5 oz Whole Wheat Rotini
- 1 cup yellow onion, diced
- 1 cup green bell pepper, diced
- 1 cup red bell pepper, diced
- 12 oz BBQ ham, beef or chicken, diced
- 1 1/2 cup ranch dressing
- 1 1/3 cup barbeque sauce
- 1/3 cup parmesan cheese, grated
- 1/4 cup scallions, minced
- Salt and pepper to taste
- My Meatless variation:
- 13.5 Whole Wheat Rotini
- 1 cup green pepper, diced
- 1 cup red pepper, diced
- 1 cup english cucumber, sliced crosswise then quatered
- 6 - 8 green onions siced with green parts
- 1 tbs mesquite liquid smoke
- 1 1/2 cup ranch dressing
- 1 1/2 cup honey barbeque sauce
- 1 1/2 cup shredded 5 cheese blend
- fresh ground pepper

Direction

- Cook the Rotini according to package directions. When pasta is "al dente", drain in colander
- Rinse pasta with cold water until cool to the touch. Drain well.
- Put pasta in large mixing bowl and add onions, pepper and meat (or cuke) and toss.
- Next mix in all remaining ingredients and blend well.
- Chill. Sprinkle with scallions (or more cheese) and serve.

126.   Fresh Greek Pasta Salad Recipe

Serving: 10 | Prep: | Cook: 35mins | Ready in:

Ingredients

- 1 box whole wheat shell pasta
- 2 boneless, skinless chicken breasts (thawed)
- 1 medium yellow onion, diced
- 1 cup grape tomatoes, quartered
- 2 large cucumbers, peeled & cut into 1-inch chunks
- 10 kalamata olives, minced
- 2 cups feta cheese, crumbled
- 1 can cannellini beans
- 1/2 cup white wine vinegar
- 2/3 cup dry white wine, plus more for deglazing
- 1/4 cup Italian dressing
- 1/8 cup milk
- 1/2 cup olive oil, plus more for browning chicken
- 1 tbsp: oregano, coriander, garlic powder, cumin
- 1 tsp: salt & freshly ground black pepper
- handful fresh flat-leaf parsley, finely chopped

Direction

- Coat the bottom of a Dutch oven with olive oil and heat. Rub chicken with seasonings and brown about 3 minutes on each side. Turn down the heat and deglaze with a splash of white wine. Add onion and cook until translucent. Stir in the white wine vinegar, Italian dressing, milk, and the rest of the white wine, and bring to a simmer. Cover and cook for about 25 minutes, or until chicken is no longer pink inside. Remove chicken to a bowl and let rest at least 5 minutes. Take the Dutch oven off of the burner and let dressing cool uncovered.

- Meanwhile, boil water in a large pot and cook pasta until "al dente". Drain in a colander and rinse with cold water; transfer to a large bowl. Add the tomatoes, cucumbers, olives. Drain and rinse the beans, add to bowl. Drizzle with a bit of olive oil and mix gently.
- Once chicken has rested, shred with two forks, and transfer to the pasta bowl.
- Once dressing has cooled, stir in feta cheese. Mix into the pasta and top with the parsley. Serve cold.

127. Fricco Crackers And Pasta Tri Color Salad With Caesar Vinaigrette Recipe

Serving: 6 | Prep: | Cook: 15mins |Ready in:

Ingredients

- 1 package (9 ounces) BUITONI® Refrigerated Three cheese tortellini prepared according to package directions
- 3/4 cup bottled caesar salad dressing divided
- 1 container (5 ounces) BUITONI® Refrigerated Freshly Shredded parmesan cheese divided
- 1 head Belgian endive separated into whole leaves
- 1 small head radicchio, separated into whole leaves soaked in cold water for 1 hour
- 2 cups (about 2 ounces total) lightly packed arugula tough stems removed

Direction

- POUR 1/2 cup dressing over prepared pasta in medium bowl. Marinate in refrigerator for 30 minutes.
- HEAT 8-inch non-stick skillet over medium heat. Sprinkle 1/3 cup cheese into pan, creating an even, lace-thin layer. Cook for 3 to 4 minutes or until top surface of cracker is pale gold. Remove skillet from heat and allow cracker to firm up for 1 minute. Carefully turn cracker over with spatula. Return to heat and

cook for 1 minute or until cracker is golden on second side. Using spatula, transfer cracker to paper towel to drain. Wipe skillet clean with paper towel and repeat 2 times with 1/3 cup cheese each time to make 3 large crackers.
- ARRANGE endive, radicchio and arugula on 6 plates. Drizzle greens with remaining 1/4 cup dressing. Top with pasta; sprinkle with remaining 3/4 cup cheese.
- BREAK crackers into smaller pieces and use as garnish. Serve immediately.
- Tip: Use a 5-ounce bag of packaged European blend salad greens in place of the endive, radicchio and arugula.

128. Fruited Turkey Pasta Salad Recipe

Serving: 4 | Prep: | Cook: 320mins |Ready in:

Ingredients

- 1 cup packaged dried rope macaroni (gemelli) or 1-1/3 cups corkscrew macaroni (4 ounces)
- 1-1/2 cups chopped cooked turkey or chicken or fully cooked turkey ham (8 ounces)
- 2 green onions, sliced (1/4 cup)
- 1/3 cup lime or lemon juice
- 1/4 cup salad oil
- 1 tablespoon honey
- 2 teaspoons snipped fresh thyme or 1/2 teaspoon dried thyme, crushed
- 2 medium nectarines or plums, sliced
- 1 cup halved fresh strawberries

Direction

- Cook pasta according to package directions. Drain pasta; rinse with cold water. Drain again.
- In a large mixing bowl combine pasta; turkey, chicken, or turkey ham; and green onions. Toss to mix.
- For dressing, in a screw-top jar combine lime or lemon juice, oil, honey, and thyme. Cover

and shake well. Pour dressing over pasta mixture; toss to coat. Cover and chill for 4 to 24 hours.

- Just before serving, stir in nectarines or plums and strawberries. Toss to mix. Makes 4 main-dish servings.

129.   GARLIC PASTA SALAD Recipe

Serving: 12 | Prep: | Cook: 15mins | Ready in:

Ingredients

- 1 POUND pasta TWISTS
- 2 green peppers, DICED
- 2 red peppers, DICED
- 2 yellow peppers, DICED
- 1 onion, CHOPPED
- 2 LARGE tomatoes DICED
- 1 LARGE, SPICY pepperoni STICK, SLICED AND QUARTERED
- CARLIFONIA STYLE garlic PEPPER(TO YOUR TASTE)
- 3 garlic AND HERB salad dressing PACKETS
- red wine vinegar
- oil AS REQUIRED FOR salad dressing

Direction

- COOK PASTA ACCORDING TO DIRECTIONS
- IN MEANTIME, CUT ALL VEGETABLES, SIZE ACCORING TO PREFERENCE.
- SLICE PEPPERONI AND THEN QUARTER SLICES.
- WHEN PASTA IS COOKED AND WELL DRAINED MIX WITH ALL OF THE VEGETABLE AND PEPPERONI.
- ADD GARLIC PEPPER TO TASTE.
- MIX ALL WITH USING RED WINE VINEGAR INSTEAD OF REGULAR. POUR ON SALAD AND TOSS WELL.
- REFRIGERATE OVER NIGHT TO ABSORB FLAVOR BEST.

130.   Gails Pasta Salad Recipe

Serving: 6 | Prep: | Cook: 10mins | Ready in:

Ingredients

- 1 12-16 oz. package pasta (bowties work well)
- 1 cup sun dried tomato halves, softened (I usually get the oil packed kind in a jar, drain them and chop them up)
- 1/3 cup pine nuts, toasted
- 3/4 cup yellow onions, julienned or chopped
- 3/4 cup spinach leaves, chopped
- 6 oz. feta cheese, crumbled
- 2 T parmesan cheese, grated
- 1/4 t. oregano
- 1/4 cup extra virgin olive oil (or more to taste)
- 1/4 cup white wine vinegar (or more to taste)
- salt & pepper to taste

Direction

- Cook pasta according to package directions. When pasta is al dente, drain well.
- Using a wooden spoon, toss pasta in colander for 2 minutes to air cool.
- In a large bowl, mix pasta with remaining ingredients.
- Adjust seasoning and serve.

131.   Gazpacho Macaroni Salad Recipe

Serving: 6 | Prep: | Cook: 10mins | Ready in:

Ingredients

- 4 ounces uncooked macaroni
- 2-1/2 cups chopped, seeded tomatoes
- 1 cup finely chopped red onion
- 1 cup finely chopped cucumber

- 1/2 cup finely chopped celery
- 1/2 cup finely chopped green bell pepper
- 1/2 cup finely chopped red bell pepper
- 3 tablespoons cider vinegar
- 2 tablespoons finely chopped black olives
- 1 bay leaf
- 2 tablespoons minced fresh parsley
- 1 tablespoons fresh thyme
- 1 clove garlic, minced
- 3-4 dashes hot sauce
- fresh ground black pepper
- Garnish: whole olives, cucumber slices and dill sprigs.

Direction

- Cook pasta according to package directions, omitting salt in water.
- Drain and rinse well under cold water until pasta is cool.
- Drain well.
- Combine pasta and remaining ingredients in a bowl.
- Cover and refrigerate for 4 hours so flavors blend.
- Remove bay leaf before serving.
- Garnish with whole olives, cucumber slices and dill sprigs.
- Makes 6-1 cup servings.

132. Gazpacho Pasta Salad Recipe

Serving: 6 | Prep: | Cook: 10mins | Ready in:

Ingredients

- 1/2 pound rotelle pasta
- 4 green onions, chopped
- 1 cup chopped green pepper
- 2 jalapeno peppers, seeded and minced
- 2 tomatoes, chopped
- 1 english cucumber, sliced(wont get soggy)
- 1/4 cup olive oil

- 1/4 teaspoon salt
- 2 cloves garlic, crushed
- 1/4 cup fresh lime juice
- 1/4 teaspoon ground black pepper
- 8 ounces hot V-8 juice
- chopped fresh cilantro

Direction

- Cook the pasta according to package directions
- Drain
- In a large bowl combine all ingredients and mix well
- Chill for about 2 hours and toss again before serving
- Sprinkle with fresh chopped cilantro (optional)

133. Georges Grilled Chicken Macaroni Salad Recipe

Serving: 20 | Prep: | Cook: | Ready in:

Ingredients

- 6 LARGE GRILLED chicken breast fillets OR 10 SMALL (CUT INTO BITE SIZE PIECES)
- 3 BOXES OF elbow macaroni
- 1 PURPLE OR yellow onion(DICED FINELY)
- 1 BUNCH green onions (CHOPPED)
- 1 YELLOW OR red bell pepper(FINELY DICED)
- 1 green bell pepper FINELY DICED
- 5-6 LARGE eggs (BOILED) EACH EGG NEEDS TO BE CUT INTO FOURTHS OR YOU CAN DICE THE EGG INTO SMALLER PIECES
- 2 CUPS OF SHREDDED cheese (YOUR CHOICE) WE USE VELEVETTA
- 2 tomatoes (CHOPPED)
- 2 CUPS celery (FINELY CHOPPED)
- 1 JAR OF HELLMAN'S OR KRAFT MAYONAISE

- seasoning (I USE NATURES seasoning, YOU CAN USE TONY'S, SLAP YA MAMA, ETC.. YOUR CHOICE)
- parsley
- black pepper (TO TASTE)

Direction

- CHOP AND DICE ALL YOUR VEGETABLES
- GRILL THE CHICKEN BREAST
- BOIL THE ELBOW MACARONI
- COMBINE ALL INGREDIENTS TOGETHER
- SERVE
- REFRIGERATE LEFTOVERS

---

134.   Ginger Peanut Pasta Salad Recipe

Serving: 6 | Prep: | Cook: 10mins | Ready in:

Ingredients

- 8 ounces corkscrew pasta
- 20 fresh pea pods with tips and stems removed
- 1 small cucumber quartered lengthwise and sliced
- 2 medium carrots cut into long thin strips
- 1 medium yellow pepper cut into thin strips
- 3/4 cup thinly sliced radishes
- 1/2 cup bias sliced green onions
- 3 tablespoons snipped fresh cilantro
- 1/3 cup chopped peanuts
- Dressing:
- 1/4 cup salad oil
- 3 tablespoons rice vinegar
- 2 tablespoons granulated sugar
- 2 tablespoons soy sauce
- 1 teaspoon grated ginger root
- 1/8 teaspoon hot pepper sauce

Direction

- Cook pasta according to package directions then during last 30 seconds add pea pods.

- Rinse with cold water and drain then combine pasta and vegetables.
- Combine dressing ingredients in a jar then cover and shake well.
- Toss salad with dressing and sprinkle with peanuts then serve.

---

135.   Graduation Macaroni Salad Recipe

Serving: 4 | Prep: | Cook: 20mins | Ready in:

Ingredients

- 1 package (7 ounces) elbow macaroni, cooked and drained
- 1 cup chopped cucumber
- 1/2 cup chopped green pepper
- 1/2 cup chopped radishes
- 2 tablespoons chopped onion
- 1/2 teaspoon salt
- 1 package (8 ounces) cream cheese, softened
- 1/4 cup mayonnaise
- 1/4 cup sweet pickle relish
- 1 tablespoon prepared mustard
- lettuce leaves and additional radishes

Direction

- In a bowl, combine the first six ingredients; set aside. In a bowl, beat cream cheese; add mayonnaise, relish and mustard. Fold into macaroni mixture. Press into a 6-cup ring mold coated with cooking spray. Refrigerate for several hours or overnight. Just before serving, unmold onto a lettuce-lined serving platter. Garnish with radishes. Yield: 12-16 servings.

136. Grand Slam Pasta Salad Recipe

Serving: 12 | Prep: | Cook: 10mins | Ready in:

Ingredients

- 1 - 16pkg. tube pasta
- 2 c. halved cherry tomatoes
- 1 -4 oz. block provolone cheese, cubed
- 1 c. chopped sweet red pepper
- 1/2 c. chopped green pepper
- 1 med. onion, chopped
- 1 - 14 oz. can pitted olives, drained
- _____
- Dressing:
- 2/3 c. veg. oil
- 1/3 c. red wine vinegar OR cider vinegar
- 3 tbsp. minced fresh basil OR 3 tsp. dried basil
- 1 garlic clove, minced
- 1 tbsp Dijon mustard
- 1-1/2 tsp. salt
- 1 tsp. sugar
- 1 tsp. onion powder

Direction

- Cook pasta, according to directions on pkg. drain, rinse w/ cold water
- Place pasta in a salad bowl
- Add tomatoes, cheese, peppers, onion, and olives
- _____
- Whisk together dressing ingredients until sugar dissolved
- Pour over pasta mixture, toss to coat
- Refrigerate until serving

137. Grandmas Macaroni Salad Recipe

Serving: 8 | Prep: | Cook: 10mins | Ready in:

Ingredients

- 2 cups cooked macaroni (cook acording package directions & cool)
- 1 can red salmon or tuna (I like the hickory smoked tuna in this too)
- 1 bunch of celery, cut up
- 1 lg cucumber, diced
- 2 Tbs minced onion
- 2 plum tomatoes diced
- salt and pepper to taste
- salad dressing - like Miracle Whip - until it looks good... (I use Mayo most ot the time)

Direction

- Combine all ingredients and refrigerate until ready to serve.

138. Greek Chicken Orzo Salad Recipe

Serving: 6 | Prep: | Cook: 25mins | Ready in:

Ingredients

- 8 ounces uncooked orzo (pasta)
- 1 can (12 ounces) Italian-herb, diced tomatoes
- 2 tablespoons olive oil
- 1/4 cup chopped fresh mint leaves or 2 tablespoons dried mint
- 2 cloves garlic, minced
- 1 can (10 ounces) white meat chicken, drained
- 1 medium unpeeled cucumber, diced
- 1/4 cup chopped, green onions
- 1/4 cup pitted canned kalamata olives, sliced
- 2 ounces feta cheese, crumbled
- 1 cup shredded, fresh spinach

Direction

- Preparation Time: Approximately 15 minutes
- Cook Time: Approximately 10 minutes
- Preparation:
- Cook orzo according to package directions without oil or salt, until al dente, or tender but firm. Drain and cool under running water.

- Drain tomatoes, reserving liquid. In a small bowl combine reserved liquid from tomatoes, olive oil, mint and garlic; set aside. In a large bowl, combine cooled pasta, with drained tomatoes, chicken, cucumber, green onions, olives and feta cheese. Toss with salad dressing mixture. Chill. Fold in spinach just before serving.
- Servings: 6
- Nutritional Information per Serving:
- Calories 270; Total fat 9g; Saturated fat 3g; Cholesterol 25mg; Sodium 520mg; Carbohydrate 34g; Fiber 2g; Protein 16g; Vitamin A 10%DV*; Vitamin C 15%DV; Calcium 8%DV; Iron 10%DV
- * Daily Value

139.   Greek Gods Pasta Salad With Marinated Chicken Breast Recipe

Serving: 6 | Prep: | Cook: 40mins |Ready in:

Ingredients

- 4 cups drained and cooled rotini
- 2 chicken breasts, grilled or sauted
- (Marinated overnight in 2 Tbsp olive oil, 2 cloves crushed garlic, 2 Tbsp lemon juice, 2 tsp oregano flakes, and ½ tsp dry mint)
- ½ cup finely chopped sweet red bell pepper
- ½ fine chopped sweet green bell pepper
- ½ cup finely chopped green onion
- 2 tsp dry basil
- 1 tsp fresh ground black pepper
- salt to taste
- 2 cloves crushed garlic
- ½ cup pitted sliced kalamata olives
- 1/3 cup good mayonnaise
- 3 Tbsp extra virgin olive oil
- 1 Tbsp fresh lemon juice
- feta cheese

Direction

- Marinate chicken breasts overnight in olive oil, garlic, lemon, oregano and mint in a covered container.
- Grill or sauté over medium heat until tender and juices run clear. Remove from heat and cool in refrigerator.
- In a large bowl, combine cooked rotini, chopped peppers, chopped green onion, and chopped olives.
- Add garlic, oregano, basil and black pepper.
- Add salt.
- Add mayonnaise, olive oil and lemon juice.
- Toss gently.
- Arrange rotini salad in a decorative shallow salad dish and decorate the top with cooked chicken breasts, which have been cut into strips.
- Crumble feta cheese over chicken
- Serve with Grecian bread and pepperoncini

140.   Greek Pasta Salad Recipe

Serving: 6 | Prep: | Cook: 120mins |Ready in:

Ingredients

- 10 ounces tri-color fusilli
- 1/2 cup extra virgin olive oil
- 1/4 cup red wine vinegar
- 1 tablespoon balsamic vinegar
- 1 tablespoon lemon juice
- 1 1/2 teaspoons garlic powder
- 1 1/2 teaspoons basil, dried
- 1 1/2 teaspoons oregano, dried
- 1 large cucumber, diced
- 1 yellow bell pepper , diced
- 15 cherry tomatoes, halved
- 3/4 cup feta cheese, crumbled
- 1/2 cup red onions, finely chopped

Direction

- In a large pot, bring lightly salted water to a boil, add rotini pasta. Cook pasta until al dente, about 8- 10 minutes; drain. Return to pot and mix in olive oil, vinegars, lemon juice, garlic powder, basil, oregano, cucumber, pepper, tomatoes, Feta cheese, onions and olives. Cover and chill for at least 2 hours, serve cold

141.   Greek Pasta Salad With Shrimp Tomatoes Zucchini Peppers And Feta Recipe

Serving: 4 | Prep: | Cook: 20mins | Ready in:

Ingredients

- Dijon Vinaigrette:
- 1/8 cup champagne vinegar
- 1 Tb Dijon mustard
- 1 clove garlic, minced
- large pinch of coarse kosher salt
- couple shakes coarse ground black pepper
- 1/3 cup EVO
- pasta Salad:
- 1 med zucchini, cut into 3/8-inch slices and quartered
- 1/2 yellow bell pepper, cut into 1-inch cubes
- salt and pepper to taste
- 1 Tb salt for pasta water
- 1/2 box penne pasta
- 1/2 12 oz beer
- 1/2 lb large shrimp
- 4 oz sweet cherry tomatoes, halved
- 1/4 cup coarsely chopped, pitted kalamata olives
- 1/2 cup feta cheese, crumbled
- 1/4 sweet onion, sliced and diced
- 1 tsp dried oregano

Direction

- For the vinaigrette, mix together the six listed ingredients in a 2 cup measure. Allow to sit.
- Chop the veggies and set aside.

- Steam the shrimp in 1/2 can of beer plus 1/2 cup water. My preference is a nice Boston Ale, but it probably doesn't matter.
- Boil the pasta in 2 qts water to which 1 Tb coarse salt has been added.
- When the pasta is done, drain well.
- Remove the steamed shrimp from steamer and cut into bite-sized chunks (thirds is a nice size).
- In a salad mixing bowl, add the pasta, zucchini, bell pepper, sweet cherry tomatoes, olives and onion. Add the shrimp. Sprinkle with oregano and add the Dijon vinaigrette. Stir to blend. Season with coarse salt and pepper.
- At this point you have a decision to make. Do you want to eat your salad warm, or cold? If this is the main course, hot is preferable. If it's a side dish, cover and place it in the refrigerator for 2 hours or so.
- Serve this salad with a dish of feta to be added if preferred.
- The flavors in this salad mature. If your shrimp are without odor (i.e., very fresh) you may overnight it. But I don't recommend keeping the salad longer than a day.

142.   Greek Pasta Salad With Shrimp And Olives Recipe

Serving: 8 | Prep: | Cook: | Ready in:

Ingredients

- 3/4 lb. tomatoes, chopped
- 1 lg red bell pepper, chopped
- 1/4 lb. feta cheese, crumbled
- 2 tbsp. dry white wine
- 1 tbsp. thyme
- 6 green onions, chopped
- 1/2 c. olive oil
- 3 lg garlic cloves, minced
- 1/2 c. kalamata olives, chopped
- 1/4 c. lemon juice

- 3/4 lb. pasta, cooked
- 3/4 lb. bay shrimp, cooked

Direction

- Mix first 10 ingredients in large bowl.
- Add pasta and shrimp and toss to blend.
- Season to taste with salt and pepper.

143.   Greek Shrimp Pasta Salad Recipe

Serving: 12 | Prep: | Cook: 10mins | Ready in:

Ingredients

- 1 lb. small pasta shells
- 1 lb. cooked salad shrimp
- 1 C. EVOO
- ¼ C. wine vinegar
- ¼ C. lemon juice
- 1 T. fresh, minced thyme
- 3 garlic cloves, minced
- 1 lb. fresh tomatoes, chopped
- 1 C. kalamata olives, quartered
- 1 large bell pepper, chopped
- 1 C. marinated artichoke hearts, drained and chopped
- 6 oz feta cheese, crumbled
- 6 green onions, chopped

Direction

- Cook pasta according to package. Drain and rinse with cold water.
- Mix the EVOO, vinegar, lemon juice, thyme, garlic and pepper, set aside.
- When pasta is cool, place in large bowl add remaining ingredients and toss with dressing.

144.   Greek Style Pasta Salad With Feta Recipe

Serving: 4 | Prep: | Cook: 25mins | Ready in:

Ingredients

- 1 red bell pepper, chopped
- 1 yellow bell pepper, chopped
- 1/2 english cucumber, chopped
- 1 medium eggplant, cubed
- 1 small zucchini, cut in 1/4 inch slices
- 6 tbsp olive oil
- 4 pc sundried tomatoes, soaked in 1/2 cup boiling water
- 1/2 c torn arugula leaves
- 1/2 c chopped fresh basil
- 2 tbsp balsamic vinegar
- 2 tbsp minced garlic
- 4 oz crumbled feta cheese
- 1 (12 oz) package bowtie pasta
- salt and pepper

Direction

- Preheat oven to 450 degrees.
- In a bowl toss the peppers, eggplant, and zucchini with 2 tablespoons of the olive oil, salt, and pepper.
- Arrange on the prepared cookie sheet and bake vegetables for 25 minutes in the preheated oven until lightly browned.
- Salt and pepper veggies once they are out of the oven.
- In the meantime put a large pot of salted boiling water, cook pasta 10 to 12 minutes, until al dente, and drain.
- Drain the softened sun-dried tomatoes and reserve the water.
- In a large bowl, toss together the roasted vegetables, cooked pasta, sun-drained tomatoes, arugula, cucumber and basil.
- Mix in remaining olive oil, reserved water from tomatoes, balsamic vinegar, garlic, and feta cheese; toss to coat.
- Season with salt and pepper to taste.

145. Greek Tacular Pasta Salad Recipe

Serving: 10 | Prep: | Cook: 10mins | Ready in:

Ingredients

- 2 1/2 cups uncooked farfalle pasta
- 1 cup greek dressing
- 2 1/2 tbs mayonnaise
- 4 radishes, finely chopped
- 1/2 cucumber, peeled & chopped
- 1 15oz can chick peas, drained
- 3/4 cup crumbled feta cheese

Direction

- Bring a medium pot of salted water to a boil. Add farfalle & cook until al dente, then strain & place in medium sized bowl.
- Stir in the Greek dressing & mayonnaise until farfalle is well coated. Fold in radishes, cucumbers, chick peas & feta. Cover & chill until ready for serving.

146. Greens Pasta Salad Recipe

Serving: 6 | Prep: | Cook: 20mins | Ready in:

Ingredients

- 1 1/2 cups (6 oz.) dried Small Shells pasta
- 3/4 cup green bell pepper cut in thin 2-in. pieces
- 3/4 cup finely chopped onion
- 3/4 cup carrots cut in thin half-moons
- 3 tbsp. extra virgin olive oil, divided
- 3/4 tsp. salt, divided
- 3/4 cup frozen green peas
- 1/4 to 1/2 tsp. hot sauce
- 1/4 to 1/2 tsp. freshly ground black pepper
- 1/4 cup lime juice

Direction

- In a medium saucepan of boiling water, cook pasta according to package directions. Drain and return to pan.
- Meanwhile, in a large frying pan over medium-high heat, cook bell pepper, onion, and carrots with 1 tbsp. olive oil and 1/4 tsp. salt, stirring often, until barely tender-crisp to the bite, about 3 minutes.
- Add onion mixture and peas to pasta mixture; stir gently to mix. In a bowl, stir remaining 2 tbsp. olive oil, remaining 1/2 tsp. salt, and 1/4 tsp. each hot sauce and pepper; pour over pasta mixture and stir until well coated. If you like, add more pepper and hot sauce to taste. Just before serving, stir in lime juice. Scrape into a serving bowl and serve warm or at room temperature.

147. Grilled Chicken Pasta Salad Recipe

Serving: 4 | Prep: | Cook: 10mins | Ready in:

Ingredients

- 2 grilled chicken breasts
- 1 bag "no yolks" wide noodles
- 1 container grape tomatoes (organic are best)
- 1 bunch basil
- red wine vinegar
- olive oil
- oregano
- parmesan cheese

Direction

- Boil pasta
- While pasta is cooking use separate bowl and add
- Tomatoes (sliced each tomato in 1/2)
- Chopped basil
- 3 T white wine vinegar
- 1 T olive oil

- Oregano to taste
- Diced chicken
- Mix all together and add hot pasta after draining
- Mix and serve topped with parmesan

---

148. Grilled Chicken Pesto Tortellini Pasta Salad Recipe

Serving: 812 | Prep: | Cook: 15mins | Ready in:

Ingredients

- 4 small Skinless, Boneless chicken breasts
- 1 small/med. red onion
- Grill seasoning (Like McCormick Montreal steak seasoning)
- olive oil
- 2 - 9 oz. pkgs. Fresh cheese tortellini
- ½ 16 oz. jar roasted red peppers
- 2 jars marinated artichoke hearts
- ½ - ⅔ c. Pesto
- ½ - ⅔ c. mayonnaise
- Splash of lemon juice or red wine vinegar
- Grated parmesan cheese, to taste

Direction

- Preheat grill to medium.
- Sprinkle chicken breasts with grill seasoning to taste. Peel and slice onion into ⅜" slices; lightly brush with olive oil. Grill chicken breasts and onions until done. Cool completely.
- Boil tortellini in plenty of salted water until al dente. Drain and rinse with cold water until cool. Drain thoroughly.
- Cut chicken into ½" – ¾" cubes, or pull apart into bite-sized pieces.
- Drain artichoke hearts and roasted red peppers.
- Chop cooled onion, artichoke hearts, and roasted red peppers.
- In a large bowl, mix pasta, chicken, and vegetables.

- Mix together equal parts of pesto and mayonnaise and the splash of lemon juice and mix into the salad mixture. Mix just a ½ cup each pesto and mayonnaise first, and mix additional ¼ cup each if you feel salad needs additional dressing.
- Sprinkle in grated parmesan cheese to taste.
- Chill well before serving.
- * You may also add some sliced, oil-packed sun-dried tomatoes as well, if you like them. They are a nice addition for something different, but I usually make it without.

---

149. Grilled Pasta Salad Recipe

Serving: 4 | Prep: | Cook: 15mins | Ready in:

Ingredients

- 2 zucchini sliced
- 2 yellow squash sliced
- 1 spanish onion cut into large chunks
- 1 package Italian herb with tomato soup mix
- 1/4 cup olive oil
- 8 ounces penne pasta cooked and drained
- 3/4 cup diced roasted red pepper
- 1/4 cup red wine vinegar

Direction

- Arrange zucchini, yellow squash and onion on grill.
- Combine soup mix and oil the brush over vegetables and grill 5 minutes turning once.
- Toss pasta, vegetables, roasted peppers and vinegar then serve warm or room temperature.

150. Grilled Sweet Pepper And Summer Vegetable Pasta Salad Recipe

Serving: 0 | Prep: | Cook: 15mins | Ready in:

Ingredients

- 6 oz whole grain spaghetti, cooked, drained, and cooled
- 1/4 C fat-free or light Italian dressing
- 1/2 lb zucchini, finely sliced and quartered
- 1/2 lb summer squash, finely sliced and quartered
- salt and pepper to taste
- 2 cloves of garlic, coarsely minced
- olive oil
- 5 small sweet peppers, grilled with skins removed and finely sliced
- parmesan cheese, for sprinkling

Direction

- 1. In a large bowl, toss together the cooked spaghetti noodles and Italian dressing. Set aside.
- 2. Lightly drizzle a frying pan with olive oil. Add in the zucchini, summer squash, and garlic. Stir to coat. Sprinkle with salt and pepper to taste. Cook over medium-high heat until zucchini and summer squash soften and start to brown. Remove from heat and cool.
- 3. Add the grilled sweet peppers to the noodles. Once zucchini and summer squash have cooled, pour entire contents of frying pan into the noodle mixture. Toss to evenly distribute the vegetables throughout the noodles.
- 4. Sprinkle with Parmesan cheese. Serve immediately or refrigerate before servings. Store all leftovers in the refrigerator.

151. Grilled Vegetable And Pasta Salad Recipe

Serving: 4 | Prep: | Cook: 20mins | Ready in:

Ingredients

- 2 squash and zucchini, cut in half and cut julienne style (large cuts)
- 1 bell pepper, sliced
- 1 cup fresh asparagus, cut in 1 inch pieces
- 1 large portebella mushroon, sliced
- 3 Tbs. olive oil
- 1 cup cherry tomatoes, quartered
- 1 package penne or rotini pasta, cooked al dente, completely cooled
- 3/4 cup green onions
- 1 cup fresh grated parmesan cheese
- Dressing:
- 1 tsp. dry mustard
- 1/2 tsp. salt
- 1/4 tsp. pepper
- 1/2 tsp. sugar
- 1 tsp. dried oregano
- 1 tsp. dried parsley (or 1/4 cup fresh)
- 2 garlic cloves, pressed
- 5 Tsp. lemon juice
- 6 Tsp. balsamic vinegar
- 1/2 cup extra-virgin olive oil

Direction

- Cup up vegetables, season with salt, pepper, and a dash of garlic powder. Coat in bowl with 3 Tsp. of olive oil. Grill in a grilling basket (or one of your choice) until done...not too soft, but cooked. Remove and let cool.
- Mix the cooked and cooled pasta with green onions and cherry tomatoes. Add a little salt and pepper. Then add dressing. Add the grilled vegetables to the pasta and top with parmesan cheese (amount to your taste). Mix well.

152. Grilled Yellow Squash And Zucchini Pasta Salad Recipe

Serving: 15 | Prep: | Cook: 45mins | Ready in:

Ingredients

- 16 oz. farfalle pasta
- 1 lb. Yellow summer squash, cut into 1-in. chunks
- 1 lb. zucchini, halved lengthwise and cut into 1-in. chunks
- 1/2 cup olive oil, divided
- 1/2 tablespoon of salt (my addition)
- 2 tbsp. champagne vinegar
- 1/2 tsp. freshly ground pepper
- 2 tbsp. chopped fresh oregano
- 1/2 cup toasted pine nuts
- 1/4 cup chopped pitted kalamata olives (Michael also said that it might be better to leave the olives whole)

Direction

- Cook pasta in a large pot of boiling water until tender, 9 to 12 minutes.
- Drain and rinse under cold water.
- Grill vegetables on grill by brushing with olive oil and sprinkle with salt and pepper. Whisk together the remaining olive oil, vinegar, salt and pepper in a small bowl.
- In a large bowl toss together pasta, vegetables, oregano, pine nuts, and olives.
- Add dressing and season with salt and pepper to taste.

153. Ham Pasta Salad Recipe

Serving: 6 | Prep: | Cook: 10mins | Ready in:

Ingredients

- INGREDIENTS
- 8 ounces ziti pasta

- 1 pound cooked ham, cubed
- 1 large red bell pepper, cut into 1 inch pieces
- 1 large green bell pepper, cut into 1 inch pieces
- 1 large red onion, coarsely chopped
- 15 small sweet pickles, chopped, juice reserved
- 1 cup cherry tomatoes, halved
- 1 cup mayonnaise
- 1/2 cup sour cream
- 2 1/2 teaspoons beef bouillon granules
- 1 tablespoon white vinegar
- 1/2 teaspoon salt
- 1/4 teaspoon ground black pepper
- 2 cloves garlic, minced
- D

Direction

- Bring a large pot of lightly salted water to a boil. Add pasta and cook for 8 to 10 minutes or until al dente; drain.
- In a large bowl, mix together the drained pasta, ham, peppers, onion, pickles and tomatoes.
- In a small bowl, whisk together the mayonnaise, sour cream, beef bouillon granules, vinegar, salt, pepper, garlic and 1/2 cup of reserved pickle juice.
- Fold into the salad and toss gently until evenly coated.
- Chill overnight to allow the flavors to blend.
- Serve near room temperature.

154. Ham And Cheese Pasta Salad Recipe

Serving: 2 | Prep: | Cook: 20mins | Ready in:

Ingredients

- 200 g mini farfalle pasta
- 1 can (310 g) corn kernels; drained, flaked
- 250 g punnet cherry tomatoes; halved
- 150 g ham slices; coarsely chopped
- 80 g (1 cup) grated Cheddar

- 1 Lebanese cucumber; coarsely chopped
- 1/2 cup Ceasar salad dressing

Direction

- Cook the pasta in a saucepan of salted boiling water following packet directions or until al dente.
- Drain.
- Combine the pasta, corn, tomato, ham, cheddar and cucumber in a large bowl.
- Add the dressing and toss until well combined.
- Store in an airtight container.
- Contributor: Australian Good Taste - February 2007, Page 53

155. Ham And Swiss Macaroni Salad Recipe

Serving: 2 | Prep: | Cook: 10mins | Ready in:

Ingredients

- 4 ounces medium shell pasta
- 1/2 pint cherry tomatoes cut in half
- 1/4 cup finely chopped red onion
- 3 tablespoons red wine vinegar
- 2 tablespoons olive oil
- 1/2 teaspoon salt
- 1/2 teaspoon freshly ground black pepper
- 1/2 cup cubed swiss cheese
- 1 cup ham chopped

Direction

- Prepare pasta according to package instructions.
- Drain and chill.
- In bowl combine pasta and remaining ingredients.
- Serve immediately or refrigerate to serve later.

156. Hawaiian Macaroni Salad Recipe

Serving: 10 | Prep: | Cook: 10mins | Ready in:

Ingredients

- 1 bag macaroni noodles
- 1 1/2 c mayo
- 3/4 c milk
- 1/2 c teriyaki sauce (see my recipe if you want to make it yourself)
- 4 carrots ~ shredded
- 1 bunch green onion ~ chopped fine
- pepper

Direction

- Mix everything together, store in the fridge overnight
- Enjoy!

157. Hawaiian Style Macaroni Salad Recipe

Serving: 10 | Prep: | Cook: 15mins | Ready in:

Ingredients

- 1 box macaroni of your choice
- 6 boiled eggs
- 1 grated carrot
- __additional add-ins may include, to your taste....
- onions finely chopped
- olives chopped
- 1 can well drained tuna
- 1 cup FROZEN petite peas
- 1/2 cup finely chopped celery
- 1 or more cups salad size cooked shrimp
- Dressing
- 1 cup MAYONAISE or more
- 2 T water
- 1/2 tsp rice vinegar (for a little tang)
- salt and pepper to taste

- **if desired
- 1/2 tsp good curry powder
- 1/2 tsp paprika
- 2 T milk
- 1 T sugar

Direction

- Cook macaroni according to package
- Rinse well and chill if possible
- Have boiled eggs prepared ahead of time
- Chop eggs and add to macaroni
- Add grated carrot to macaroni and any additional add-ins you desire
- Chill while mixing dressing
- Mix all dressing ingredients together, adding more mayonnaise or water as needed MAYONAISE IS A MUST!!!
- Mix all together well, keep chilled and serve

---

158.   Incalata Con Pasta Rapido Y Facile Recipe

Serving: 8 | Prep: | Cook: 20mins |Ready in:

Ingredients

- The salad:
- • 1 lb uncooked pasta. I usually use three color rotini but any short pasta type will do.
- • 2 – 3 cups frozen mixed veggies, to taste. I use the carrot, green bean, pea and corn mix.
- • 2 – 3 Tbs chopped ripe olives, to taste.
- • 2 – 4 sliced fresh mushrooms, depending on size.
- The dressing:
- • 1 cup real mayonnaise.
- • 1 tsp Dijon mustard, to taste.
- • 2 Tbs dry white wine or vinegar, to taste.
- • A pinch of sweet basil.
- • A sprig of cilantro, chopped.
- • 1 tsp chili powder, to taste.
- • Salt and fresh ground pepper to taste.

Direction

- 1. Cook the pasta just al dente, rinse with cold water and drain
- 2. Mix all of the Dressing ingredients together until smooth and creamy.
- 3. Mix all of the salad ingredients and the dressing in a large bowl and toss until well mixed.
- You can garnish this with a few sprigs of parsley or cilantro.

---

159.   Italian Antipasta Cold Pasta Salad Recipe

Serving: 12 | Prep: | Cook: 30mins |Ready in:

Ingredients

- 1 package of Wacky Macroni (tri-color pasta mix)
- 2 pints of grape tomatoes
- 1 (8 oz) fresh mozzerella, cubed
- 1 pkg of smoked mozzerella or provolone cheese cubed
- 1 red pepper chopped
- 1 green pepper chopped
- 1 small red onion chopped
- 1 zucchini cubed
- 1 small can of sliced black olives
- 1 small can of sliced green olives
- hard salami, cubed (I used half of a stick)
- 1 to 1-1/2 pkgs of Hormel Mini Peppperoni slices (or used stick and cube)
- Dressing:
- 3/4 cup olive oil
- 3/4 cup red wine vinegar
- 1/4 cup balsamic vinegar
- 2 garlic cloves minced well
- 1 tsp salt
- 1 tsp pepper
- 1 tsp dried basil
- 3 tbsp shredded parmesan/romano cheese mix
- 1/2 tsp oregano
- 1/2 tsp italian seasoning

Direction

- In bowl, mix dressing ingredients all together, cover and shake well to mix flavors (use a jar if you wish)
- In large bowl, put all other ingredients in
- Pour dressing over top and mix well
- Cover and refrigerate overnight
- Before serving, top with fresh basil

160.   Italian Antipasto Pasta Salad Recipe

Serving: 12 | Prep: | Cook: 15mins | Ready in:

Ingredients

- 12 ounces (one box) plain or tricolor rotelli pasta
- 8 oz Italian dressing
- 1 t dry Italian herb seasoning
- 8 ounces genoa salami, cubed
- 8 ounces provolone, cubed
- 1 green bell pepper, chopped
- 1/2 red onion, chopped
- 1 – 2 oz can sliced black olives

Direction

- In a large pot of salted boiling water, cook pasta until al dente, drain and rinse under cold water. In a large bowl, add the pasta, salami, provolone, bell pepper, olives and onion. Slowly add Italian dressing and stir well to evenly coat. You may not need all 8 oz. of Italian dressing, but may need to add more before serving. Mix in the Italian herb seasoning. Allow to chill before serving.
- Variation – Try replacing the salami and provolone with julienned pepperoni slices and freshly shredded parmesan.

161.   Italian Bowtie Pasta Salad Recipe

Serving: 8 | Prep: | Cook: 30mins | Ready in:

Ingredients

- 1 Package Bowtie pasta
- 1 Cup   feta cheese Crumbles
- 1 Cup   Chopped Mozerella cheese (I use string cheese)
- 1 Cup   black olives
- 1 Cup   green olives
- 1 Cup   Sun dried tomatoes
- 2 Tbsp   red wine vinegar
- 2 Tbsp   lemon juice
- 2 Tbsp   italian seasoning
- 1 Tbsp   lemon pepper seasoning
- 2 tsp   garlic powder
- 1/4 Cup extra virgin olive oil

Direction

- Cook pasta according to directions on box.
- In a small bowl, combine all other ingredients.
- Cool pasta and place in large bowl.
- Mix in other ingredients and enjoy! :)

162.   Italian Market Pasta Salad Recipe

Serving: 4 | Prep: | Cook: 15mins | Ready in:

Ingredients

- 4 ounces packaged dry mafalda, large bow tie, or campanelle pasta
- 6 cups mesclun or other spring greens
- 1 cup grape tomatoes or cherry tomatoes, halved lengthwise
- 1/2 cup crumbled gorgonzola, blue, or feta cheese (2 ounces)
- 3 tablespoons olive oil
- 3 tablespoons white wine vinegar or balsamic vinegar

- salt and freshly ground black pepper
- 1/4 cup pine nuts, toasted

Direction

- If using mafalda, break into irregular pieces, 2 to 3 inches long. Cook pasta according to package directions. Drain, rinse with cold water, and drain again.
- In a large salad bowl, combine cooked pasta, mesclun or other spring greens, tomatoes, and cheese. Drizzle with olive oil and vinegar, tossing to coat. Season to taste with salt and freshly ground pepper.
- Divide salad evenly among four dinner plates. Sprinkle with pine nuts. Makes 4 LARGE main course servings.

163.   Italian Organic Basil Tomato And Pasta Salad Recipe

Serving: 16 | Prep: | Cook: 15mins | Ready in:

Ingredients

- CHILL 4 TO 24 HOURS
- 1/2 cup red wine vinegar
- 2 tablespoons dijon-style mustard
- 1/4 teaspoon black pepper
- 2 cloves garlic, minced
- 1/2 cup olive oil
- 1/2 cup slivered fresh basil
- 8 ounces dried pasta (such as rotini, bow ties, shells, cavatelli, or penne)
- 2 9-ounce packages frozen cut green beans
- 6 medium tomatoes, cut into thin wedges
- 1 cup sliced pitted kalamata olives or ripe olives
- 2 cups loosely packed fresh basil leaves
- 3/4 cup (3 oz.) finely shredded parmesan cheese
- 3 tablespoons snipped fresh parsley

Direction

- For dressing, in a small bowl whisk together vinegar, mustard, pepper, and garlic. Gradually whisk in oil. Stir in the slivered basil. Set dressing aside.
- Cook pasta according to package directions; drain. Rinse with cold water; drain again.
- Meanwhile, in a large saucepan cook frozen beans according to package directions; drain. Rinse with cold water; drain again.
- Toss one-third of the dressing with the cooked pasta; place pasta in the bottom of a very large salad bowl. Layer ingredients on top of the pasta in the following order: cooked green beans, tomatoes, and olives. Top with remaining dressing. Sprinkle with the basil leaves, the Parmesan cheese, and parsley. Cover and chill for 4 to 24 hours. To serve, toss lightly to combine.

164.   Italian Orzo Salad Recipe

Serving: 12 | Prep: | Cook: 30mins | Ready in:

Ingredients

- 6 c chicken broth
- 1 pkg (16 oz) orzo pasta
- 1/3 c olive oil
- 1/4 c red wine vinegar
- 2 TB lemon juice
- 1 TB honey
- 1/2 tsp salt
- 1/2 tsp pepper
- 2 c chopped plum tomatoes
- 1 c chopped,seeded,peeled cucumber
- 1 c fresh basil leaves,thinly sliced
- 4 green onions,chopped
- 1/2 c fresh baby spinach
- 1-3/4 c (7 oz) crumbled feta cheese
- 1/2 c pine nuts,toasted

Direction

- In large saucepan, bring broth to a boil; add pasta. Return to boil. Cook, uncovered, for 10-

12 mins or till pasta is tender. Meanwhile, in small bowl, whisk oil, vinegar, lemon juice, honey, salt and pepper.

- In large bowl, combine tomatoes, cucumber, basil, onions, and spinach.
- Drain pasta; add to tomato mixture. Drizzle with dressing; toss to coat. Chill till serving.
- Just before serving, stir in cheese and pine nuts.

165. Italian Pasta Salad For 50 Recipe

Serving: 50 | Prep: | Cook: 30mins | Ready in:

Ingredients

- 2 1/2 cups cider vinegar
- 2 1/2 tbsp salt
- 2 1/2 tbsp (about 7-8 cloves) garlic, fresh, minced (essential that it is very fine)
- 1 tbsp plus 1/4 tsp dry mustard
- 2 1/4 tsp dried oregano
- 1 1/2 tbsp ground black pepper
- 1 3/4 cups oil, preferably an olive oil blend
- 4 lbs 6 oz rotini pasta, uncooked
- 5 lbs 12 oz broccoli bunches (about 5-6 bunches)
- 2 lbs carrots, sliced
- 3 lbs (about 18) plum tomatoes, diced or coarsely chopped
- 1 1/2 cups olives, sliced
- 4 oz (1 cup) parmesan cheese, grated (good quality)

Direction

- Mix vinegar, salt, garlic, mustard, oregano and pepper in a bowl. Slowly pour in oil and whisk to combine.
- Steam the pasta for about 15 minutes or JUST until tender but still firm (DO NOT OVERCOOK; time will be determined by intensity of steamer). Drain. Rinse under cold water until pasta is cold. (Cool from 140 to 70

degrees F within 2 hours and from 70 to 41 degrees F within 4 hours OR Cool from 140 to 41 degrees F within 4 hours)

- Mix the pasta with the rest of the dressing to prevent sticking.
- Cut broccoli crowns into small florets. If you are using the stems, remove 1-2 inches from the tough ends and discard. Peel the remaining stems and slice thinly.
- Steam broccoli, together with the stems if using them, until slightly tender but still bright green on the firm side, about 3 minutes. (CCP: Heat to 140 degrees F or higher.)
- Run under cold water until well chilled. Drain well and add to pasta. (CCP: Cool from 140 to 70 degrees F within 2 hours OR Cool from 70 to 41 degrees F within 4 hours.)
- JUST BEFORE SERVICE:
- Toss pasta with the remaining dressing, broccoli, carrots, plum tomatoes, olives and Parmesan cheese. If necessary, up to 1/2 cup water may be added per 100 servings. (Tossing right before service prevents the pasta from absorbing the dressing and becoming dry.) (CCP: Hold for cold service at 41 degrees F or lower.)

166. Italian Pasta Salad Recipe

Serving: 6 | Prep: | Cook: 10mins | Ready in:

Ingredients

- 1 packet Italian dressing or 1 bottle Wishbone Italian dressing
- 16 oz. multi-colored rotini pasta
- 1 large can of sliced olives
- 2 tomatoes diced
- 1 jar artichoke hearts
- 3/4 can red kidney beans
- Optional:
- 1 diced red bell pepper
- 1/2 to 1 pound cheese mozz – cubed
- 1/2 to 1 cup diced salami

Direction

- Cook pasta according to package directions. Rinse under cold water to stop cooking and drain well.
- If using packaged dressing, prepare 1 packet of Italian dressing as directed.
- Place pasta in large salad bowl, add dressing and toss gently to coat.
- Add remaining ingredients to pasta and mix gently.
- Cover and refrigerate at least 4 hours to blend all flavors.

167.   Italian Salami Pasta Salad Recipe

Serving: 16 | Prep: | Cook: 45mins | Ready in:

Ingredients

- 1 tbsp olive oil
- 1 cup diced vidalia onion
- 2 large garlic cloves, minced
- 1 tsp garlic powder
- 3 cups broccoli florets
- 1 red bell pepper, cut into 3/4" pieces
- 1 zucchini, cut into 3/4" cubes
- 1/4 cup dry white wine
- 3/4 lb black pepper salametti, cut into 3/4" cubes
- 1 pint halved grape tomatoes
- 1 pound tri-color rotini
- 1 tbsp salt
- 1/4 cup drained chopped black olives, optional
- 1/2 cup lemon-parmesan-vinaigrette.html">Lemon Parmesan Vinaigrette

Direction

- Heat oil in a skillet over medium high heat.
- Add onion and garlic; sauté until translucent, about 5 minutes.

- Add broccoli, red pepper, zucchini and wine; sauté until vegetables are just tender, about 4 minutes.
- Add salami and tomatoes; toss until heated through, about 2 minutes. Transfer to large bowl.
- Cook pasta in a large pot of water with the 1 tbsp. salt. Drain and immediately add to the vegetables.
- Add olives and dressing. Stir to coat well and season with salt and pepper to taste.

168.   Italian Tuna Pasta Salad Recipe

Serving: 4 | Prep: | Cook: 11mins | Ready in:

Ingredients

- 8 oz medium shell pasta
- 2 cans water-packed tuna, drained
- 1 can white beans (northern, canellini, etc.), drained and rinsed
- 1 small onion, minced (1/2 cup)
- 1/2 cup chopped celery
- 12 kalamata or similar olives, roughly chopped
- 1 T capers
- 2 T fresh basil, chopped (I used lemon basil) - or more, to taste
- 1/4 cup olive oil
- 1 T lemon zest, minced
- 1 lemon, juiced
- 1 t coarse ground or cracked pepper
- 1 t dried dill weed
- salt, to taste

Direction

- Bring pot of water to a boil, add pasta and cook to desired tenderness.
- In the meantime, mix tuna, beans, onion, celery, olives, capers and basil in a large bowl.
- Whisk together olive oil, lemon zest, lemon juice, pepper and dill weed.

- Drain pasta, run under cold water and add to bowl w/ tuna mixture.
- Pour dressing over and toss well. Salt to taste.
- Note: you could add blanched (or frozen, thawed) green beans or parsley for more flavor and color.

---

169.   JKs Monterey Jack Pasta Salad Recipe

Serving: 6 | Prep: | Cook: 45mins | Ready in:

Ingredients

- 1 lb rigatoni noodles
- 12 oz grape tomatoes
- 8 oz watercress (leaves only)
- 1/4 c chopped basil
- 1 small shallot
- 1 clove garlic
- 2 lemons
- 1/2 c olive oil
- 8 oz monterey jack cheese
- salt & pepper

Direction

- Bring water to boil and salt
- Add pasta
- While pasta boils, prepare watercress, basil & dressing
- Remove watercress & basil leaves and set aside
- Mince garlic & shallot and add to a large mixing bowl
- Add olive oil & juice of 2 lemons & whisk
- Add grape tomatoes and stir
- Add watercress and basil and stir
- When noodles are al dente, drain and immediately toss with dressing and vegetables
- Cover with saran wrap and let greens wilt
- Place cold Monterey jack cheese in freezer
- When greens are wilted remove cheese from freezer and dice in to small cubes

- Toss cheese with pasta, cover with saran wrap and let come to room temperature

---

170.   Jos Pasta Salad Recipe

Serving: 6 | Prep: | Cook: 15mins | Ready in:

Ingredients

- 2 - CANS OF canned chicken (WHITE MEAT) OR YOU CAN USE THE MEAT OF A CHICKEN YOU HAVE BOILED AND DEBONED.
- 1-LARGE CAN OF black olives.
- 1-BUNCH OF green onions
- 1-1/2 CUP OF cheddar cheese OR MOTZERELLA
- 2TSP. OF GALIC-BUY THE JAR OF GALIC PACKED IN olive oil OR CHOP YOUR OWN garlic
- 2 MEDIUM tomatoes
- 1/2 green pepper AND 1/2 A red pepper
- 1-1/2 CUP OF MAYONAISE.
- use a little black pepper to taste.
- a bag of whole wheat pasta in any shape . can use regular pasta if you prefer

Direction

- Chop chicken and vegetables place in bowl set aside and boil up the pasta, drain, cool and then place in bowl with vegetables and chicken.
- Make your dressing for the salad with mayonnaise thinned by milk or water till it will pour. Put the garlic and pepper in the sauce and pour over your salad. Mix well. Cut up cheese in to small sq. mix into salad also. Mix well place in refrigerator to chill or serve at once which ever you prefer.
- Hope you enjoy this salad. You can add other vegetables to your liking.

171.   Joys Moms Pasta Salad Recipe

Serving: 12 | Prep: | Cook: 10mins | Ready in:

Ingredients

- 1 lb box of linguini
- cherry tomatoes or grape tomatoes
- green & black olives sliced
- green pepper chopped
- red pepper chopped
- broccoli
- Fresh sliced mushrooms
- Any other vegetables of choice
- feta cheese
- Ken's LITE only LITE Caesar Dressing
- McCormick Salad Supreme seasoning

Direction

- Cook and drain linguini
- Mix Caesar dressing and half bottle of Salad supreme together in bowl
- While pasta is hot toss dressing mixture and vegetables
- Refrigerate at least 12 hours

172.   Jp's "secret Pasta Salad" Shhhhh! Recipe

Serving: 0 | Prep: | Cook: 45mins | Ready in:

Ingredients

- 1lb Tri-Color-rotini pasta
- 1 of each red, green, yellow, and orange bell peppers
- 4 roma tomatos
- 2 garlic cloves(pressed)
- 1/2 medium red onion
- 1/4 cup of sliced black olives
- 1/2 lb genoa salami
- Pinch of salt
- Pinch of black pepper

- Pinch of garlic salt
- 1 tsp crushed red pepper
- 2 cups Newmans own family recipe Italian dressing
- Any Italian herb that you like feel free to be creative
- 1/4 cup of fresh grated parmesan or romano cheese
- garnish with fresh parsley

Direction

- Cook pasta, according to directions, al dente. Drain, rinse with cool water. (I always do a little olive oil in my warm pasta)
- Caramelize onions and garlic
- In a large size bowl
- Add Pasta, onions and garlic
- Julienne cut all vegetable ingredients including the salami (try to cut salami so the bit size pieces will be on every fork) and add to bowl, salt and peppers, black olives, Italian dressing and any herbs you like on Italian food.(I have some that just love)
- Combine (toss) in bowl add parmesan or Romano atop your creation with a few parsley leafs and "Viva la Italy" you now have a great salad that your friends will just eat up at parties....
- Enjoy

173.   KFC Macaroni Salad Copycat Recipe

Serving: 6 | Prep: | Cook: 10mins | Ready in:

Ingredients

- 7 ounces Box elbow macaroni, cooked according to directions
- 2 Ribs celery minced fine
- 1 tablespoon Dry minced onion
- 1/3 cup Diced sweet pickles
- 1 1/2 cups Fat free Miracle Whip
- 1/2 cup Fat free mayo

- 1/4 teaspoon black pepper
- 1/4 teaspoon dry mustard
- 1 teaspoon sugar
- salt to taste

Direction

- Combine everything just as listed.
- Refrigerate salad tightly covered several hours before serving.

---

174.   Katiedyd's Easy Tortellini Salad Recipe

Serving: 0 | Prep: | Cook: 20mins | Ready in:

Ingredients

- One Bag Italian Mixed frozen vegetables.
- One pound bag of frozen cheese tortellini.
- One bottle of Italian salad dressing,regular or low/no fat.
- Parmesan cheese to taste (optional).
- Salt and pepper to taste.

Direction

- Bring three quarts of salted water to the boil.
- Add tortellini and vegetables to boiling water, stir.
- Cook to package directions, about 7 to 10 minutes (DON'T overcook!)
- Drain in colander and run cold water over pasta and veggies.
- After drained well, pour into large salad bowl, and toss with about three quarters of the Italian dressing, stir.
- Garnish with freshly grated Parmesan cheese.
- Refrigerate if served cold, also good served warm after 20 minutes standing time.
- Season to taste with salt and pepper.

175.   Kentucky Fried Chicken Secret Macaroni Salad Recipe

Serving: 8 | Prep: | Cook: 12mins | Ready in:

Ingredients

- 8 Oz of elbow macaroni
- 2 Ribs celery minced fine
- 1/4 cup thinly diced carrots (very thin!)
- 1 tablespoon Dry minced onion
- 1/3 cup Diced sweet pickles
- 1 1/2 cups Miracle Whip
- 1/2 cup Hellmans Mayonaise
- 1/4 teaspoon black pepper
- 1/4 teaspoon dry mustard
- 1 teaspoon sugar
- salt to taste

Direction

- Cook elbow macaroni to package directions, drain well and let cool.
- Combine remaining ingredients in a mixing bowl and mix well.
- Fold mixture into macaroni and toss to combine. Cover and let chill for several hours.

---

176.   Kitchen Sink Pasta Salad Recipe

Serving: 12 | Prep: | Cook: 60mins | Ready in:

Ingredients

- 1 pound pasta that will hold the dressing
- 1/4 pound genoa salami, chopped
- 1/4 pound pepperoni sausage, chopped
- 1/2 pound asiago cheese, diced *
- 1 (6 ounce) can black olives, drained and chopped
- 1 red bell pepper, diced
- 1 can green beans
- 1 cup artichoke hearts
- 1/2 cup chopped red onion

- 1 16 ounce container grape tomatoes halved
- 1 (.7 ounce) package dry Italian-style salad dressing mix
- 3/4 cup extra virgin olive oil
- 1/4 cup red wine vinegar
- 1/4 cup chopped fresh basil
- 1/4 cup grated parmesan cheese (NOT the stuff in the can, please)
- salt and ground black pepper to taste

Direction

- Cook the pasta in a large pot of salted boiling water until al dente. Drain, and cool under cold water.
- In a large bowl, combine the pasta, salami, Asiago cheese, black olives, red bell pepper, artichoke hearts, red onion, green beans and tomatoes. Stir in the envelope of dressing mix. Cover, and refrigerate for at least one hour.
- To prepare the dressing, whisk together the olive oil, red wine vinegar, fresh basil, Parmesan cheese, salt and pepper.
- Just before serving, pour dressing over the salad, and mix well.
- * I'll usually use whatever white cheese I've got on hand. Fresh mozzarella is nice.

177.   Krab Pasta Salad Recipe

Serving: 20 | Prep: | Cook: 10mins | Ready in:

Ingredients

- 1# pasta-I like small seashells
- 1 package "Krab" meat
- 1 chopped onion
- 2 chopped carrots
- 1 rib celery chopped
- about a cup of frozen peas
- 1/2 c. mayo
- 1/2 c. ranch dressing
- other chopped veggies as desired (please suggest any and all!)

Direction

- Chop veggies while pasta water heats up
- Cook pasta
- Put peas and carrots into colander
- Drain pasta over peas and carrots to thaw/blanch
- Rinse well with cold water to halt cooking
- combine all ingredients in a large bowl and chill until time to serve (an hour or so is best-if you need to chill longer, dress no more than an hour before serving or be prepared to add more dressing)

178.   Leftover Macaroni And Pea Salad Recipe

Serving: 8 | Prep: | Cook: 120mins | Ready in:

Ingredients

- Here's what I had:
- 1/2 cup uncooked salad pasta or macaroni (I actually used 2 cups, because that was the serving size I broke my huge bag of macaroni into!!)
- 1 lb. can of sweet (English) peas (I used the rest, probably about 1 cup of my Publix brand grocery store frozen bag of peas!!)
- 1 small onion, chopped fine
- 2 slices american, cheddar or any favorite cheese, cut into small cubes (I used the rest of my Publix brand grocery store shredded cheddar cheese, maybe 1/2 to 1 cup, or so)
- salt and pepper, to taste
- Here's what I needed and had to buy:
- 2 stalks celery, chopped fine (only because I ran out!!) :(
- 1/4 cup Miracle Whip or mayonnaise (I used about 3/4 to 1 cup of mayo, due to the amount of pasta, also I use Duke's brand mayo, it's my favorite, much better than anything else I've tried!!) (also ran out of this....figures!!)
- Here's what I added into some of the left-over macaroni salad:

- 1/2 cup Durkee brand french fried onions
- 1/2 jalapeno pepper, chopped fine
- also, 1 dash or so of cayenne pepper

Direction

- Cook pasta according to package directions. Cool (maybe about 20 minutes or so, so the mayo won't get cooked.)
- Blend together the rest of the ingredients with cooled pasta.
- Cool again (that's what the 120 minutes is for. It will also be nice and chilled and the vegetables will be so crunchy!!!! Mmmmmmmmmm!!
- If you would like to add some meat, add some chopped cooked chicken or some cubed ham or even salami would be great..... Don't forget about pepperoni!!!
- If adding the Durkee onions, add at the very possible last minute you can get away with or they will get soggy!!
- Enjoy!!

179. Lemon Basil Pasta Salad Recipe

Serving: 8 | Prep: | Cook: 10mins | Ready in:

Ingredients

- 1 pound farfalle (bow-ties) pasta
- 4 plum tomatoes, cut into 1 inch dice (or grape tomatoes cut in half)
- 8 basil leaves, cut into chiffonade
- 1 lemon, juiced
- 1/4 cup extra-virgin olive oil
- 1/2 teaspoons salt or to taste
- fresh basil leaves, for garnish

Direction

- Cook pasta according to directions on box.
- Drain the pasta and rinse under cold water to cool down.

- Put the pasta in a large serving bowl and add the tomatoes, basil, lemon juice, olive oil and salt.
- Toss well and garnish with fresh basil leaves.

180. Lemon Shrimp Pasta Salad Recipe

Serving: 12 | Prep: | Cook: 10mins | Ready in:

Ingredients

- 3 cups (8 oz.) farfalle (bow-tie pasta), uncooked
- 1lb. fresh asparagus spears, cut into 2-inch lengths
- 1 cup Light Zesty Italian Reduced Fat Dressing
- 1 tsp. dried oregano leaves
- 1 tsp. grated lemon peel
- 1 lb. cooked large shrimp (20 to 25 count)
- 1 cup halved cherry tomatoes
- 1 pkg. 2% milk colby & monterey jack cheese Crumbles

Direction

- COOK pasta as directed on package, adding asparagus to the cooking water for the last 3 min. of the pasta cooking time; drain. Rinse with cold water; drain well.
- MEANWHILE, mix dressing, oregano and lemon peel.
- PLACE pasta mixture in large bowl. Add dressing mixture, shrimp, tomatoes and cheese; mix lightly. Serve immediately. Or, cover and refrigerate until ready to serve.
- Kitchens Tips Substitute:
- Prepare as directed, substituting linguini, broken in half, for the farfalle. Variation - Easy Pasta Salad with Asparagus. Prepare as directed, omitting the shrimp and increasing tomatoes to 2 cups. How to Use Fresh Shrimp Substitute 1 lb. cleaned raw large shrimp for the cooked shrimp. Cook shrimp with 1 Tbsp. Zesty Italian dressing in large non-stick skillet

on medium-high heat for 3 to 4 min. or until no longer pink, stirring occasionally. Continue as directed.

181. Light Summer Pasta Salad Recipe

Serving: 8 | Prep: | Cook: 15mins | Ready in:

Ingredients

- 10 oz colourful pasta, cooked (omit any salt and oil)
- 2 Tbs olive oil
- 3 Tbs white wine vinegar
- 2 cloves garlic, minced
- 1 tsp salt
- 1/2 tsp sugar
- pepper to taste
- 1 Tbsp chopped fresh basil
- 1/2 tsp crushed pepper flakes
- 1 cup cubed fresh mozzarella
- 1 1/2 cups, halved cherry tomatoes
- green onions to garnish

Direction

- Combine all ingredients except pasta in a large bowl. Stir until combined.
- Add pasta and stir well.
- Garnish with green onions.
- Chill.

182. Lightly Lime Pasta Salad Recipe

Serving: 10 | Prep: | Cook: 12mins | Ready in:

Ingredients

- SALAD
- 7 oz uncooked small pasta shells

- EVOO
- kosher salt
- 11/2 c seedless green grapes
- 11/2 c cantalope cubes
- 2 bananas
- 2 c halved fresh strawberries
- DRESSING
- 1/2 c sour cream (or lowfat sour cream)
- 3 T thawed limeade concentrate
- 1/8 t salt

Direction

- Cook pasta in water salted with generous pinches kosher salt and EVOO, until al dente
- Drain well and rinse pasta with cold water to cool
- Drain well
- ** Cut bananas into small bowl and drizzle with juice from the lemon to prevent browning
- Meanwhile in large bowl mix grapes, cantaloupe and bananas
- In small bowl mix dressing ingredients until well blended
- Gently stir cooled cook pasta and dressing into salad
- Gently stir in strawberries
- ** I always drain a can of pineapple, packed in its own juice, and cut any bananas or apples that I am using into that juice. It's works better than lemon to prevent browning, and I take the pineapple in my lunch, etc.

183. Linguini Pasta Salad Recipe

Serving: 6 | Prep: | Cook: 24mins | Ready in:

Ingredients

- 16 oz. Linguini pasta
- 6 cloves garlic crushed
- 6 tablespoons sugar
- 6 tablespoons oil

- 6 tablespoons rice vinegar
- 6tablespoons soy sauce
- 2 tablespoons sesame oil
- sesame seed and scallion for garnish

Direction

- Prepare the linguini according to the directions on its box
- Boil all the ingredients on the stove top until the sugar dissolves
- Pour the sauce over the pasta while the pasta is still hot
- Mix until the pasta is well coated
- Before serving, you can add sesame seed and/or scallions for added color and garnish

---

184. Lisa's Roasted Tomato Salad With Israeli Couscous Recipe

Serving: 8 | Prep: | Cook: 2hours | Ready in:

Ingredients

- 1 cup Israeli couscous
- 2 cups chicken stock
- 1 1/2 pounds cherry tomatoes, sliced in half
- 1 large purple onion, chopped into large chunks
- 3-4 cloves garlic, unpeeled
- 3 Tbs fresh lemon juice
- 2 Tbs olive oil (the best you have)
- salt, to taste
- pepper, to taste
- kalamata olives (about 1/2 cup or so, chopped)
- feta cheese, crumbled (2-4 oz. should do it)
- fresh basil, finely shredded (chiffonnaded?)

Direction

- Preheat oven to 300 degrees.
- Spread the onions and tomatoes on a large, foil-lined baking sheet. Season with salt and pepper, then drizzle the olive oil over everything. Toss to coat, then place the garlic cloves in a corner of the sheet.
- Place the sheet in the oven and set the timer for an hour.
- Meanwhile, prepare the couscous by placing it in a saucepan with the chicken stock. Simmer for 7-8 minutes until the stock is absorbed and the couscous is al denté. Rinse the couscous in cold water to stop the cooking and set aside to drain.
- Keep an eye on the roasting veggies, especially when your whole kitchen starts to smell like heaven. You want the tomatoes to reduce and dry somewhat, and you want the onions to wilt and brown a little, but not burn. Count on this taking an hour or so.
- Take the sheet out of the oven and let everything cool off. When it gets to room-ish temperature, it's time to make the dressing.
- Squeeze the flesh of the garlic cloves into a food processor or blender. Add about 1/2 to 3/4 cup of the tomato/onion mixture, lemon juice, salt and pepper to taste, and a touch of olive oil if you wish. Whir away until it's a smooth, orange-y mass.
- Mix the remaining tomato/onion batch with the couscous and toss. Add the Kalamatas, feta, and basil. Pour the dressing over the top, toss, adjust seasonings, and enjoy! Looks great, tastes yummy! Serve at room temp or chilled.

---

185. Loris Italian Pasta Salad Recipe

Serving: 8 | Prep: | Cook: 10mins | Ready in:

Ingredients

- 1 lb. box of bow tie pasta (cooked and drained according to the package)
- 1 sm. can of sliced black olives drained
- 1 jar (about 12 oz) of roasted red peppers (drained and sliced into strips

- 1 jar (about 12 oz) of marinated artichokes (drained and rough chop)
- 1 pt. of grape or cherry tomatoes rinsed and halved
- 1 sm. container of boccacini mozzerella (small mozz. balls) drained from their liquid
- 1/4 lb. genoa salami cut into small strips
- 1/4 lb. chunk of provolone cheese cut into small chunks (or more if desired)
- 1/2 (8 oz) bottle of balsamic vinegrette
- 1/2 (8 oz) bottle of House Italian dressing (I like Newmans)
- fresh basil

Direction

- Toss pasta with all ingredients except the fresh basil. Use more or less dressing to taste.
- I usually make this salad the day before serving and add more dressing as needed as the pasta absorbs some dressing overnight.
- Add chopped fresh basil before serving.
- Enjoy!

---

186.   MACARONI FRUIT SALAD Recipe

Serving: 8 | Prep: | Cook: 10mins |Ready in:

Ingredients

- 2 c. macaroni, uncooked (use elbow, shells or twists)
- 1 c. celery, sliced
- 1 lg. apple, diced & toss with lemon juice
- 1 c. seedless white grapes
- 1 (15 oz.) can pineapple chunks
- 1 (11 oz.) can mandarin orange segments, well drained
- 1 c. mini white marshmallows
- 1/2 c. mayonnaise or salad dressing
- 1/2 c. sour cream
- 1 tsp. sugar
- 1/8 tsp. nutmeg

- lettuce leaves
- .

Direction

- Cook macaroni, rinse and drain well.
- In large bowl, combine all ingredients except lettuce, mix well. Cover and chill thoroughly.
- When ready to serve you can place lettuce leaf on plate and fill with salad.

---

187.   MACARONI SALAD Recipe

Serving: 5 | Prep: | Cook: 8mins |Ready in:

Ingredients

- Ingredients
- 2 cups uncooked elbow macaroni
- 4 hard-cooked egg, chopped fine
- 1 med onion, chopped fine
- 3 stalks celery, chopped
- 1 small red bell pepper, seeded and chopped
- 2 tablespoons dill pickle relish
- 2 cups creamy salad dressing (e.g. Miracle Whip)
- (I use 3/4 c Miracle Whip, the rest mayo)
- 3 tablespoons prepared yellow mustard
- 3/4 cup white sugar
- 2 1/4 teaspoons white vinegar
- 1/4 teaspoon salt
- 3/4 teaspoon celery seed

Direction

- Bring a pot of lightly salted water to a boil.
- Add macaroni, and cook for 8 to 10 minutes, until tender.
- Drain, and set aside to cool.
- In a large bowl, stir together the eggs, onion, celery, red pepper, and relish.
- In a blender, mix the salad dressing, mustard, white sugar, vinegar, salt and celery seed.

- Pour over the vegetables, and stir in macaroni until well blended.
- Cover and chill for at least 2 hour before serving.

188. Macaroni And Ham Salad Recipe

Serving: 6 | Prep: | Cook: 30mins | Ready in:

Ingredients

- 2 cups elbow macaroni
- 1 1/2 cups diced cooked ham
- 2 chopped hard boiled eggs
- 6 sliced stuffed olives
- 2 tablespoons chopped parsley
- 2 tablespoons chopped pimentos
- 1 teaspoon salt
- 1/8 teaspoon pepper
- 1/2 cup mayonnaise

Direction

- Cook and drain macaroni following directions on package. Rinse, drain and chill. Combine all ingredients, blending thoroughly. May be served on lettuce leaves; topped with tomato slices.

189. Macaroni Chicken Salad Recipe

Serving: 12 | Prep: | Cook: 25mins | Ready in:

Ingredients

- 500g elbow macaroni, uncooked
- 2 pieces chicken breast
- 100g chopped celery
- 1 large carrot, chopped or shredded
- 2 tbsp pickle relish

- 1 apple, sliced into small cubes
- 4 pieces pineapple rings, sliced
- 1 big jar of mayonnaise
- 1/2 cup condensed milk
- 4 tbsp raisins
- 1 cup all purpose cream or heavy cream
- 2 cups grated cheese
- salt and ground black pepper to taste

Direction

- Boil water in a pot with a little salt and cooking oil. Put the elbow macaroni in boiling water and cook until it is firm to the bite (al dente). Drain.
- Boil the chicken breast in slightly salted water until tender. Drain and let it cool, then shred the chicken breast and discard the bones.
- In a large bowl, combine the cooked macaroni, shredded chicken, chopped celery, carrot, pickle relish, apples, pineapple slices and raisins. Season to taste with fine salt and ground black pepper.
- Add the mayonnaise, all-purpose cream and condensed milk. Lastly, add the cheese and mix well. Adjust the seasonings according to your taste.
- Refrigerate for a few hours to chill. Serve cold.

190. Macaroni Salad Recipe

Serving: 6 | Prep: | Cook: | Ready in:

Ingredients

- 2 cups elbow macaroni, uncooked
- 2 cups creamy salad dressing (e.g. Miracle Whip)
- 3 hard-cooked eggs, diced
- 3 stalks celery, diced
- 2 tbsp dill pickle relish
- 1 small onion, diced
- 1 small red bell pepper, seeds removed and diced
- 3 tbsp prepared yellow mustard

- 3/4 tsp celery seed
- 2 1/4 tsp white vinegar
- 3/4 cup white sugar
- 1/4 tsp salt

Direction

- Boil a pot of lightly salted water, add macaroni and cook for 8-10 minutes, until tender. Then, drain, and place aside to cool.
- Combine the eggs, celery, relish, onion, and red pepper in a large sized bowl. In a small bowl, mix together the salad dressing, mustard, vinegar, sugar, celery seed and salt. Pour the mixture onto the vegetables, and mix in macaroni until blended well. Cover and place in the refrigerator to chill for at least 1 hour prior to serving.

191.   Macaroni Shrimp Salad Recipe

Serving: 4 | Prep: | Cook: 10mins | Ready in:

Ingredients

- 12 ounce package salad macaroni
- 1 pound salad size shrimp
- 1/4 cup mayonnaise
- 3 teaspoons prepared mustard
- 1 teaspoon chili powder
- 1 teaspoon pappy seasoning
- 1 large stock celery chopped
- 2 tablespoons white onion chopped
- 8 ounces canned sliced olives
- 1 teaspoon salt

Direction

- Cook macaroni according to directions then drain in colander and rinse with cold water.
- Mix mayonnaise and mustard together to taste then add remaining ingredients and mix well.
- Chill in refrigerator several hours before serving.

- Keep refrigerated until ready to eat.

192.   Macaroni Supper Salad Recipe

Serving: 6 | Prep: | Cook: 10mins | Ready in:

Ingredients

- 1 8 oz. package small shell macaroni
- 2 cups diced cooked ham or ham luncheon meat
- 1/2 c. coarsely grated carrot
- 1/4 cup chopped onion
- 1/4 cup chopped green pepper
- 1 tsp salt
- 1 cup mayonaise
- 1 8 oz can tomato sauce

Direction

- Cook, drain and rinse macaroni according to package directions.
- Mix ham, carrots, onion, and green pepper and salt in large bowl.
- Blend Mayonnaise and tomato sauce
- Pour over salad ingredients: toss lightly to mix
- Chill thoroughly.
- Serve on crisp salad greens

193.   Macaroni Tuna Salad Recipe

Serving: 4 | Prep: | Cook: 5mins | Ready in:

Ingredients

- 12 ounces canned water packed albacore tuna drained and flaked
- 8 ounce package small shell macaroni
- 2 hard boiled eggs finely chopped
- 1/4 cup green or red pepper chopped

- 2 stalks celery chopped
- 1 bunch green onions chopped
- 1 cup frozen green peas cooked and cooled
- 3/4 cup mayonnaise
- 2 tablespoons pickle relish
- 1 teaspoon salt
- 1 teaspoon freshly ground black pepper

Direction

- Cook macaroni according to package directions then drain and rinse with cold water. Allow to cool then add tuna, eggs, pepper, celery, onions and peas and mix well.
- In a small bowl mix together mayonnaise, pickle relish, salt and pepper.
- Add to the macaroni and mix well then place in refrigerator several hours before serving.

---

194. Macaroni And Shrimp Salad Recipe

Serving: 14 | Prep: | Cook: 10mins | Ready in:

Ingredients

- 16 oz. bag salad or elbow macaroni
- 1 cup celery, diced fine
- 1 cup green onions, chopped (include some of the green part)
- 1/2 cup green pepper, diced fine
- 1 lb. salad shrimp, cooked and shelled
- 1 cup mayonnaise
- 5 Tbs. Dijon mustard
- 1 tsp. celery seed
- 1 tsp. horseradish
- 2 to 3 Tbs. sweet pickle juice from a jar of pickles
- salt and pepper to taste
- 5 hard boiled eggs

Direction

- Cook the pasta according to package directions. Rinse so that pasta is cool. Drain well.
- Place the celery, green onions and green pepper in a large bowl. Add the cooked and drained pasta. Stir to evenly incorporate celery, onions and pepper.
- Add the shrimp and mayonnaise and evenly stir in.
- Add the mustard, celery seed, horseradish, pickle juice and salt and pepper. Stir until all is well combined. Chill overnight.
- Peel and slice hard boiled eggs and place on top of salad before serving.

---

195. Make Ahead Pasta Salad Recipe

Serving: 6 | Prep: | Cook: 180mins | Ready in:

Ingredients

- 1 1/2 cups medium size macaroni shells, freshly cooked
- 1 tablespoon vegetable oil
- Dressing:
- 1 cup mayonnaise
- 1/2 cup sour cream
- 2 teaspoons Dijon mustard
- 1/4 cup sliced green onions
- 1/2 teaspoon salt
- 1/2 teaspoon freshly ground pepper
- 2 cups shredded iceberg lettuce
- 3 hard cooked eggs, sliced
- pepper to taste
- 1 ounces of ham, cut in thin slices
- or 1 cup each of thin strips ham
- and hard salami
- 10 ounces frozen tiny green peas, thawed
- 1 cup coarsely shredded monterey jack cheese
- For garnish: 2 tablespoons chopped parsley

Direction

- Rinse the cooked macaroni shells
- Drain the cooked macaroni.
- Toss macaroni with oil to prevent shells from sticking.
- Mix all dressing ingredients in a small bowl until thoroughly blended.
- Put lettuce in one layer in a 3 quart bowl.
- Clear glass or plastic bowl is best to show off the layered effect.
- Top with cooled macaroni.
- Next add the egg slices.
- Sprinkled with pepper.
- Add in layers the ham, peas, and cheese.
- Spread dressing carefully over the top to bowl's edge.
- Cover tight with plastic wrap.
- Refrigerate overnight.
- Before serving, sprinkle with parsley.

196.   Marinated Antipasto Pasta Salad Recipe

Serving: 6 | Prep: | Cook: 120mins |Ready in:

Ingredients

- Dressing:
- 2 cloves garlic
- 2/3c white balsamic vinegar or white wine vinegar
- 2Tbs Dijon mustard
- 1tsp salt
- 1/2tsp sugar
- 1c extra virgin olive oil
- pasta Salad:
- 4 oz. uncooked ziti or mostaccioli pasta
- 6oz genoa salami,diced
- 6oz. provolone or mozzarella,diced
- 12 kalamata olives
- 12 cherry tomatoes
- 4 bottled pepperoncini peppers,seeded and sliced
- lettuce leaves
- basil leaves,chopped

Direction

- Dressing: Drop garlic through food processor feed tube with motor running. Process till garlic minced
- Add vinegar, mustard, salt and sugar; process to blend. With motor running, slowly pour oil through feed tube; process till thickened. Cover; refrigerate 2 hours or up to 1 month
- Salad: Cook pasta according to directions; drain and rinse with cold water.
- Combine pasta, salami, cheese, olives, tomatoes and pepperoncini in med. bowl. Add dressing; toss well
- Cover; refrigerate 2 hours or up to 2 days. Serve on lettuce leaves. Sprinkle with basil.

197.   Mediterranean Chicken Pasta Salad Recipe

Serving: 4 | Prep: | Cook: 20mins |Ready in:

Ingredients

- 8 oz pasta (farfalle or penne works well)
- 4 chicken breast halves, skinless and boneless
- 8 oz blue cheese, crumbled
- 16 sun-dried tomato slices, soaked in olive oil or water
- 1 bunch arugula (about 1/2 the size of a head of lettuce)
- 4 oz fresh basil
- 4 oz black olives (preferably not canned)
- 2 cloves garlic
- 3 tsp salt
- 2 tsp pepper, freshly ground
- 1 tsp thyme
- 2 T extra virgin olive oil

Direction

- Pasta Preparation
- 1. Boil water in large pot, adding 1 tsp. salt to flavor

- 2. Add pasta and boil until done, about 10 minutes.
- Chicken Preparation
- 3. Cut chicken into 1/2 inch strips, like fajita strips
- 4. Rub chicken with salt, pepper, and thyme. Fry in olive oil and garlic until golden brown on the outside and cooked throughout.
- Salad Preparation
- 5. Mix pasta, arugula and basil on 4 plates.
- 6. Add chicken, blue cheese, olives and sun-dried tomatoes.
- 7. Sprinkle fresh-ground pepper on top, mix and serve with a nice red or white wine.

---

198. Mediterranean Pasta Salad Recipe

Serving: 8 | Prep: | Cook: 40mins | Ready in:

Ingredients

- Vinaigrette:
- 1/4 cup red wine vinegar
- 1 tbsp. lemon juice
- 2 cloves garlic, minced
- 2 tsp. dried oregano
- salt and freshly ground pepper to taste
- 2/3 cup extra-virgin olive oil
- Salad:
- 2 cups uncooked penne pasta (I use whole-wheat)
- 1 19 oz. can chick peas, drained or 1 cup channa dall (split chickpeas cooked in boiling water for 30 min. or until tender)
- 10 cherry tomatoes, cut in half
- 1 small red onion, coarsely chopped
- 1 yellow pepper, coarsely chopped
- 1 red pepper, coarsely chopped
- 1/2 english cucumber, sliced
- 1/2 cup pitted olives, sliced
- 1/2 cup feta cheese, crumbled

Direction

- To make the Vinaigrette:
- In a small bowl, whisk together the red wine vinegar, lemon juice, garlic, oregano, salt and pepper and olive oil until combined. Set aside until ready to use.
- To assemble the salad:
- Bring a pot of salted water to boil. Add the pasta and cook until just tender. Drain and rinse under cold running water until cooled.
- If you are using Chana Dal instead, put measured amount in water on saucepan on the stove and bring to a boil. Turn down the heat and cook until tender, approximately 1/2 hour.
- Place the pasta in a large bowl and add the chickpeas (or the Chana Dal), tomatoes, feta cheese, red onion, yellow and red peppers, cucumber and olives.
- Pour on the vinaigrette and toss the salad well. This can be done ahead of time and stored, covered with plastic wrap and refrigerated for a few hours.

---

199. Mediterranean Salad Recipe

Serving: 6 | Prep: | Cook: 15mins | Ready in:

Ingredients

- • 3 tablespoons extra-virgin olive oil, plus 1/4 cup
- • 2 cloves garlic, minced
- • 1 (1-pound) box Israeli couscous (or any small pasta)
- • 3 cups chicken stock
- • 2 lemons, juiced
- • 1 lemon, zested
- • 1/2 teaspoon salt
- • 1/2 teaspoon freshly ground black pepper
- • 1 cup chopped fresh basil leaves
- • 1/2 cup chopped fresh mint leaves
- • 1/4 cup dried cranberries
- • 1/4 cup slivered almonds, toasted

Direction

- In a medium saucepan, warm 3 tablespoons of the olive oil over medium heat. Add the garlic and cook for 1 minute. Add the couscous and cook until toasted and lightly browned, stirring often, about 5 minutes. Carefully add the stock, and the juice of 1 lemon, and bring to a boil. Reduce the heat and simmer, covered, until the couscous is tender, but still firm to the bite, stirring occasionally, about 8 to 10 minutes. Drain the couscous.
- In a large bowl, toss the cooked couscous with the remaining olive oil, remaining lemon juice, zest, salt, and pepper and let cool. Once the couscous is room temperature, add the fresh herbs, dried cranberries, and almonds. Toss to combine and serve.

200.   Mega Egga Macaroni Salad From Big Daddys House Recipe

Serving: 6 | Prep: | Cook: 12mins | Ready in:

Ingredients

- 2 pounds elbow noodles
- 12 hard boiled eggs, peeled and diced
- 1/2 onion, finely diced
- 4 celery stalks, finely diced
- 1/4 cup pickle relish (dill)
- 3 cups heavy mayonnaise (Kraft real mayo)
- 2 tablespoons salt
- 1 teaspoon coarsely cracked black pepper
- Dash hot sauce
- 1 tablespoon worcestershire sauce

Direction

- Directions
- In a large pot with salt, boil pasta for 12 to 15 minutes until cooked. Stir often.
- Drain and cool.
- Refrigerate for 30 minutes.

- In a large pot with a dash of salt, add eggs on medium high heat. Bring to a boil.
- Cover and remove from heat.
- Let eggs sit for 6 to 7 minutes.
- Remove eggs and shock in ice water.
- Once thoroughly cooled, peel eggs and roughly dice.
- Place pasta in a large bowl.
- Add onions, celery, eggs, relish, mayonnaise, salt and pepper, hot sauce and Worcestershire.
- Mix until well combined.

201.   Mexican Pasta Salad Recipe

Serving: 8 | Prep: | Cook: | Ready in:

Ingredients

- 12 ounces corkscrew pasta cooked and cooled
- 4 ounces green chilies chopped
- 16 ounce can red kidney beans drained
- 1/2 green pepper chopped
- 8 ounce can whole kernel corn drained
- 1/2 cup celery chopped
- 1/4 red onion chopped
- 2 teaspoons fresh chopped parsley
- 1 teaspoon chili powder
- 1/2 teaspoon ground cumin
- 1 cup mayonnaise

Direction

- Mix pasta, chilies, beans, pepper, corn, celery, onion and parsley together and set aside.
- Mix together chili powder, cumin and mayonnaise then pour over pasta mixture.
- Chill overnight and if desired add chopped tomato right before serving.

202. Mexican Street Corn Pasta Salad Recipe

Serving: 8 | Prep: | Cook: 40mins | Ready in:

Ingredients

- 1 pound rotini pasta
- 6 ears of corn, husks removed
- 1 cup roughly chopped cilantro
- ¾ cup chopped green onion
- 1 cup grated cotija cheese
- 1 cup regular Hellman's mayonnaise
- ½ cup sour cream
- Zest and juice of one lime
- 1 garlic clove, minced
- 1-2 dashes of chipotle chili pepper
- Salt and pepper to taste

Direction

- Cook pasta per package instructions. Drain thoroughly then place pasta in a large bowl and set aside.
- Preheat grill.
- Once grill is nice and hot place corn directly on grates.
- Cook corn for 3-4 minutes per side until corn begins to char.
- Once all sides have been slightly charred, remove from grill.
- Remove corn off the cob standing corn firmly up on a cutting board and with a sharp nice carefully removing kernels.
- Alternatively place a small bowl upside down inside a large mixing bowl. Hold corn standing up on top of inverted bowl and carefully run a down the side of the corn to remove the kernels.
- Reserve about ¾ cup of the kernels and place the remaining kernels in a large bowl along with cooked pasta.
- Add ½ cup cilantro and ½ cup green onion to pasta.
- In a medium bowl mix together grated Cotija cheese, mayonnaise, sour cream, lime zest and

juice, garlic and a dash or two of chipotle chili pepper until blended.
- Season sauce with a pinch of salt and pepper to taste.
- Pour sauce in with pasta and corn and toss to coat.
- Transfer pasta to a serving bowl and top with reserved corn and remaining ½ cup cilantro and ¼ cup green onion.
- Refrigerate until ready to serve.

203. Mexican Tuna Noodle Salad Recipe

Serving: 5 | Prep: | Cook: 20mins | Ready in:

Ingredients

- 1 - 8oz package macaroni noodles
- 3 - cans tuna in water, drained
- 8 oz mixed vegetables
- 1 - 14.5 oz can diced tomatoes with green chiles, drained
- 1 bunch green onions, chopped
- 1 cup mexican crema
- 1/2 cup mayonnaise
- 1 teaspoon latin seasoning
- 1/2 teaspoon fresh cracked black pepper
- 1/2 teaspoon salt

Direction

- 1. Cook noodles as directed. Drain and place noodle in bowl. Add remaining ingredients to bowl and mix well. Store in the fridge or serve immediately.

204. Minestrone Pasta Salad Recipe

Serving: 4 | Prep: | Cook: 10mins | Ready in:

Ingredients

- 7 ounces shell pasta cooked
- 1 cup carrots sliced
- 1 cup bell peppers chopped
- 1 can dark red kidney beans drained
- 1 can garbanzo beans drained
- 1 can diced tomatoes drained
- 1/2 cup parmesan cheese
- 2/3 cup Italian salad dressing

Direction

- In mixing bowl combine cooked pasta, carrots, bell peppers, beans, tomatoes, parmesan cheese and salad dressing. Mix well then chill several hours before serving.

205.   Mini Wheels Pasta Salad Recipe

Serving: 8 | Prep: | Cook: 30mins | Ready in:

Ingredients

- 1 16oz. box Barilla Piccolini Mini Wheels
- 4 T. extra virgin olive oil, divided
- 2 cups frozen green peas
- 1 pound chicken breast diced
- 6 slices bacon cut into strips
- 2 cups cherry tomatoes, halved
- 1 cup fresh mozzarella cubed
- 2 T. lemon juice

Direction

- Cook pasta for 6 minutes; drain and drizzle with 2 Tablespoons olive oil and spread on cookie sheet to cool.
- Boil peas in salted water for 5 minutes, drain and cool.
- In a skillet over medium heat, cook chicken in remaining olive oil for 4-5 minutes or until cooked through, season with salt and pepper.(I used seasoned salt) Allow to cool.

- Cook bacon until crispy, drain fat.
- Combine all ingredients, let sit 30 minutes before serving.

206.   Minnesota Pasta Pea Salad Recipe

Serving: 0 | Prep: | Cook: 2hours | Ready in:

Ingredients

- 8 oz cooked medium shell pasta; cooked al dente', drained and rinsed under cold water
- 1¼ cups frozen peas; cooked, drained and rinsed under cold water
- 1 egg, hard boiled and chopped
- 1/4 cup green onions, sliced; white and light green parts only
- 1/2 cup celery, chopped
- 1/2 cup mayonnaise, increase to 3/4 cup if adding a meat option
- 1/2 cup sour cream, increase to 3/4 cup if adding a meat option
- 1 cup sharp cheddar cheese, shredded
- 1/2 teaspoon dried dill weed, use up to 1 teaspoon if desired
- Dry roasted sunflower seed kernels, salted variety
- Make it a meal by adding one of the following options when adding the pasta to the mixing bowl:
- 1 cup cooked chicken, chopped
- 1 cup cooked ham, cut into small cubes
- 8 ounce can of albacore tuna that's packed in water, drained and flaked
- 8 ounce package of imitation crab meat, the ready-to-eat variety

Direction

- In a large bowl, blend the mayonnaise and the sour cream together. Stir the celery, chopped egg, onion and dill weed into the mayonnaise/sour cream mixture. Fold the cooked pasta into the bowl, followed by folding in any meat option. Fold in the cheese and then gently fold in the cooked peas. Cover and chill for at least 1 hour or up to 4 hours before serving. After 4 hours you may need to add more mayonnaise/sour cream mixture. Top each serving with 2 teaspoons of sunflower kernels.

207.   Mixed Herbed Pesto Dressed Pasta Salad With Garden Greens Recipe

Serving: 8 | Prep: | Cook: 35mins | Ready in:

Ingredients

- 1 Can of Organic black pitted olives
- ½ Cup of brine from the olives
- 1 Package of Organic Fussily pasta
- 6 Organic radishes
- 4 Hard boiled eggs quartered
- 3 Cups of Organic Greens
- 2 cloves of Organic garlic
- 2 Cups of Organic basil
- 1 tablespoon of nutritional yeast
- 6 Organic Lemon sage leaves
- ½ Cup of Organic walnut halves
- 4 Organic tarragon leaves
- 1 Cup of Organic parsley
- 1/4 cup Organic olive oil
- 4 tablespoons of Organic apple cider vinegar
- ½ teaspoon of Organic crushed red pepper flakes
- 4 tablespoons of sea salt
- Fresh Organic black pepper to taste

Direction

- Boil the Fusilli drain and shock it in an Ice water bath to cool it down and prevent it from over cooking
- Directions for Pesto:
- Combine the Olive oil, Brine, the Red pepper flakes in a measuring cup

- Remove all of the leaves from the herbs and rinse well, add to food processor
- Remove the skins of the garlic and chop, add to food processor
- Pulse the processor until a paste is formed
- Add the oil and brine mixture in a stream until blended smooth
- Add the Nutritional yeast and pulse for a few seconds
- In a large Bowl add the Pasta, Radishes, Olives and the Greens, Walnut halves and toss.
- Add the Pesto dressing and toss to coat the pasta evenly.
- Place a generous mound of Salad onto a plate
- Shave the Romano Cheese onto each plate
- Add the Egg quarters
- Enjoy

208.   My Lomaglio Pasta Salad Recipe

Serving: 10 | Prep: | Cook: 1mins | Ready in:

Ingredients

- 2 Pounds Spiral tri-color pasta (not noodles)
- (or 2 boxes 12 oz same as above)
- 1-Large jar roasted red peppper
- 1-Medium can sliced black olives
- 1-Medium jar green olives with pimentos
- 1-or 2-Jars marinated artichoke hearts
- (Can add pepperoni - your choice)
- 1/4-Cup onion (sweet)
- 3-tsp Chopped garlic
- (Can add 1 can/jar marinated mushrooms - your choice)
- Cheese: feta, Provolone, Mozzarella (amount your choice)
- or....you can use any cheese of your own choosing)
- 1-1/2 Bottle Italian dressing (Kens) or your choice
- (Note: Also tastes good with Cesear Dressing)

Direction

- Boil large pot of water adding some olive oil and salt
- Add past - cook on medium heat only until pasta is soft NOT mushy
- Remove from pot and drain
- Pour cold water over pasta and drain again
- Set aside until Past cools down
- After Pasta is totally cooled add all the other ingredients
- Make sure to cut everything up very small (not shredded)
- Add garlic and onion
- Add cheese last (also cut up small or can be shredded-your choice)
- Add salad dressing and toss entire salad
- After tossing sprinkle some parmesan cheese on top
- Refrigerate at least 3 hours to allow the flavors to set.
- Serve: As a side dish, on a picnic, to a church group, sports event or whenever you think this dish might go!
- Enjoy my wonderful childhood pasta salad dish!

209.   My Macaroni Salad Recipe

Serving: 8 | Prep: | Cook: 10mins | Ready in:

Ingredients

- 8 ounces elbow macaroni
- 8 ounce package sharp cheddar cheese crumbles
- 1/2 cup mayonnaise
- 10 grape tomatoes
- 1/2 cup chopped sweet pickles
- salt to taste
- pepper to taste

Direction

- Cook macaroni according to package directions. Mine called for 10 minutes and that is the "cook time" shown.
- Drain macaroni and run cool water over it until it cools off. Set your colander over paper towels to drain while you prepare your other ingredients.
- Slice tomatoes lengthwise, then cut each half into 3 or 4 pieces.
- Chop pickles. Today I used the little tiny whole sweet pickles.
- Place drained macaroni in a large bowl and season with salt and pepper as desired.
- Add the mayonnaise and stir to coat the macaroni evenly.
- Add cheese and mix, then stir in pickles and tomatoes.
- Chill at least a couple hours, or overnight if possible.
- Stir before serving. Add additional mayonnaise if needed, or additional salt and pepper.

210.   My Simple Macaroni Salad Recipe

Serving: 8 | Prep: | Cook: 10mins | Ready in:

Ingredients

- 8 oz. (dry) cooked salad macaroni (you can use whatever pasta you prefer)
- Chopped roma tomatoes (I only had 2, but 3 would be better)
- 1/3 cup chopped sweet onion (approx. - I don't measure, sorry)
- bunch of ciilantro (leaves only) chopped (about 1/3 cup)
- 1 small can sliced black olives (drained)
- 1 tsp minced garlic
- 1/2 cup mayonnaise (more/less)
- 1 Tbls yellow mustard (Frenchs, I just squirted it in)

- 1/2 tsp dill weed - approx. (or you can use dill relish, or if you prefer, sweet)
- salt and pepper to taste
- olive oil (I drizzle with just before serving because it seems to soak up the mayo while in the fridge, just to moisten, and stir)

Direction

- Add chopped tomatoes, onions, cilantro, olives, and garlic to large bowl
- Add cooked macaroni (or pasta)
- Add mayo and mustard, stir in
- Add dill weed (or relish), salt and pepper
- Adjust seasoning and mayo to taste

211.   Nannas Pasta Salad Recipe

Serving: 8 | Prep: | Cook: 12mins |Ready in:

Ingredients

- 1 12-16 oz. bag of spiral pasta
- 1 cup Miracle Whip
- 1/2 can sweetened condensed milk
- 2 medium carrots; shredded
- 1 small green pepper; diced
- 1 small onion ; diced
- salt and pepper to taste

Direction

- Boil pasta till al dente. Rinse under cold water.
- Add the rest of the ingredients and chill for at least 3 hours.
- Serve cold.
- Right before serving - add a 1 Tbs. each of Miracle Whip and sweetened condensed milk.

212.   Natures Table Pasta Salad Recipe

Serving: 4 | Prep: | Cook: 20mins |Ready in:

Ingredients

- 1 each cucumber -- diced
- 2 each tomatoes -- diced
- 1 cup broccoli florets
- 1 cup carrots -- shredded
- 1/2 cup black olives -- sliced
- 2 pounds rotini -- tri-colored
- 1 1/4 cups canola oil
- 1 teaspoon pepper
- 3/4 cup red wine vinegar
- 1 tablespoon dried oregano
- 1 tablespoon dried basil
- 1 tablespoon garlic -- granulated
- 3 tablespoons Spike all purpose seasoning
- 1/2 cup romano cheese -- grated
- 1/4 cup mayonnaise

Direction

- To make dressing, mix canola oil, pepper, red-wine vinegar, oregano, basil, garlic, all-purpose seasoning, cheese and mayonnaise in blender container and blend until smooth; set aside.
- Cook pasta according to package directions.
- Drain and rinse in cold water.
- Fold together pasta and vegetables.
- Fold in dressing.
- Garnish with additional Romano cheese
- Will keep a week in the Refrigerator- flavors improves with age

213.   Never Fail Macaroni Salad Recipe

Serving: 12 | Prep: | Cook: 20mins |Ready in:

Ingredients

- 1 pound tri colored spriral pasta
- 5 hard boiled eggs
- 2 medium carrots shredded
- 1 large green pepper, diced
- 1 bunch green onions, chopped
- 3 stalks celery, chopped
- 1 envelope Good Season's Italian salad dressing mix
- 1 quart mayonnaise

Direction

- Cook pasta per package
- Boil eggs and cool
- Mix all ingredients in a large bowl
- Refrigerate 3 to 8 hours

---

214. New England Pasta Salad With Ricotta And Feta Recipe

Serving: 6 | Prep: | Cook: 10mins | Ready in:

Ingredients

- 1 pound penne pasta
- 2 medium cucumbers peeled seeded and sliced
- 1 cup olives pitted and halved
- 1 teaspoons red pepper flakes
- 3/4 cup ricotta cheese
- 3/4 cup crumbled feta cheese
- 1 ounce crumbled feta cheese for garnish
- Dressing:
- 1/2 large red onion finely chopped
- 1/4 cup plus 2 tablespoons fresh lemon juice
- 1/4 cup finely chopped fresh oregano leaves
- 3 tablespoons finely chopped fresh dill
- 2 tablespoons red wine vinegar
- 1/2 cup extra-virgin olive oil
- 1 teaspoon salt
- 1 teaspoon freshly ground black pepper

Direction

- Bring 3 quarts of water and 1 tablespoon of kosher salt to a boil then add the pasta and cook for 10 minutes.
- Drain and let cool to room temperature stirring occasionally.
- When cool place in a large bowl and add the dressing.
- For the dressing combine all ingredients except for oil, salt and pepper.
- Slowly whisk in the oil until it is thoroughly combined.
- Season with salt and pepper.
- Allow to stand at least 30 minutes.
- Using a wooden spoon gently mix salad until dressing is well distributed.
- Add remaining ingredients except 1 ounce feta for garnish.
- Let stand for 1/2 hour.
- Mix well and top with feta and serve.

---

215. Old Bay Pasta Salad Recipe

Serving: 8 | Prep: | Cook: 10mins | Ready in:

Ingredients

- 1 (16 oz.) pkg. rotini pasta
- 1 (6 oz.) can sliced black olives.
- 1 large cucumber.
- 8 oz. monterey jack cheese.
- 3 3/4 tsp. Old Bay Seasoning
- 1 cup Zesty Italian dressing.

Direction

- Cook Rotelle pasta according to the package directions until tender, but slightly firm.
- Rinse with cold water, drain well.
- Using a large bowl, mix together the Monterey Jack cheese, dressing, olives, and the diced cucumber.
- Add seasoning and toss well with cooled pasta, all above ingredients.
- Mix together well.

- Refrigerate several hours or preferably overnight.
- Serve and ENJOY!

216. Olive Pasta Salad Recipe

Serving: 4 | Prep: | Cook: 10mins | Ready in:

Ingredients

- 1 1/2 Cups elbow macaroni or pasta of your choice
- Jar of olives (I used Guiliano brand olives)
- 2 cloves of garlic
- parmesan cheese (grated, fresh is best)
- 3 tablespoons balsamic vinaigrette (I used Newman's Own)
- 1 dash italian seasoning
- 1/2 Cup peas or cooked soy beans
- salt and pepper

Direction

- Boil your pasta and drain, add to a large bowl.
- Dice up a handful of olives or as many as you'd think you like.
- Mince garlic
- Mix in all ingredients, don't forget to add a splash of olive juice from the jar or tub for an extra kick of flavor!
- Refrigerate and enjoy for a nice snack when it's too hot!

217. Over The Top Macaroni Salad Recipe

Serving: 8 | Prep: | Cook: 30mins | Ready in:

Ingredients

- 5 ounces small Sea shell macaroni
- 1 almost ripe avocado, cut in ½" dice
- 4 slices bacon, fried crispy

- 2 ounces cheddar cheese, cut in ¼" chunks
- 2 hard boiled eggs, cut in ¼" chunks
- 2 roma tomatoes, seeded and cut in small chunks
- 2 Tbsp. sweet yellow onion, chopped fine
- 2 Tbsp. chopped Italian parsley
- ½ cup mayonnaise
- ¼ cup sour cream
- ¼ teas. celery salt
- pepper to taste

Direction

- Boil macaroni according to directions on package. Drain and rinse in cold water. Set aside.
- Combine bacon, cheese, eggs, tomatoes, onion and parsley. Add macaroni and stir to combine.
- Mix together mayonnaise and sour cream with celery salt and pepper. Add to salad and stir.
- Lastly add avocado and stir gently to combine. Refrigerate until ready to serve. Having avocado in this salad, it should be consumed the same day or the avocado discolors.
- Also, using an avocado that is almost ripe works best. If they are too ripe, it just goes to mush when you mix it in the salad.

218. PESTO PASTA SALAD Recipe

Serving: 10 | Prep: | Cook: | Ready in:

Ingredients

- 1 package (16 ounces) spiral pasta, cooked, drained and cooled
- 1 cup julienned fully cooked ham
- 1 cup julienned carrots
- 1 cup thinly sliced celery
- 1 cup frozen peas, thawed
- 1 cup sliced fresh mushrooms
- 1 cup julienned zucchini
- 1 cup cubed monterey jack cheese

- 1/2 cup grated parmesan cheese
- 1/2 cup thinly sliced green onions
- 1/3 cup chopped radishes
- 1 can (6 ounces) medium pitted ripe olives, drained and halved
- 1 jar (2 ounces) chopped pimientos, drained
- ***
- PESTO DRESSING:
- ******************************
- 3 to 5 garlic cloves
- 2 cups loosely packed fresh basil leaves
- 3/4 cups grated Parmesan or romano cheese
- 1/4 cup slivered almonds
- 3/4 teaspoon salt
- 1/2 teaspoon dried tarragon
- 1/4 teaspoon pepper
- 1/8 teaspoon sugar
- 1 cup olive oil
- 1/2 cup white wine vinegar
- 1 cup whole almonds, toasted

Direction

- In a large bowl, combine the first 13 ingredients; set aside.
- For dressing, process garlic in a blender or food processor until finely chopped.
- Add basil, cheese, slivered almonds, salt, tarragon, pepper and sugar.
- Process 15-30 seconds or until coarsely chopped.
- With the motor running, gradually add oil until mixture is smooth. Add vinegar and process until blended.
- Pour over salad; toss to coat.
- Just before serving, add whole almonds.

---

219.   PRONTO PASTA SALAD Recipe

Serving: 6 | Prep: | Cook: 10mins |Ready in:

Ingredients

- Ingredients:
- 1 cup Hellman's Best Foods real mayonnaise
- ¼ cup milk
- 1 Tbs. vinegar
- 1 tsp. dried basil
- 1 package KNORR vegetable soup and Recipe Mix
- 1 package (10-oz) frozen broccoli florets, thawed
- 8-oz Prince rotini pasta, cooked and drained as package directs.

Direction

- In a large bowl combine mayonnaise, milk, vinegar, basil and soup mix. Add broccoli and macaroni; toss to coat well. Cover; chill 2 hours. Makes 6 cups.
- Variation: Substitute I medium tomato, chopped, for broccoli florets.

---

220.   Parmesan Pasta Salad Recipe

Serving: 8 | Prep: | Cook: 12mins |Ready in:

Ingredients

- 1 small box/bag of tri-color pasta (3 1/2 cups cooked)
- 2 eggs; hard boiled and sliced
- 1 cucumber; peeled and sliced
- 2 medium tomatoes; wedged
- 1/2 purple onion - diced
- 4 cloves garlic - crushed
- 6 radishes - sliced
- 1 small can sliced black olives - rinsed
- 1 small jar parmesan 4 cheese dressing
- 1/3 cup olive oil
- 1/2 bag Real Sargento Salad Creations - or italian blend
- salt and pepper to taste

Direction

- Cook pasta till al dente. Drain and rinse under cold water.
- Mix the rest of the ingredients except for eggs.
- Top with sliced eggs.
- Chill for at least 2 hours.

221. Pass It To Me Pasta Salad Recipe

Serving: 4 | Prep: | Cook: 5mins | Ready in:

Ingredients

- 1 1/2 pkgs. spiral pasta
- 1 jar (26 oz.) pasta sauce, any variety
- 1/2 cup olive oil and vinegar salad dressing
- 2 1/2 cups broccoli florets
- 1 cup diced carrots
- 1 cup peas
- 1 cup olives
- 1/2 cup scallions

Direction

- Cook pasta according to package directions
- Mix pasta, broccoli, carrots, green peppers, peas, onions and olives in a large salad bowl
- Add pasta sauce and salad dressing
- Toss and refrigerate for at least 3 hours
- Serve at room temperature

222. Pasta Buffet Salad Recipe

Serving: 0 | Prep: | Cook: 9hours | Ready in:

Ingredients

- 2 cups broccoli
- 2 cups cauliflower
- 2 cups carrots
- 2 cups celery
- 2 cups zucchini

- 1 cup red pepper
- 1 cup green pepper
- 1 large bottle Italian salad dressing (your favorite)
- 1 1/2 lbs. pasta, spirals
- 1 bottle chili sauce
- 2 T. lemon juice
- 6 T. dill dip mix
- 1-4 oz. can sliced olives (opt.)

Direction

- Cut up all the vegetables into bite size pieces. In a large bowl, marinate vegetables in Italian dressing overnight.
- The next day, prepare pasta according to the package instructions. Drain and rinse with cold water. Drain marinade from vegetables, reserving 1/2 cup of dressing.
- Combine chili sauce, lemon juice and dill mix in a small bowl. Pour over pasta and vegetables and toss to coat. Add remainder of Italian marinade to taste.
- Refrigerate until thoroughly chilled and serve.

223. Pasta Pesto Salad Recipe

Serving: 4 | Prep: | Cook: 10mins | Ready in:

Ingredients

- 8 oz. dried Orzo pasta
- 8 oz. ripe cherry tomatoes,quartered
- Pesto Dressing{SEE BELOW}
- About1/4 cup pine nuts,lightly toasted
- Fresh basil sprigs
- About 1 cup fresh basil leaves
- 2 garlic cloves,peeled
- about1/4 cup of pine nuts
- 3 tablesspoons xtr-virgin olive oil
- 1/4 cup freshly grated good Parmeson cheese
- 3 tblsp. of half & half

Direction

- Cook pasta as directions indicate, tender but firm
- Drain, rinse with cold water, and drain again.
- In a bowl, put orzo and add the tomatoes.
- PESTO DRESSING:
- Combine basil leaves, garlic, pine outstand oil in a blender.
- Process till smooth.
- Turn into a bowl and beat in cheese and the half & half.
- Stir dressing into pasta mixture.
- Transfer into a serving dish and sprinkle with the toasted pine nuts.
- Garnish with Basil sprigs.

224. Pasta Potato Salad With Variations Recipe

Serving: 10 | Prep: | Cook: 20mins | Ready in:

Ingredients

- 1 cup elbow macaroni cooked
- 2 large redskinned potatoes, unpeeled, cubed and cooked
- 1 carrot coarsely shredded
- 2 tbs. minced red onion
- 1 stalk celery fine diced
- 1 cup of mayonasise or enough to bind
- salt and pepper to taste
- Variations:
- tuna/seafood:
- Add 2 cans albacore tuna/seafood drained
- turkey/chicken
- Add 2 cups diced cooked poultry
- Other Options:
- 1/2 cup cooked green peas
- fresh chopped parsley or herbs to taste
- chopped dried cranberries esp with the chicken

Direction

- Make basic pate potato salad and add variations as you like.
- Makes a large bowl serving 8 to 10.
- The pasta and potato combination is very delicious.
- A nice change from basic macaroni or potato salad!

225. Pasta Primavera Salad Recipe

Serving: 8 | Prep: | Cook: 7mins | Ready in:

Ingredients

- 1/2 lb ziti (before cooking)
- 5 tomatoes, coarsely chopped
- 2 green peppers, chopped
- 1 Tbsp chopped fresh basil or 1 tsp dried basil leaves
- 2/3 cup Wishbone Robusto Italian dressing
- 1 pkg. (8oz) mozzarella cheese (diced)
- 1/2 cup grated parmesan cheese
- pepper to taste

Direction

- Cook macaroni according to pkg. directions. Drain and rinse with cold water.
- In large bowl, combine tomatoes, green peppers, basil and Italian Dressing.
- Add cheeses, ziti and pepper to taste; toss lightly, then chill.
- You can also add cubed summer sausage or pepperoni.

226. Pasta Salad For A Crowd Recipe

Serving: 0 | Prep: | Cook: 45mins | Ready in:

Ingredients

- 2 - Boxes Bowtie pasta
- Red, Yellow, orange & green bell peppers - Diced
- 2 - Bushels of chives - Minced
- 2 - Containers of garlic & herb feta cheese
- 1 - Small can of pitted black olives
- 16-20 oz of your favorite Italian dressing (I use two of the good seasons Italian packets)
- Fresh cracked black pepper
- Freshly Grated parmesan cheese

Direction

- Boil the Bowtie Pasta until just al dente
- While the pasta is boiling cut up all the bell peppers and set aside
- Prepare dressing if you are making your own or using the packets
- Once the pasta is ready, drain and drizzle with a little bit of olive oil to prevent the pasta from sticking together, and allow to cool.
- Once the pasta has cooled, transfer it to a very large Pasta Bowl.
- Combine the pasta and half of the dressing, tossing to make sure all the pasta is coated, and add lots of fresh cracked pepper.
- Top the pasta with the Feta Cheese, Diced Bell Peppers, Minced Chives, Black Olives and Freshly Grated Parmesan in that order.
- Cover and let chill for at least 1 hour.
- Right before serving pour on the remaining dressing, toss & serve!
- Enjoy!

---

227.   Pasta Salad Primavera Recipe

Serving: 6 | Prep: | Cook: 180mins | Ready in:

Ingredients

- 8 ounces pasta of your choice (I like tricolor rotini)
- 14 1/2 ounce can diced tomatoes (drained, save juice for other use)

- 2 cups assorted chopped vegetables of your choice (onions, peppers, carrots, green onions etc--I like a little broccoli too)
- 1 cup Italian salad dressing.

Direction

- Cook pasta according to package directions, drain and cool.
- Combine pasta with all other ingredients in a large serving bowl
- Cover and refrigerate for at least 3 hours, overnight if you wish.

---

228.   Pasta Salad Recipe

Serving: 0 | Prep: | Cook: 25mins | Ready in:

Ingredients

- 1 cup medium pasta shells
- 1/4 cup Kraft Italian salad dressing
- 1/2 cup (or to taste) Kraft Mayo
- 1/2 cup finely chopped onion
- 1-2 small tomatoes, chopped
- 1/2 cup grated cheddar cheese
- 3 green onions, chopped
- parsley or chives

Direction

- Cook pasta shells in water in saucepan until al dente or how you like them. Drain, rinse and cool.
- Put pasta shells in a serving bowl and add the Italian dressing, Mayo, onion, tomatoes and grated cheese.
- Mix well. Garnish with green onions, parsley or chives. Set in refrigerator to chill for an hour or so before serving.
- Yummy!

229. Pasta Salad Supreme Recipe

Serving: 10 | Prep: | Cook: 12mins | Ready in:

Ingredients

- 1 box rotini pasta, or Veggie rotini pasta
- olive oil
- kosher salt
- 1/2-3/4 red onion, chopped
- 3/4 small package prewashed/cut borcolli florets, stems cut off, and cut into smaller pieces
- 1 small jar mushroom slices, drained (optional)
- 3/4 can jumbo ripe olives, drained, cut in half lengthwise
- 1 small tub grape tomatoes, cut in half lengthwise
- 1 T. pimentos, or a chopped, roasted red pepper (optional)
- 2 T. chopped garlic
- garlic pepper
- seasoned salt
- 2 - 3 T. Salad Supreme seasoning
- 1 c. fresh grated parmesan
- 1 c. Shredded mozzerella
- 1 Bottle Good Italian dressing (Ken's 3 cheese Northern Italian is good)

Direction

- Add Olive Oil and 2 pinches Kosher salt to pot of boiling water
- Add pasta, and cook until al dente
- Drain and rinse with cool water (yeah, I know...the chefs on FN say not to rinse, but, I hate that starchiness, was taught to rinse and I can tell it when I don't; also, rinsing with cool water helps cool it down to mix in with your other ingredients...but if you prefer to not rinse, go for it.)
- In large mixing bowl, add all ingredients except dressing & pasta
- Add pasta
- Add about 3/4 bottle dressing
- Toss well

- Place in fridge overnight.
- Taste the next morning, stir, and add more dressing/seasoning if needed.

230. Pasta Salad With A Twist Recipe

Serving: 6 | Prep: | Cook: 15mins | Ready in:

Ingredients

- cheese tortellini
- baby spinach
- Cardini Ceasar salad dressing(or any creamy ceasar dressing)
- Crumbled feta
- grape tomatoes(optional)

Direction

- Mix all together and serve.
- Great BBQ dish!

231. Pasta Salad With Creamy Red Wine Vinaigrette Recipe

Serving: 0 | Prep: | Cook: 15mins | Ready in:

Ingredients

- 1/2 pound vegetable radiatore or other short cut pasta, cooked according to package & cooled
- 1 cup carrots, sliced or diced
- 1 cup cucumbers, diced (I used little Persians with the skin still on)
- 1 cup tomatoes, diced (I used mini red vine), seeded
- 1/2 cup black olives, sliced
- 1/2 cup red wine vinaigrette
- 1/4 cup mayo
- 1/2 cup Parmesan, grated

- sea salt & black pepper, freshly ground - to taste

Direction

- Combine vinaigrette and mayo and mix well. In a large bowl toss the mixture with the pasta and veggies. Add cheese and toss well. Season with salt & pepper to taste.

---

232. Pasta Salad With Grilled Tuna And Roasted Tomatoes Recipe

Serving: 8 | Prep: | Cook: 45mins | Ready in:

Ingredients

- 8 plum tomatoes, about 1 1/4 lb. total, halved
- lengthwise
- 2 Tbs. plus 1/2 cup olive oil
- salt and freshly ground pepper, to taste
- 1 lb. pasta shells
- 2 lb. tuna fillets, each about 3/4 inch thick
- 1 cup loosely packed fresh basil leaves
- 3 Tbs. red wine vinegar
- 1 lb. fresh mozzarella cheese, finely diced
- 1/4 cup chopped fresh flat-leaf parsley

Direction

- Preheat an oven to 450°F. Prepare a hot fire in a grill.
- Place the tomatoes on a baking sheet and toss with 1 Tbs. of the olive oil. Arrange them, cut sides up, on the sheet and season with salt. Roast until tender, about 20 minutes. Let cool, then cut in half crosswise.
- Meanwhile, bring a large pot three-fourths full of salted water to a boil over high heat. Add the pasta and cook until al dente (tender but firm to the bite), about 10 minutes. Drain, rinse under cold running water and drain again. Set aside.

- Brush both sides of the tuna fillets with 1 Tbs. of the oil. Season well with salt and pepper. Place on the grill rack 4 to 6 inches above the fire and grill until lightly browned, about 3 minutes. Turn and cook for 3 to 4 minutes more for medium, or until done to your liking. Transfer to a cutting board, let cool and cut into 3/4-inch cubes.
- In a food processor or blender, combine the basil leaves and the remaining 1/2 cup oil. Pulse or blend until chopped to a coarse puree. Add the vinegar and season with salt and pepper. Pulse or blend until combined.
- In a large bowl, combine the pasta, tomatoes and any accumulated juices, tuna, mozzarella, parsley and basil dressing. Toss gently and serve. Serves 8.

---

233. Pasta Salad With Grilled Tuna And Roasted Tomatoes Recipe

Serving: 6 | Prep: | Cook: 20mins | Ready in:

Ingredients

- 8 plum tomatoes halved lengthwise
- 2 tablespoons olive oil plus 1/2 cup olive oil
- 1 teaspoon salt
- 1 teaspoon freshly ground black pepper
- 1 pound pasta shells
- 2 pounds tuna fillets
- 1 cup fresh basil leaves loosely packed
- 3 tablespoons red wine vinegar
- 1 pound fresh mozzarella cheese finely diced
- 1/4 cup chopped fresh flat leaf parsley

Direction

- Preheat oven to 450.
- Prepare a hot fire in a grill.
- Place the tomatoes on a baking sheet and toss with 1 tablespoons of the olive oil.

- Arrange them cut sides up on the sheet and season with salt.
- Roast for 20 minutes then let cook and cut in half crosswise.
- Meanwhile bring a large pot three-fourths full of salted water to a boil over high heat.
- Add the pasta and cook until al dente about 10 minutes.
- Drain and rinse under cold running water and drain again then set aside.
- Brush both sides of the tuna fillets with 1 tablespoon of the oil.
- Season well with salt and pepper.
- Place on the grill rack 4 to 6 inches above the fire and grill until lightly browned.
- Turn and cook for 4 minutes more for medium or until done to your liking.
- Transfer to a cutting board then allow to cool and cut into cubes.
- In a food processor or blender combine basil leaves and the remaining 1/2 cup oil.
- Pulse or blend until chopped to a coarse puree.
- Add vinegar and season with salt and pepper.
- Pulse or blend until combined.
- In a large bowl combine pasta, tomatoes and any accumulated juices, tuna, mozzarella, parsley and basil dressing.
- Toss gently and serve.

---

234. Pasta Salad With Mixed Vegetables Recipe

Serving: 8 | Prep: | Cook: 12mins | Ready in:

Ingredients

- 12 ounces farfalle (bow tie) pasta
- 1 tablespoon olive oil
- 1/4 cup low-sodium chicken broth
- 1 garlic clove, chopped
- 2 medium onions
- 1 can (28 ounces) unsalted diced tomatoes in juice
- 1 pound mushrooms, sliced

- 1 red bell pepper, sliced
- 1 green bell pepper, sliced
- 2 medium zucchini, shredded
- 1/2 teaspoon basil
- 1/2 teaspoon oregano
- 8 romaine lettuce leaves

Direction

- Fill a large pot 3/4 full with water and bring to a boil.
- Add the pasta and cook until al dente (tender), 10 to 12 minutes, or according to the package directions.
- Drain the pasta thoroughly.
- Place pasta in a large serving bowl.
- In a large skillet, heat the chicken broth over medium heat.
- Add the garlic, onions and tomatoes.
- Sauté until the onions are transparent, about 5 minutes.
- Add the remaining vegetables and sauté until tender crisp, about 5 minutes.
- Stir in the basil and oregano.
- Add the vegetable mixture to the pasta.
- Toss to mix evenly.
- Cover and refrigerate until well chilled, about 1 hour.
- Place lettuce leaves on individual plates.
- Top with the pasta salad and serve immediately.

---

235. Pasta Salad With Sea Scallops Recipe

Serving: 5 | Prep: | Cook: 240mins | Ready in:

Ingredients

- 1 teaspoon finely shredded orange peel
- 1/3 cup orange juice
- 1/4 cup white wine vinegar
- 2 tablespoons powdered fruit pectin
- 1 tablespoon sugar

- 6 ounces dried medium shell macaroni
- 8 ounces fresh or frozen sea scallops
- 2 cups water
- 4 cups torn fresh spinach
- 1 cup frozen peas
- 1/2 cup coarsely chopped red onion
- 1/2 cup thinly sliced celery
- 1/3 cup chopped red sweet pepper

Direction

- For dressing, in a small bowl stir together the orange peel, orange juice, vinegar, pectin, and sugar until smooth. Cover and chill at least 3 hours or up to 24 hours.
- Cook macaroni according to package directions; drain. Rinse with cold water; drain again.
- Meanwhile, thaw scallops, if frozen. Cut any large scallops in half. Bring water to boiling; add scallops. Return to boiling. Simmer, uncovered, for 1 to 3 minutes or until scallops are opaque. Drain. Rinse under cold running water.
- For salad, in a large bowl toss together cooked macaroni, cooked scallops, spinach, peas, onion, celery, and sweet pepper. Stir dressing; pour over salad. Toss to coat

236. Pasta Salad With Smoked Cheese Recipe

Serving: 6 | Prep: | Cook: 30mins | Ready in:

Ingredients

- 8 oz. elbow noodles
- 1 jar of pimentos including juice
- 1/3 cup of chopped scallions
- 1/2 cup of chopped brocolli florets
- 4 oz. smoked cheddar cheese - cut into 1/4 inch cubes
- 3 T olive oil
- 1 whole lemon zest and juice
- 1/2 cup chopped walnuts

- 1 tsp salt
- 1 tsp black pepper
- 1 tsp garlic salt
- 1 tsp garlic powder

Direction

- Boil pasta until al dente. Place in medium sized serving bowl.
- Fold in balance of ingredients. Taste and adjust seasoning if necessary.
- You can substitute broccoli with any vegetable you prefer or have on hand: asparagus or green beans would be excellent subs.
- Serve room temp or cold. Enjoy!

237. Pasta Salad With Spinach Olives And Mozzarella Recipe

Serving: 6 | Prep: | Cook: 25mins | Ready in:

Ingredients

- 1 pound orecchiette or conchiglie pasta
- 8 ounces fresh mozzarella cheese, drained, small dice
- 3 ounces baby spinach (about 4 cups), thoroughly washed and dried
- 1 1/2 cups pitted and halved kalamata olives
- 1 cup finely grated parmesan cheese
- 3 tablespoons red wine vinegar
- 2 teaspoons kosher salt
- 1 teaspoon freshly ground black pepper
- 6 tablespoons olive oil

Direction

- Bring a medium pot of heavily salted water to a boil over high heat. Cook pasta according to the package instructions, or until al dente.
- Drain, then rinse under cold water until cool.
- Transfer pasta to a large bowl and add mozzarella, spinach, olives, and Parmesan. Toss to combine.

- In a separate, nonreactive bowl, combine vinegar, salt, and pepper.
- Whisking constantly, slowly add oil by pouring in a thin stream down the side of the bowl. Whisk until completely incorporated.
- Pour vinaigrette over salad, and toss until pasta is coated. Taste, adjust seasoning as desired, and serve.

238. Pasta Salad With Capers Recipe

Serving: 8 | Prep: | Cook: 30mins | Ready in:

Ingredients

- 8 oz bowtie pasta
- 6 Tb olive oil
- 2 Tb red wine vinegar
- 1 Tb lemon juice
- 1 clove minced garlic
- 1/2 tsp salt
- 1/2 tsp pepper
- fresh basil, sliced
- 8 oz salami, sliced
- 2 Tb capers
- 1 can artichoke hearts, drained and chopped
- fresh mozzarella cheese, diced
- 1/2 c kalamata olives, pitted
- cherry tomatos, halved

Direction

- Boil pasta 14 minutes.
- Drain pasta and toss with dressing while still hot.
- Whisk together oil, vinegar, lemon juice, garlic, salt, pepper, basil.
- Refrigerate 30 minutes.
- Add remaining ingredients.

239. Pasta Salad With Proscuitto And Feta Cheese Recipe

Serving: 10 | Prep: | Cook: 10mins | Ready in:

Ingredients

- coarse salt and ground pepper
- 1 pound elbow macaroni
- 2 ounces thinly sliced prosciutto, cut into strips
- 4-5 green onions (sliced thin)
- 1/2 cup red-wine vinegar
- 1 clove of garlic
- 1 teaspoon Dijon mustard
- 1/4 cup extra-virgin olive oil
- 1 medium tomato, chopped
- 1/2 cup crumbled goat or feta cheese (2 ounces)
- 1/4 cup pitted kalamata olives (or your favorite olives), sliced
- 2 tablespoons capers (optional)
- 1/4 cup chopped fresh parsley
- ½ small jar of roasted peppers (cut into strips)
- Small jar of marinated artichoke hearts (cut in half)

Direction

- In a large pot of boiling salted water, cook macaroni until al dente. In a small skillet, cook prosciutto over medium until crisp; discard fat.
- Combine vinegar, mustard, and garlic in a large bowl; whisk in oil in a slow, steady stream – add salt and pepper to taste.
- Add tomato, cheese, prosciutto, olives, roasted peppers and artichoke hearts (and capers).
- Drain pasta; add to bowl with tomato mixture, and toss. Add parsley; season with salt and pepper.
- Cool to room temperature, and serve.

240. Pasta Salad With Summer Ale Vinaigrette Recipe

Serving: 6 | Prep: | Cook: 15mins | Ready in:

Ingredients

- 2 red bell peppers, seeded, and roasted
- 2 zucchini, grilled and diced
- 2 summer squash, grilled and diced
- 2 red onions, quartered and grilled
- 1lb. rotini pasta, cooked according to instructions
- 1/2 cup olive oil
- 2 1/2 tbls. cider vinegar
- 1 1/2 tsp rosemary, dried
- 2/3 cup summer ale (I use Sam Adams)
- 1 tsp lemon juice
- Salt and pepper to taste
- 1 pinch sugar
- Grated parmesan and chopped olives for garnish

Direction

- In blender, put red peppers, olive oil, cider vinegar, rosemary, beer, lemon juice, salt, pepper and sugar
- Blend until smooth
- Add vegetables to pasta
- Stir in vinaigrette
- Garnish with black olives and parmesan cheese.

241. Pasta And Pepper Salad Recipe

Serving: 4 | Prep: | Cook: 40mins | Ready in:

Ingredients

- 3 each of orange and yellow bell peppers
- 1 lb. uncooked farfalle (bow tie) pasta
- 2 lemons
- 2/3 c. bottled or homemade balsamic dressing

- 8 oz. mozzarella or Fontina cheese, cubed
- 1 pt. cherry tomatoes, cut in half
- 3/4 c. each of basil and mint, stacked and cut into narrow strips

Direction

- Remove broiler pan from broiler and preheat broiler.
- Bring a large pot of salted water to boil. While the water comes to a boil, cut peppers in half lengthwise, remove stems and seeds. Place cut side down on broiler pan and broil until the skin is charred. Remove, place in a medium bowl and cover, let stand until cool enough to handle.
- When the water boils, add pasta and cook according to package directions. Drain and rinse with cold water. Grate 2 tsp. of peel from lemons and squeeze 3 TB. juice; mix with balsamic dressing
- Slip skins off peppers and cut into narrow strips. Transfer pasta to a large serving bowl. Add pepper strips, cheese, tomatoes, basil, mint and balsamic dressing. Toss to mix. Chill until ready to serve.

242. Patriotic Pasta Salad Recipe

Serving: 12 | Prep: | Cook: 10mins | Ready in:

Ingredients

- 1/4 cup mayonnaise
- 1/4 cup sour cream
- 1/4 cup blue cheese, crumbled
- 1 1/2 teaspoons milk
- 1/2 teaspoon salt
- 1/2 teaspoon white vinegar
- 1/4 teaspoon garlic powder
- 1/2 teaspoon honey mustard
- 1/4 teaspoon ground black pepper
- 1/8 teaspoon cayenne pepper

- 8 ounces penne or zita pasta, cooked and cooled
- 1 clove garlic, minced
- 1/4 teaspoon dried basil, or to taste
- 2 tablespoons vegetable oil
- 1 cup cherry tomatoes, cut in half
- 3 green onions, thinly sliced
- 1/4 cup red bell pepper, diced
- 4 ounces mozzarella cheese, shredded

Direction

- Whisk together mayonnaise, sour cream, blue cheese, milk, salt, vinegar, garlic powder, honey mustard, black pepper and cayenne.
- In large bowl, toss together remaining ingredients.
- Pour dressing over and toss to coat.
- Cover and chill several hours.

243. Paula Deens Shrimp N Pasta Salad Recipe

Serving: 10 | Prep: | Cook: 10mins | Ready in:

Ingredients

- 1 cup mayonnaise
- 1 cup sour cream
- 1/2 cup onion, minced
- 1/4 cup celery, minced
- 3 tablespoons ketchup
- 4 teaspoons fresh lemon juice
- 3 teaspoons horseradish, prepared
- 1 teaspoon seasoned salt, Crazy Salt
- 3/4 teaspoon pepper
- 1 1/2 pounds shrimp, medium - cooked, peeled and deveined
- 16 ounces macaroni, cooked and drained (gluten-free macaroni will make this gf)
- Old Bay seafood seasoning (not in original recipe, just a nice addition)

Direction

- In a large bowl, combine sour cream, mayo, onion, celery, ketchup, lemon juice, horseradish, Crazy Salt and pepper. Stir in shrimp and macaroni. Cover and chill for at least 4 hours before serving.
- Sprinkle Old Bay over each individual serving.
- NOTE: To make this gluten-free, simply use gluten-free macaroni. BiAglut is the best by far. Stays nice and firm and does NOT get mushy!

244. Pea Pasta Ravioli Salad Recipe

Serving: 4 | Prep: | Cook: 20mins | Ready in:

Ingredients

- FILLING
- 200g frozen creamed spinach, thawed and drained
- 200 g ricotta cheese
- 20g grated parmesan cheese
- 2ml ground nutmeg
- pea pasta
- 300g flour, sifted
- pinch salt
- 12eggs
- 10 ml olive oil
- 220g cooked peas, pureed

Direction

- For filling just combine all ingredients, set aside
- To make Ravioli Pasta
- Sift flour and salt onto work surface and make well in centre
- Blend remaining ingredients with a fork
- Pour into well
- Gradually work all flour into centre of well
- Flour hands and work surface
- Knead pasta for 15min
- Let rest 15 min.

- Makes 600g
- Roll out half the dough to 3mm thick
- Cut into 40mm squares
- Spoon a little filling into middle of each square
- Brush edges with beaten egg
- Roll remaining dough and place over filling
- Press firmly around edges and cut
- Cook in boiling salted water for five to seven min.

245. Pea Pod And Pasta Salad Recipe

Serving: 8 | Prep: | Cook: |Ready in:

Ingredients

- 10 oz Tri color pasta (rigatoni type)
- 8 oz snow peas (blanched)
- 1/2 cup onion (diced)
- 1/4 cup pepper (red bell diced)
- 1/2 cup celery (diced)
- 1 cup tomato (grape, cut in half)
- 1/2 cup carrot chopped
- 1 packet herb and garlic dressing mix (good seasons -mix as directed on package)

Direction

- Cook Pasta in well-seasoned water - to blanch the pea pods - I just throw them in with the pasta for the last 5 minutes - when you drain the pasta and pea pods - throw 2 cups of ice on top to stop the cooking - leave the colander over top of a pot to drain as the ice melts. (Make sure to remove any unmelted ice cubes after 10 minutes)
- Add diced vegetables to the pasta and pea pods - add your dressing and place in the fridge for at least one hour before serving. This is one of those salads that you could add anything to - cheese, mushrooms, artichokes, if you like it you could add it. Enjoy

246. Peanut Sesame Pasta Salad Recipe

Serving: 6 | Prep: | Cook: 10mins |Ready in:

Ingredients

- pasta Salad:
- 12 oz. dry bowtie pasta
- 1 medium red bell pepper, cut into 1/8-inch strips
- 1 medium yellow bell pepper, cut into 1/8-inch strips
- 1 cup thinly sliced or chopped snow peas
- 1 medium carrot, cut into 1-inch matchstick-size pieces
- 4 green onions, thinly sliced
- 1/2 Cup Chopped peanuts for garnish
- 3 tablespoons sesame seeds, toasted
- peanut Dressing:
- 1/2 cup creamy peanut butter
- 1/4 Cup light soy sauce
- 1/3 cup warm water
- 2 tablespoons rice vinegar
- 1 tablespoon honey
- 2 teaspoons sweet chili sauce
- 1 Tbs minced garlic

Direction

- FOR PASTA SALAD:
- PREPARE pasta according to package directions. Drain under cold running water.
- FOR PEANUT DRESSING:
- Place peanut butter, soy sauce, water, ginger, vinegar, sweet chili sauce, honey and garlic in blender; cover. Blend until smooth. Transfer to large serving bowl. Refrigerate.
- ADD pasta, bell peppers, snow peas, carrot, green onions and sesame seeds to dressing; toss to combine.
- Garnish with chopped peanuts.

247. Pears Pasta And Pecan Salad Recipe

Serving: 8 | Prep: | Cook: 10mins | Ready in:

Ingredients

- pasta Ingredients:
- 4 ounces (1 cup) uncooked dried gemelli (double twist pasta) or small pasta shells
- salad dressing Ingredients:
- 1/4 cup sour cream
- 1 teaspoon freshly grated lime peel
- 3 tablespoons lime juice
- 3 tablespoons olive or vegetable oil
- 2 tablespoons honey
- Salad Ingredients:
- 1/4 cup coarsely chopped pecans, toasted
- 2 ribs (1 cup) celery, sliced
- 1 medium pear, sliced, quartered
- 1 medium apple, sliced, quartered
- 2 tablespoons chopped green onions

Direction

- Cook gemelli according to package directions. Rinse with cold water; drain.
- Meanwhile, combine all salad dressing ingredients in small bowl.
- Just before serving, toss together cooked pasta and all remaining salad ingredients in large bowl. Drizzle with dressing; toss gently to coat.

248. Penne Pasta Salad Recipe

Serving: 4 | Prep: | Cook: 10mins | Ready in:

Ingredients

- 16 ounces penne pasta - cooked and drained
- 8 ounces feta cheese - crumbled (use sun dried tomato flavor!)
- 2 ripe tomatoes, large - chopped
- 1/4 cup capers

- 1/4 cup parsley - chopped
- 3 ounces package of sun dried tomatoes , chopped
- Your favorite Zesty Italian dressing
- salt and pepper to taste

Direction

- Cook pasta according to package directions, drain and put into a large bowl.
- While pasta is cooking, prepare salad dressing and pour over the warm, drained pasta. Let cool before adding the rest of the ingredients.
- Add drained capers, crumbled feta cheese, chopped parsley, and chopped sun dried tomatoes.
- Add salt and pepper to taste.
- Refrigerate for 4 to 6 hours so ingredients absorb the flavors.
- Just before serving, add the tomatoes. Instead of using capers, chopped Kalamata olives can be substituted.
- To use this as an entrée, add one chicken breast per person. This recipe doubles and triples easily.

249. Pepper Olive Pasta Salad Recipe

Serving: 10 | Prep: | Cook: 10mins | Ready in:

Ingredients

- 3 - cups pkg dried small pasta penne and radiatore together.
- 1/4 - cup olive oil
- 2 - tablespoons balsamic vinegar
- 1/2 - teaspoon finely shredded lemon peel
- 2 - tablespoons lemon juice
- 1 - tablespoons sugar
- 1 tablespoon dijon-style mustard
- 1 - teaspoon snipped fresh basil or (1/2 tsp of dried basil crushed)
- 1 - teaspoon snipped fresh thyme (or 1/2 teaspoon dried thyme crushed)

- 1/2 - teaspoon snipped fresh marjoram (or 1/2 teaspoon dried marjoram crushed)
- 1/4 - teaspoon black pepper
- 2 - bell peppers red and yellow (or green) cut into thin strips
- 1/2 - cup pitted green olives, drained and halved
- 1/2 - cup thinly sliced green onions

Direction

- In a large saucepan cook the pasta according to directions on pkg.
- Drain, rinse with cold water; drain again and set aside
- For the dressing in a screw top jar combine olive oil, balsamic vinegar, lemon peel, lemon juice, sugar, mustard, basil, thyme, marjoram, black pepper.
- Cover and shake well to mix.
- Note; I always make double the dressing the pasta soaks it up. I add as needed and it taste so good. Try it first.
- In a large bowl, combine the pepper strips, olives, green onions, and pasta, add dressing; toss gently to coat.
- Makes 8 to 10 servings......

---

250. Pepperoni Pasta Salad Recipe

Serving: 8 | Prep: | Cook: | Ready in:

Ingredients

- 12 oz package tricolor rotini noodles
- 1 medium onion, chopped
- 1/2 cup black olives, sliced
- 1 1/2 cups sharp cheddar cheese, cubed (about 8 oz)
- 4 oz sliced pepperoni
- 1 cup frozen peas, thawed
- 1/2 tsp salt
- 1/4 tsp black pepper
- Dressing:

- 1 Tbsp Italian vinegar & oil dressing base
- 1 Tsp Italian herb mix
- 1/2 tsp minced garlic
- 1 Tbsp water
- 2/3 cup vegetable oil
- 1/3 cup vinegar

Direction

- Cook the pasta according to package directions. In small bowl, mix the dressing base, herb mix and garlic with water and let sit 5 minutes. When the pasta is done, drain and rinse briefly. Add onion, olives, cheese, pepperoni, peas, salt, and pepper to the pasta. For the dressing, mix the spices with the oil and vinegar. Whisk well. Pour the dressing over the pasta salad and mix well.

---

251. Peppery Monterey Jack Pasta Salad Recipe

Serving: 4 | Prep: | Cook: 10mins | Ready in:

Ingredients

- 6 ounces uncooked acini di pepe pasta (about 1 cup)
- 2 1/4 cups diced plum tomato (about 14 ounces)
- 1/3 cup capers, rinsed and drained
- 1/4 cup finely chopped red onion
- 1/4 cup sliced pickled banana peppers
- 1/4 cup chopped fresh parsley
- 2 tablespoons cider vinegar
- 1 tablespoon extra-virgin olive oil
- 1/2 teaspoon dried oregano
- 1/8 teaspoon salt
- 2 ounces monterey jack cheese, cut into 1/4-inch cubes
- 1 (16-ounce) can navy beans, rinsed and drained
- 1 ounce salami, chopped
- 1 garlic clove, minced

Direction

- Preparation
- 1. Cook pasta according to package directions, omitting salt and fat. Drain.
- 2. Combine tomato and remaining ingredients in a large bowl. Add pasta to tomato mixture, tossing well to combine.
- Asiago breadsticks: Combine 1/2 cup grated Asiago cheese, 1 tablespoon sesame seeds, and 1 teaspoon freshly ground black pepper in a small bowl. Separate 1 (7-ounce) can refrigerated breadstick dough to form 8 sticks; roll each breadstick in cheese mixture. Bake according to package directions.

252. Pesto Pea And Pasta Salad Recipe

Serving: 8 | Prep: | Cook: 10mins | Ready in:

Ingredients

- 1 cup pesto sauce
- 10 ounce box frozen baby sweet peas or equal in fresh peas
- 1 lb. farfalle (bow tie) or fusilli (cork screw) pasta, cooked to al dente
- 2 ounces shaved Parmessan cheese
- salt and pepper to taste
- 12 fresh basil leaves, cut in slivers

Direction

- Steam fresh peas for 2 minutes and then pour into a colander and sit in a bowl of ice water to chill and retain the fresh green color - or - if using frozen peas, run under warm water for a couple minutes in a colander and then allow to drain.
- Combine peas, pasta and pesto and stir to combine. Season with salt and pepper. Chill for at least 1 hour.
- Add shaved Parmesan and slivered basil, stir gently.

253. Pizza Pasta Salad Recipe

Serving: 6 | Prep: | Cook: 10mins | Ready in:

Ingredients

- 1/2 container grape tomatoes
- 1 medium red onion
- 10 fresh button mushrooms, sliced
- 1 green pepper, chopped
- 1 package pepperoni
- 1 lb fresh mozzarella cheese
- 20 leaves of basil, thinly sliced
- 3 gloves minced garlic
- 1 lb wagon wheel pasta, cooked and drained
- salt and pepper
- Dressing
- 1 teaspoon oregano
- 2 tablespoons red wine vinegar
- 1/2 cup extra virgin olive oil

Direction

- Combine tomatoes, onion, garlic, mushrooms, bell pepper, pepperoni, cheese, pasta and basil in a big bowl.
- Whisk salt, oregano, vinegar, olive oil and salt and pepper together. Pour over pasta and chill.

254. Polynesian Shrimp Salad Recipe

Serving: 6 | Prep: | Cook: 30mins | Ready in:

Ingredients

- 1 can (20 ounces) pineapple chunks
- 2 teaspoons cornstarch
- 1 teaspoon curry powder
- 1/8 teaspoon salt

- 1/8 teaspoon pepper
- 1/2 cup mayonnaise
- 1/2 cup lite sour cream
- 1 pound cooked medium shrimp, peeled and deveined
- 3 cups cooked medium pasta shells
- 1 can (8 ounces) sliced water chestnuts, drained
- 1/4 cup chopped sweet red pepper

Direction

- Drain pineapple, reserving 3/4 cup juice; set pineapple aside. In a small saucepan, combine the cornstarch, curry powder, salt, pepper and reserved pineapple juice until smooth. Bring to a boil; cook and stir for 1 minute or until thickened. Remove from the heat; cool to room temperature. Stir in mayonnaise and sour cream.
- In a large bowl, combine the shrimp, pasta, water chestnuts, red pepper and reserved pineapple. Add dressing and toss to coat. Cover and refrigerate for at least 2 hours before serving.

255.   Pot Luck Pasta Salad Recipe

Serving: 6 | Prep: | Cook: 10mins |Ready in:

Ingredients

- 16 ounces pasta (your choice of type)
- 1/2 cup green onion, chopped
- 1/4 cup green pepper, chopped
- 1/2 each cucumber, chopped
- 1 dozen cherry tomato, halved
- 1/4 cup broccoli, chopped
- 1 cup mayonnaise
- 2 stalks celery, peeled and chopped
- 4-5 slices bacon, fried crisp and crumbled
- salt and pepper, to taste

Direction

- Bring pot of water to a boil, pour in pasta and cook till tender. Drain in colander, cool and put in large mixing bowl.
- Prep and chop all other ingredients. Mix all dry ingredients except tomato into pasta. Add mayonnaise and mix together.
- Finally add tomatoes and mix gently to keep from crushing them. Salt and Pepper to taste.
- Cover and refrigerate until time to serve. [Can be done the day before]
- Add crumbled bacon on top just before serving to keep it crisp.

256.   Premio Italian Sausage Pasta Salad Recipe

Serving: 6 | Prep: | Cook: 28mins |Ready in:

Ingredients

- 16oz Premio italian sausage
- 2tbsp margarine
- 6oz Italian dressing
- 16oz angel hair pasta
- 1 Sliced tomato
- Pinch of garlic

Direction

- Cook sausage in butter. Let sausage cool.
- Toss sausage with cooked pasta and Italian dressing.
- Serve chilled on a warm day with cold lemonade or white wine.

257.   Ramen Noodle Salad Recipe

Serving: 0 | Prep: | Cook: |Ready in:

Ingredients

- ramen noodlE SALAD
- 1 lg. head cabbage, cut fine
- 4 tbsp. sesame seeds
- 1 c. slivered almonds
- 2 pkg. ramen noodles (chicken flavored)
- 3/4 c. green onions & tops
- Brown seeds and almonds. Do separately as one brown faster. Smash noodles with rolling pin.
- DRESSING:
- 1 tsp. salt
- 1/4 tsp. pepper
- chicken flavor packets from soup
- 4 tbsp. sugar
- 6 tbsp. vinegar (or rice wine vinegar if you like, but is more expensive)
- 1 c. oil

Direction

- Toss dressing, onions, cabbage and noodles, 2-3 hours before serving. Add almonds and seeds right before serving. You can cut cabbage, mix dressing, etc., the day before.

---

258.   Ranch Bacon Pasta Salad Recipe

Serving: 10 | Prep: | Cook: 20mins | Ready in:

Ingredients

- 1 pound corkscrew pasta (I like multi colored)
- 1 cup frozen peas, thawed
- 1 cup carrots, blanched, peeled and diced
- 1/2 cup celery, finely sliced
- 1 medium cucumber, peeled and diced
- 1 large red pepper, diced
- 1 red onion, diced
- 1 cup grape tomatoes, sliced in half
- 2 slices turkey bacon, cooked and crumbled
- 2 oz. sliced black olives (heck... I use about a cup and I just halve them.)
- 3/4 cup non-fat or low-fat mayonnaise

- 1 0.4-ounce packet of dry ranch salad dressing mix
- 1/4 cup prepared barbecue sauce (I use about 1/2 cup)

Direction

- Cook pasta according to package directions for al dente. Drain in a colander. Transfer to a large bowl. Add in the peas, carrots, celery, cucumber, red pepper, onion, tomatoes, bacon and olives. Gently mix. In a small bowl, whisk together the mayonnaise, ranch salad dressing mix and barbecue sauce.
- If making ahead, store the pasta salad and the dressing in separate sealed containers in the fridge until ready to serve. Just before serving, pour the dressing over the pasta salad and toss to combine. Serve cold.
- Makes 10 to 12 servings.
- Per serving (based on 10): 240 calories, 8 g fat (1 g saturated fat), 35 mg cholesterol, 35 g carbohydrate, 2 g fiber, 8 g protein, 61% vitamin A, 42% vitamin C, 3% calcium, 13% iron

---

259.   Ranch Macaroni Salad Recipe

Serving: 8 | Prep: | Cook: 1hours | Ready in:

Ingredients

- 1 box mini penne, cooked according to package directions, I like mine el dente
- 1 small tomato, seeded and chopped
- 1-2 stalks celery, chopped
- 4-6 radishes, chopped
- 1/4 cup cucumber, chopped
- 2 scallions, chopped up to light green
- 1/2 small bell pepper, any color and chopped
- 1 8 oz. bottle ranch dressing
- salt and pepper to taste

Direction

- In large mixing bowl, combine all ingredients
- If I have any cooked bacon on hand I crumble it into the salad but that's not often around here....never any bacon leftover!!!

260. Ranch Noodle Salad Recipe

Serving: 8 | Prep: | Cook: 30mins | Ready in:

Ingredients

- pasta elbow noodles or your choice, ranch dressing pack of Hidden Valley Homemade packages.Or your choice of Ranch, peas, shredded carrots, bacon bits from jar or cooked & diced/chopped. Shredded cheddar cheese & white Mozzarella shredded cheese.

Direction

- In a pot boil pasta ever so gently until done don't overdo it, al dente. Put into a colander & run cool water over it, put aside. In a big mixing bowl add pasta & cooled steamed shredded carrots & peas. Toss gently. In another bowl mix Hidden Valley ranch dressing, mayo, milk & stir or shaker method in bottle jar, it is good to make this one a day ahead enhanced flavor blended. Add bacon bits to dressing. Then add this ranch dressing to the pasta/veggie mix. Stir & chill in frig. Ahead of dinner. To leave enough time for chilling.

261. Ranch Pasta Salad

Serving: 0 | Prep: | Cook: | Ready in:

Ingredients

- 3 cups uncooked tricolor spiral pasta
- 1 cup chopped fresh broccoli florets

- 3/4 cup chopped seeded peeled cucumber
- 1/2 cup seeded chopped tomato
- 1 bottle (8 ounces) ranch salad dressing
- 1/2 cup shredded Parmesan cheese

Direction

- Cook pasta according to package directions; drain and rinse in cold water. In a large bowl, combine the pasta, broccoli, cucumber and tomato. Drizzle with salad dressing; toss to coat. Sprinkle with cheese.
- Nutrition Facts
- 3/4 cup: 285 calories, 17g fat (3g saturated fat), 8mg cholesterol, 317mg sodium, 27g carbohydrate (2g sugars, 1g fiber), 6g protein.

262. Ravioli Pasta Salad Recipe

Serving: 4 | Prep: | Cook: 7mins | Ready in:

Ingredients

- 1/2 pound ricotta-stuffed ravioli
- 1 bunch thin asparagus, cut on deep bias (angle)
- 10 ounce bag frozen peas, thawed overnight in refrigerator
- 3 - 4 big handfuls baby spinach, washed (any stems removed - optional)
- a couple splashes of extra-virgin olive oil
- 1/2 cup pine nuts, toasted
- fine grain sea salt
- parmesan cheese, for garnish

Direction

- Prep all of your ingredients ahead of time - cut asparagus, wash spinach, etc.
- Into an extra-large pot of well-salted boiling water add the raviolis. After a few minutes, when a couple of the raviolis begin to float, add the asparagus and peas. You'll need to cook them only for about a minute - really

quick, just enough to brighten up the peas and give the asparagus a touch of tenderness.

- Drain everything into a large colander. Immediately transfer to a large bowl, add the spinach and pine nuts, and gently toss with a couple big splashes of olive oil and a pinch or two of salt. Serve in a big bowl or on a simple platter with a bit shaved Parmesan crumbled on top.

263. Roasted Pepper Chicken Pasta Recipe

Serving: 8 | Prep: | Cook: 45mins | Ready in:

Ingredients

- 12 ounce package of small shell pasta
- 1 cup of diced roasted sweet peppers, packed in oil
- 1/2 cup of grape tomatoes, sliced
- 1 1/2 cups cooked chicken breast (I cheated and used canned)
- 1 stalk of celery, diced
- 1 small onion, chopped
- 1 cup of raw spinach, cut into small bits
- 1 clove of garlic, crushed (optional)
- 1/2 cup of parsley, cut into small pieces
- 1/4 tsp pepper
- Dash of ginger
- Salt to taste
- 1/2 cup sour cream
- 1/4 cup mayonnaise

Direction

- Cook and drain pasta. Rinse well. Set aside.
- Prepare other ingredients and add.
- Mix well. Chill to blend flavors.
- If it's too dry, additional mayonnaise can be added.

264. Roman Spaghetti Salad Recipe

Serving: 8 | Prep: | Cook: 10mins | Ready in:

Ingredients

- 3 large garlic cloves, minced
- 5 Tbsp olive oil
- A handful of fresh mint leaves (spearmint is best), minced
- 5 Tbsp fresh orange juice
- 12 black olives
- 6 anchovy fillets
- 1 small jar marinated mushrooms in oil
- salt to taste
- 1 1/2 lbs. spaghetti

Direction

- Fry garlic gently in the oil until golden. Add the mint and take off the heat. Pour in the orange juice. Chop the olives and anchovies roughly and stir into the pan, then add the mushrooms. Season with salt and mix all together.
- Cook the spaghetti in lots of boiling water, till al dente. Drain and pour onto a large platter. Mix in the sauce and spread out to cool. When cool, transfer to a nice rustic bowl to serve outside :)

265. SANTA FE CHICKEN PASTA SALAD Recipe

Serving: 4 | Prep: | Cook: 360mins | Ready in:

Ingredients

- Ingredients:
- 12-oz uncooked spiral pasta
- 2 cups cooked chicken breast cubes
- 1 medium zucchini or yellow squash, cut in half lengthwise, then crosswise

- 1 cup GILTLESS GOURMET Green tomatillo Salsa
- 1 cup drained and coarsely chopped artichoke hearts
- ½ cup chopped green onions
- ½ cup Medium Black pitted olives sliced
- lettuce leaves
- fresh dill sprigs (optional)

Direction

- Method;
- 1) Cook pasta according to package directions; drain. Place cooked pasta in a non-metal bowl; add chicken, zucchini, tomatillo salsa, artichoke hearts, onions and olives. Toss lightly. Refrigerate at least 6 hours before serving.
- 2) To serve, line the serving platter with lettuce leaves (any type). Garnish with dill sprigs, if desired.
- Calories per serving: 413

266.　　Sadies Macaroni And Shrimp Salad Recipe

Serving: 6 | Prep: | Cook: 120mins | Ready in:

Ingredients

- 1-1/2 cups uncooked elbow macaroni
- 1 lb shrimp
- 1/2 cup chopped green onions
- 1/2 cup celery; sliced fine
- 1/2 cup sliced black pitted olives
- 1/4 cup dill pickles; chopped fine
- 1/2 teaspoon salt
- 1/2 teaspoon fine ground white pepper
- 6 hard boiled eggs; coarsely chopped
- 1 cup Sadie's Salad Dressing; * See Recipe

Direction

- Cook the eggs and refrigerate until needed.

- Cook, and peel the shrimp. Refrigerate until ready to mix.
- Cook macaroni, chill in iced water to cool, then drain.
- In a large bowl, mix macaroni, shrimp, onions, celery, olives, pickles, salt and pepper and toss well, then add chopped eggs and gently toss to mix.
- Spoon on the dressing and gently toss to mix thoroughly. Refrigerate until ready to serve.
- Note: Sadie is from Natchitoches, Louisiana, is pronounced [NAK-ah-dish]. I never met her but her salad is a real crowd pleaser.

267.　　Salami Pasta Salad Recipe

Serving: 4 | Prep: | Cook: 10mins | Ready in:

Ingredients

- 7 ounces small pasta shells uncooked
- 1 cup cherry tomatoes sliced in half
- 1 cup ripe olives sliced in half
- 6 ounces mozzarella cheese cut into thin strips
- 4 ounces salami cut into thin strips
- 1/2 cup bell pepper chopped
- 4 green onions chopped
- 1/3 cup vegetable oil
- 3 tablespoons red wine vinegar
- 1 teaspoon salt
- 1 teaspoon dried basil
- 1 teaspoon dried oregano
- 1/4 teaspoon garlic powder

Direction

- Cook pasta shells according to package directions then drain and rinse in cold water.
- Place in large bowl then add tomatoes, olives, mozzarella cheese, salami, bell pepper and onions.
- Combine vegetable oil, vinegar, salt, basil, oregano and garlic powder and mix well.

- Pour over salad and toss to coat then refrigerate 1 hour before serving.

---

268.   Salmon Pasta Salad Recipe

Serving: 4 | Prep: | Cook: | Ready in:

Ingredients

- 4 cups small shell pasta
- 1/4 cup of chopped celery (I add how much I like)
- 1 cup peas
- 1 can (7.5 oz) sockeye salmon, drained
- 1/2 cup low fat plain yogurt
- 1/3 cup finely diced red onion
- 1/4 cup light mayo
- 6 radishes, thinly sliced
- 2 tbsp chopped fresh dill or 2 tsp dried dill
- salt, pepper and a dash of hot sauce
- 12 romaine lettuce leaves (I skip this part- I do not like lettuce in my pasta salad)

Direction

- Boil your pasta as directed on the package. In the last minutes of cooking add your peas
- Drain and rinse under cold water
- In a small bowl, flake your salmon and mash away!!
- In a large bowl, stir together yogurt, onion, mayo, radishes, dill, salt, pepper and hot sauce
- Add the salmon and pasta to the dressing and gently stir until combined
- If you have lettuce spoon onto lettuce leaves.

---

269.   Salmon Pasta Salad A La Northwest Recipe

Serving: 8 | Prep: | Cook: 10mins | Ready in:

Ingredients

- 3/4 lb. cooked salmon fillet, flaked into 1" pieces
- 8 oz. rotini pasta, cooked and drained
- 1 smaller cucumber, peeled, seeded and diced
- 1 green onion, thinly sliced (optional)
- 1/3 cup mayonnaise
- 3 Tbps. buttermilk or plain yogurt
- 1 Tbsp. lemon juice
- 1 teas. lemon zest
- 2 Tbsp. chopped fresh dill weed
- 2 tsp. chopped chives
- salt & pepper to taste

Direction

- In a small bowl, combine mayonnaise, sour cream (or yogurt), lemon juice, lemon zest, dill, chives, salt and pepper. Whisk until well combined.
- In a larger salad bowl, combine salmon, pasta, cucumber and green onion. Stir together gently so the salmon remains in chunks. Add dressing and stir together again. Place in fridge and allow to chill 2 hours.

---

270.   Salmon Pasta Salad With Pesto Recipe

Serving: 10 | Prep: | Cook: 15mins | Ready in:

Ingredients

- 1 box Rotinni
- 1lb. salmon steak
- 6-8 green onions (or one med.-sized purple or sweet onion), sliced
- 1 red bell pepper, diced
- 1 large or 2 small ripe avocado, cut in large dice
- 1 small can sliced black (ripe) olives
- 1/2 Cup pesto (I used Scearley's recipe from this site)
- olive oil, high quality virgin

- salt and pepper to taste

Direction

- Cook pasta to al dente according to package directions, then rinse in cold water and drain.
- Brush salmon lightly with some pesto or olive oil.
- Broil or bake salmon until it flakes easily with a fork (about 10-15 minutes at 350 degrees). Cool briefly, then flake entire salmon steak and refrigerate.
- Thin the pesto with a little olive oil (about 2-3 Tbs.)
- Gently mix all ingredients.
- Refrigerate until served. Best when refrigerated overnight.

---

271. Salsa Cruda Pasta Salad Recipe

Serving: 4 | Prep: | Cook: 10mins | Ready in:

Ingredients

- 4oz farfalle or rotini pasta
- 1/4 c EVOO
- 2 tbs balsamic vinegar
- 1 3/4 lb mixed red, yellow, and green tomatoes, seeded and coarsely diced
- 1/3 c thinly sliced green onions
- 1/3 c thinly slicked mixed fresh herbs such as basil and orgeano
- 1/2 tsp coarse salt
- 1/2 tsp pepper
- 2 oz shaved ricotta salata or romano cheese

Direction

- Cook pasta accord to package directions. Drain and return to pot.
- Meanwhile, whisk oil and vinegar in med bowl. Stir in tomatoes, green onion, herbs, salt and pepper.
- Stir tomato mixture into pasta, tossing to mix

- Serve warm or at room temp, sprinkled with cheese.

---

272. Santa Fe Pasta Salad Recipe

Serving: 4 | Prep: | Cook: | Ready in:

Ingredients

- 16 ounce package bow tie pasta
- 5 quarts water
- 1/2 cup grated parmesan cheese
- 1/2 cup cooked yellow corn kernels
- 1/3 cup chopped cilantro
- 1/4 cup chopped green onions
- 2 tablespoons diced red bell pepper
- 2 tablespoons diced green bell pepper
- 1 chicken breast fillet cooked and diced
- Dressing:
- 1-1/4 cup vegetable juice
- 1-1/2 tablespoons olive oil
- 1 tablespoon red wine vinegar
- 1-1/2 teaspoons chili powder
- 3/4 teaspoon paprika
- 1/2 teaspoon salt
- 1/4 teaspoon freshly ground black pepper

Direction

- Prepare pasta by bringing water to a rolling boil in a large saucepan.
- Add pasta to pan and when water begins to boil again cook for 10 minutes.
- Whisk all dressing ingredients together in a small bowl then cover and chill.
- When pasta is done pour it into a large bowl then add dressing and toss well.
- Add remaining ingredients to pasta and toss until combined.
- Cover and chill for several hours before serving.

273.   Satay Chicken Pasta Salad Recipe

Serving: 6 | Prep: | Cook: 30mins | Ready in:

Ingredients

- 8 oz bowtie pasta, uncooked
- 1 cup Lite Asian vinaigrette salad dressing (I like sesame dressings)
- 1 inch fresh ginger Root, finely grated
- 2 cloves garlic, minced
- 1/4 tsp cayenne pepper
- 2 Tbsp peanut butter
- 2 medium carrots, julienned
- 1 red bell pepper, cut in strips
- 1/2 cup dry-roasted peanuts, chopped
- 1 cup fresh basil, julienned
- 2-3 Tbs peanut oil, or canola, or olive...
- 3 cups chicken, diced (about 1 lb)
- 1 clove garlic, minced
- 1 Tbsp ginger, finely grated
- garnish (suggest basil leaves or decoratively cut carrots and peppers)

Direction

- Cook pasta according to package directions and taste. Drain, rinse, set aside.
- In small deep bowl, combine salad dressing, garlic, ginger, and peanut butter and vigorously whisk till combined.
- Heat oil in wok to med-high. Add chicken and stir fry quickly for 2-3 minutes. Add ginger and garlic, stir fry 2 more minutes, till chicken is done.
- In large bowl combine pasta, chicken, carrots, peppers, basil, peanuts and dressing. Toss well.
- Garnish with basil leaves.
- Serve immediately.

274.   Shrimp And Macaroni Salad Recipe

Serving: 8 | Prep: | Cook: 15mins | Ready in:

Ingredients

- 1 c. mayonaise (not Helman's)
- 1 tsp. seasoned salt
- 1 tsp. celery seed
- 1 tsp. salt
- 1/2 tsp. pepper
- 3 tblsp. spicy brown mustard
- 3 ribs celery, chopped
- sm. container grape tomatoes or halved cherry tomatoes
- small bunch of green onions, chopped
- 1 1/2 lbs. jumbo shrimp shelled and cooked
- 16 oz. shell macaroni (cooked in salted water)

Direction

- Combine mayo, seasonings, and mustard in a large bowl. Mix well. Add celery, tomatoes, and green onions. Mix well. Add the shrimp and macaroni, and mix well. Refrigerate for about 2 hours before serving.

275.   Shrimp Macaroni Salad Recipe

Serving: 1012 | Prep: | Cook: | Ready in:

Ingredients

- 2 1/2 cups of cooked shell macaroni
- 1 1/2 lb small cooked shrimp
- 2/3 cup chopped celery
- 1 medium chopped onion
- 1 cup mayo
- 3/4 cup catsup
- 1/2 cup sweet pickle relish
- 2-3 tabs. lemon juice
- 2 dashes hot sauce
- 1/2 teaspoon salt

- 1/4 teaspoon pepper

Direction

- Put first 4 ingredients in a large bowl
- Mix next 7 ingredients and Blend well, then pour over salad and stir. Ref until chilled.
- When I serve this, I sometimes put it in a large bowl with a center small bowl that I fill with cocktail sauce, and hang some whole shrimp off the sides of the small bowl. Put on a platter and put crackers around the bowl.

276.   Shrimp Pasta Salad Recipe

Serving: 4 | Prep: | Cook: | Ready in:

Ingredients

- 2-1/2 cups shell pasta cooked al dente then drained and cooled
- 1 red bell pepper seeded and diced
- 6 green onions including some tender green tops sliced
- 2 celery stalks sliced
- 2 avocados peeled pitted and cut into bite sized pieces
- 2 tablespoons lemon juice
- 1/2 pound cooked small bay shrimp
- 1 teaspoon salt
- 1 teaspoon freshly ground black pepper
- lettuce leaves for lining plates
- 3 hard cooked eggs quartered
- Creamy Italian Dressing:
- 1/4 cup extra virgin olive oil
- 1/2 cup mayonnaise
- 1/2 cup buttermilk
- 3 teaspoon fresh lemon juice
- 1/4 teaspoon dried basil crumbled
- 1/4 teaspoon dried rosemary crumbled
- 1/4 teaspoon dried oregano crumbled
- 1/4 teaspoon garlic powder
- 1/4 teaspoon salt

- 1 teaspoon freshly ground black pepper

Direction

- In bowl combine pasta, bell pepper, onion and celery then stir well.
- In separate bowl toss avocados with lemon juice and add to salad along with shrimp.
- Cover and refrigerate several hours.
- Combine all ingredients and whisk well until blended.
- Add 1 cup dressing, salt and pepper then mix well 1 hour before serving.
- Line a platter with lettuce and mound salad on top then garnish with eggs and serve immediately.

277.   Shrimp Pasta Salad With Feta Recipe

Serving: 4 | Prep: | Cook: 20mins | Ready in:

Ingredients

- 12 oz. Rotelli pasta
- 2 Tbs olive oil
- 1 bunch green onion, diced
- 2 clove garlic, crushed
- 3/4 lb. medium shrimp, shelled and deveined
- 1/4 cup black olives, sliced
- 1/2 cup oyster sauce
- 2 Tbs lemon juice
- 1/2 lb feta cheese, crumbled
- 1 Tbs fresh oregano, minced
- 1/4 tsp pepper

Direction

- 1. In a large pot of boiling water, cook rotelli until just tender but still firm, about 8-10 mins. Drain well and keep warm.
- 2. Meanwhile, in a sauté pan, heat olive oil. Add onion and garlic, cook until softened, 2-3 mins. Add shrimp and cook, until pink 2-3 mins longer.

- 3. Add olives, oyster sauce, and lemon juice. Reduce heat and cook 2 minutes to slightly reduce. Add the feta, oregano and pepper. Cook until cheese melts about 1 min.
- 4. Add hot pasta and toss to mix.

278.   Shrimp Salad Recipe

Serving: 10 | Prep: | Cook: 20mins | Ready in:

Ingredients

- 4 cups small cooked pasta shells
- 1 pound cooked and peeled shrimp cut into thirds
- 1 cup frozen peas
- 1/2 cup chopped green onions
- 1 T dried parsley or 1/4 cup fresh chopped
- 1 small container of plain yogurt
- 1 cup mayo
- 1/4 lemon juice
- Healthy sprinkle of dill

Direction

- In large bowl combine pasta, shrimp, peas, onions and parsley.
- Mix up well.
- In small bowl mix other ingredients.
- Pour sauce into large bowl.
- Mix well, chill.

279.   Shrimp And Macaroni Salad Recipe

Serving: 10 | Prep: | Cook: 10mins | Ready in:

Ingredients

- 1 lb. small shell macaroni, cooked al dente
- ½ lb. small fresh salad shrimp, rinsed and drained

- ½ cup chopped celery
- ½ cup chopped green pepper
- ½ cup chopped red onion
- 1 small jar pimento pieces
- 2 hard boiled eggs, chopped
- 3 Tbsp. chopped fresh dill
- 2 Tbsp. chopped fresh parsley
- 1 teas. season salt
- ½ teas. fresh ground pepper
- 1 cup mayonnaise
- 2 Tbsp. milk

Direction

- Put first eight ingredient is large salad bowl.
- In a small bowl mix together Season salt, pepper, mayonnaise and milk. Mix well and pour over salad ingredients. Stir to combine and cover with plastic wrap. Refrigerate for at least 4 hours for flavors to blend.

280.   Simple Pasta Salad Recipe

Serving: 8 | Prep: | Cook: 15mins | Ready in:

Ingredients

- one pound tri-colour pasta spirals
- one medium red onion julienned
- 4 large carrots grated
- 1 cup slice black olives
- 1/2 cup oil
- 1 cup white vinegar
- 1/2 cup water
- 1/2 tsp salt
- 1/2 tsp pepper
- 1 tsp italian herb mix
- 1 pkg Good Seasons Italian dressing mix (or fav)
- optional: other veg or beans when handy

Direction

- Prepare pasta per instructions on package, drain and cool under cold water, drain, set aside
- In bowl combine vinegar, water, salt, pepper, dressing blend, herbs.
- Into bowl add all veg and toss to coat.
- Combine pasta and vinegar/veg mix and toss.
- Add oil at end and toss to mix thoroughly.
- Great for making ahead, flavours improve and vinegar mellows.
- Keep refrigerated

281. Smoked Ham And Veggies Pasta Salad Recipe

Serving: 6 | Prep: | Cook: 30mins | Ready in:

Ingredients

- 1 pound box bowtie pasta
- 1-2 cups smoked ham, diced
- 1 cup shredded cheddar cheese
- 1 cup frozen peas, thawed slightly
- 1 large cucumber, peeled and chopped
- ½ bell pepper, diced
- 1-2 cups grape tomatoes
- 1 Cup buttermilk Ranch Dressing

Direction

- Cook pasta according to package directions. Drain in colander and pour running cold water over pasta, while stirring, until completely cooled. Allow to drain fully before pouring in large bowl.
- Add all other ingredients and stir until well combined.
- Cover and refrigerate until ready to serve. Keeps well for three days in refrigerator.

282. Smoked Mozzarella Pasta Salad Recipe

Serving: 6 | Prep: | Cook: 12mins | Ready in:

Ingredients

- 1 (6 ounce) jar marinated artichoke hearts
- 1 (8 ounce) package rotini pasta, cooked
- 1 (7 ounce) jar roasted red bell peppers, drained and cut into strips
- 1/2 pound smoked mozzarella cheese, cut into 1/2-inch cubes
- MAY USE SMOKED GOUDA OR cheddar cheese INSTEAD
- 1/2 (5 ounce) bag baby spinach leaves (about 1-1/2 cups)
- 1/2 of a 4 ounce can chopped green chilies, drained
- 1/2 cup mayonnaise
- 1/2 cup grated parmesan cheese
- 1/4 cup pine nuts, toasted
- 1 garlic clove, minced
- 1/2 teaspoon black pepper
- MAY GARNISH WITH tomato WEDGES, OR baby spinach leaves
- OPTIONAL: chopped fresh green onions

Direction

- Drain the artichokes, reserving marinade
- Cut artichokes into strips
- Place in a large bowl
- Add pasta and next 4 ingredients, gently tossing
- STIR together reserved artichoke marinade, mayonnaise, and next 4 ingredients until blended
- Add to the pasta mixture, stirring to combine
- Cover and chill
- May garnish before serving

283. Smoked Salmon Dill Salad With Pasta Shells Dated 1964 Recipe

Serving: 4 | Prep: | Cook: | Ready in:

Ingredients

- 7 ounces smoked salmon
- 8 ounces sea shell pasta cooked
- 3 tablespoons chopped shallots
- 1 teaspoon finely chopped fresh dill
- 1/4 cup plain yogurt
- 1/4 cup mayonnaise

Direction

- Flake salmon with fork then toss into dressing made of mayonnaise, yogurt, shallots and dill.
- Mix carefully with the pasta then refrigerate salad for several hours.

284. So Easy Pasta Salad Recipe

Serving: 68 | Prep: | Cook: 10mins | Ready in:

Ingredients

- 1 pkg. tricolor rotini pasta
- 2 tomatoes, diced
- 1 cucumber, diced
- 1 bell pepper, diced
- salt & pepper
- bottle of Zesty Fat Free Italian dressing

Direction

- Boil rotini according to pkg. directions
- Drain well
- Add the rest of the ingredients and toss well.
- Either eat right away or let it sit in fridge for about 30 mins.
- Kids love it!

285. Soba Salad With Chicken In Sake/Onion Dressing Recipe

Serving: 0 | Prep: | Cook: 60mins | Ready in:

Ingredients

- 2 lbs. of chicken breast meat
- 1 tsp. each of chopped garlic and ginger
- 2 tsp. of Chinese five spice
- 1/4 cup of light oil
- 3 tbls. of sweet teryaki sauce
- ---SALAD---
- 12 oz. of soba noodles (made from buckwheat)
- 1 large carrot
- 1 large cucumber
- 1 cup of baby corn
- Half a small napa cabbage
- 1 bunch of scallions
- 5 oz. of the ubiquitous shitake mushrooms
- 1 large red bell pepper
- ---DRESSING---
- 1/3 cup of rice vinegar
- 2 tbls. of soy sauce
- 2 tsp. sugar
- 3 tsp. of sake
- 1 smaller sized white onion
- 1 tsp. of ginger (minced very finely)
- 2/3 cup of very good quality vegetable oil
- 2 tbls. of sesame oil
- salt, white pepper

Direction

- FOR THE SALAD: Marinate the chicken in the four ingredients listed right beneath it above. Char grill it and cut it into short but wide thin pieces. If that makes sense.
- Cook the noodles to whatever your definition of al dente is – keeping in mind though that they should be fully cooked but firm. Cool them at once beneath running water and drain them well.
- Shred the carrot into a very thin julienne. Cut the cucumber into thin slices and then those

slices into thin strips. Cut the cabbage likewise into a thin shred. The scallions, cut at a long bias and the mushrooms need be de-stemmed and sliced thinly. Plunge both the cabbage and mushrooms into boiling water for a few minutes to simplify them slightly and cool them also at once as you did the noodles. Clean the pepper and cut it in fashion to match the carrots. Cut the baby corn into quarters, lengthwise.

- FOR THE DRESSING: Chop the onion very small. Deeply caramelise it in some of the vegetable oil.
- Simply whisk everything which is not oil into that which is oil to create only a loose emulsification. Season with the salt (light) and the white pepper.
- TO FINISH: Completely integrate the chicken and the vegetables into the noodles and keep the lot chilled. No more than 20 minutes before being served should you massage the dressing into the salad.

286.   Southwest Chicken Pasta Salad Recipe

Serving: 8 | Prep: | Cook: 10mins | Ready in:

Ingredients

- 8 oz rotini pasta
- 1 C. frozen corn
- 3 C. roasted garlic salsa
- ¼ C. extra virgin olive oil
- juice from 1 lime
- ½ tsp kosher salt
- ¼ C. cilantro or parsley, chopped
- 1 C. red and green bell pepper, chopped
- ½ C. green onion, chopped
- 2 C. cooked chicken, diced
- 1 can black beans, drained, rinsed
- 1 can sliced black olives, drained

Direction

- Cook pasta as directed on package. Add corn to pasta just before draining. Drain, rinse with cold water.
- In a large bowl, stir together salsa, olive oil, lime juice and salt. Stir in pasta and remaining ingredients.
- Cover and refrigerate for at least 2 hours.

287.   Southwestern Pasta Salad Recipe

Serving: 8 | Prep: | Cook: 10mins | Ready in:

Ingredients

- 16 oz pasta (Spirals work best)
- 1 green bell pepper
- 1 can of corn
- 2 minced garlic cloves
- 1 small can sliced black olives
- 1 can of kidney beans (washed and strained)
- 1 diced avacado
- 1 lemon or lime (juicies work just as well)
- 16 oz salsa (You determine how spicy this gets)
- 1/2 cup of sour cream
- 3/4 tsp cumin
- 1/2 tsp salt

Direction

- Boil Pasta
- Dice avocado and cover in lemon/lime juice to prevent browning in a side bowl.
- In a large bowl mix the pasta, cut bell pepper, and other ingredients.
- Add avocado and remaining lemon/lime juice for added kick.
- Serve cold and enjoy!

288. Spaghetti Confetti Pasta Salad Recipe

Serving: 12 | Prep: | Cook: 1hours | Ready in:

Ingredients

- 3/4 box angel hair pasta
- 8-10 oz. sour cream or Greek yogurt
- 8 - 10 oz. mayonaise
- 1 package dill harvest ranch dip mix
- 1/2-1 package ranch dip mix powder
- 2 heads of broccoli (just the florets trimmed off)
- 1/2 to 1 cup match-stix carrots, diced finely
- 1 large cucumber, julienned and chopped
- 1 bunch of green onions, chopped finely
- 2-3 tablespoons dried chives
- 1 tomato, seeded and finely diced

Direction

- Mix the sour cream and mayo with the powder mixes and dried chives. Place in the fridge to chill.
- Prepare all the veggies and mix together. (The broccoli florets should be JUST the flowers, not the stalks!)
- Now, boil the spaghetti, making sure to add salt to the pasta water. This will be the only time you can salt the spaghetti. Boil for around 5-7 minutes, or as package directs. You DO NOT want to overcook the pasta.
- Once the spaghetti is done, drain WELL and rinse in cold water.
- Place all ingredients into a large bowl and mix well.
- Refrigerate overnight or at least 4 hours, to get the best taste!
- Can be kept in the fridge up to 1 week!
- ENJOY!!!!

289. Spaghetti Salad Dated 1966 Recipe

Serving: 6 | Prep: | Cook: 10mins | Ready in:

Ingredients

- 1 pound thin spaghetti cooked rinsed and drained
- 3 tomatoes diced in large pieces
- 3 cucumbers halved quartered and sliced
- 1 bottle salad supreme
- 6 ounce bottle Italian dressing
- 1 medium red onion diced

Direction

- While spaghetti is still warm add seasoning mix, salad dressing and onions.
- Mix well then add tomatoes and cucumbers and refrigerate overnight.

290. Spaghetti Salad Recipe

Serving: 8 | Prep: | Cook: 10mins | Ready in:

Ingredients

- 1 small box of thin spaghetti
- salt
- 1 - 16 oz bottle of Italian dressing
- 1 c parmesan cheese, grated
- 2 cucumbers, cut into small pieces
- 1 tomato, cut into small pieces
- 1 green pepper, cut into small pieces
- 1 onion, cut into small pieces

Direction

- Cook spaghetti per package directions with desired amount of salt.
- Mix remaining ingredients and toss with spaghetti.
- Refrigerate.

291. Spaghetti Squash And Avocado Salad Recipe

Serving: 4 | Prep: | Cook: 20mins | Ready in:

Ingredients

- 1   medium spaghetti squash
- 6   mushrooms, sliced
- 1/2   each red and green bell pepper, julienned
- 1   can (4 ounces) sliced black olives, drained
- 2   avocados, seeded, peeled and sliced
- >
- >
- >
- avocado oil Vinaigrette:
- ------------------------
- 3/4 cup   avocado oil or light vegetable oil
- 1/4 cup   white wine vinegar
- 2 to 3   cloves garlic, crushed
- 1 tsp   each oregano, sweet basil, rosemary, dry mustard and
- worcestershire sauce
- salt and pepper to taste
- Shake all ingredients together in tightly covered container. Let
- vinaigrette stand at least 24 hours.

Direction

- Prepare Avocado Oil Vinaigrette at least 24 hours before serving time.
- Halve squash lengthwise, scoop out seeds.
- Place halves cut side down in large saucepan; add water to a depth of two inches; cover and bring to a boil.
- Reduce heat; simmer squash 20 minutes.
- Drain off water; cool squash and shred into strands & chill.
- Mix squash, mushrooms, peppers, olives and avocados in serving bowl.
- Pour Vinaigrette over, toss gently and serve.

292. Spaghetti Squash And Avocado Salad Recipe

Serving: 4 | Prep: | Cook: 30mins | Ready in:

Ingredients

- 1 medium spaghetti squash
- 6 mushrooms sliced
- 1/2 each red and green bell pepper julienned
- 4 ounce can sliced black olives drained
- 2 avocados seeded peeled and sliced
- avocado oil Vinaigrette:
- 3/4 cup avocado oil
- 1/4 cup white wine vinegar
- 3 cloves garlic crushed
- 1 teaspoon oregano
- 1 teaspoon sweet basil
- 1 teaspoon rosemary
- 1 teaspoon dry mustard and
- 1 teaspoon worcestershire sauce
- 1/2 teaspoon salt
- 1 teaspoon freshly ground black pepper

Direction

- Halve squash lengthwise and scoop out seeds.
- Place halves cut side down in large saucepan then add water to a depth of 2".
- Cover and bring to a boil then reduce heat and simmer for 20 minutes.
- Drain off water and cool squash then shred into strands.
- Mix squash, mushrooms, peppers, olives and avocados in serving bowl.
- Combine avocado oil, vinegar, garlic, herbs and Worcestershire sauce in jar with lid.
- Season with salt and pepper and shake several times to mix well.
- Refrigerate vinaigrette at least 2 hours.
- When ready to serve pour vinaigrette over salad then toss gently and serve.

293.　　Spicy Peanut Noodle Salad Recipe

Serving: 4 | Prep: | Cook: 15mins | Ready in:

Ingredients

- 8 ounces fresh chinese noodles (or any other fresh pasta)
- For the Dressing:
- 1/2 cup all natural peanut butter
- 3 tablespoons soy sauce
- 3 tablespoons Sriracha, more or less to taste
- 1 tablespoon fresh lime juice
- 1 tablespoon rice wine vinegar
- 1 tablespoon toasted sesame seed oil
- 1 clove garlic, grated on a microplane grater
- 1 jalapeño peppers, seeds and ribs removed, finely minced
- sugar and honey, to taste
- 3 tablespoons hot water
- To Assemble:
- 2 large red, orange, or yellow bell peppers, sliced into thin strips
- 1 large cucumber, seeded and sliced into fine julienne
- 1 cup mung bean sprouts
- 1/2 cup loosely packed fresh basil, mint, or cilantro leaves
- 4 scallions, sliced
- 1 red thai bird chilis, finely minced (optonal)
- 1/2 cup roasted peanuts, roughly crushed

Direction

- Cook noodles according to package directions. Drain and rinse with cold water to cool down noodles. Set aside while you make the dressing.
- In a large bowl, combine all dressing ingredients. Whisk until homogeneous. Add drained cooled noodles to bowl. Add bell peppers, cucumber, bean sprouts, herbs, scallions, and bird chilies (if using). Toss to combine. Allow to chill in fridge for at least an hour. Serve topped with roasted peanuts.

294.　　Spinach And Basil Pesto Pasta Salad Recipe

Serving: 8 | Prep: | Cook: 8mins | Ready in:

Ingredients

- 3/4 cup walnuts, toasted
- 2 cloves garlic, roasted and mashed
- 1 pound fusilli - I use gluten-free fusilli
- 1/4 cup extra-virgin olive oil
- 2 cups fresh basil leaves, packed
- 2 cups fresh spinach, packed
- freshly ground black pepper, lots!
- 1/8 teaspoon cayenne
- 1/2 lemon, juiced
- 1 cup parmesan cheese, freshly grated
- 6 tablespoons mayonnaise, NOT salad dressing!
- 1/4 cup warm water

Direction

- Cook pasta to al dente, drain, toss with 1 T. olive oil and cool while making dressing.
- In bowl of food processor, combine nuts, garlic, basil, spinach, pepper, cayenne, lemon juice, and remaining oil. Process until smooth and creamy. Add parmesan, warm water and mayo, whirl until well combined. Toss pasta and sauce. Serve warm or chilled.
- NOTE: This is gluten-free when you use gluten-free pasta.

295.　　Spinach And Pasta Salad Recipe

Serving: 6 | Prep: | Cook: 10mins | Ready in:

Ingredients

- 9 ounce package linguine
- 7 ounce package pesto with basil

- 5 cups shredded fresh spinach leaves
- 1 cup chopped fresh tomato
- 1 cup halved thinly sliced red onion
- 1/4 cup pine nuts toasted
- 3 tablespoons lemon juice
- 1/4 teaspoon salt

Direction

- Cook linguine according to package directions then rinse and drain.
- Combine pasta, spinach, tomato, onion and pine nuts in large bowl.
- Combine pesto, lemon juice and salt in small bowl then add to pasta and toss well.
- Serve immediately or refrigerate.

---

296. Spinach Artichoke Pasta Salad Recipe

Serving: 6 | Prep: | Cook: 5mins | Ready in:

Ingredients

- kosher salt
- 1 pkg cheese tortellini
- 1/2 lb fresh baby spinach
- 1 can baby artichoke hearts in water, drained and chopped
- 1 roasted red pepper, drained and chopped
- 1/2 small red onion, chopped
- 1 garlic clove
- 1 lemon, zested
- 2 tsp fresh lemon juice
- 2 Tbs red wine vinegar
- 1/2 cup EVOO
- 1 Tbs fresh thyme leaves, chopped (or 1/2 tsp dried)
- pepper
- handful sundried tomatoes, packed in oil, chopped

Direction

- Bring pot of water to boil and add pasta

- Cook 3-4 minutes
- Drain and cool pasta
- Chop spinach
- Combine with artichoke pieces, roasted red pepper and onion
- Chop garlic, add salt to it and make into a paste with the back of your spoon or a flat knife
- Transfer garlic paste to small bowl and add lemon zest, lemon juice and vinegar
- Whisk in oil, thyme and pepper
- Add pasta and sun-dried tomatoes
- Dress salad and gently toss
- Serve or refrigerate!
- **you could add cubed or shredded rotisserie chicken and make it a meal! Fabulous!!

---

297. Spinach Pasta Salad Recipe

Serving: 10 | Prep: | Cook: 12mins | Ready in:

Ingredients

- 10 oz penne pasta
- half pint red cherry tomatoes, halved
- half pint yellow cherry tomatoes, halved
- **I don't always have both colors, all red is fine**
- 4 oz baby spinach leaves - stems chopped off
- 1 can jumbo ripe olives, drained, slice olives in half lengthwise
- about 1/4 c chopped roasted red pepper
- 1/4 med red onion, chopped fine
- About 1/2 a keilebasa, diced small
- half pound thick cut bacon, cut into small pieces and fried crisp
- 4 oz mozzerella cheese, cut into small cubes, or, bite size balls, halved
- 1 bottle good Italian dressing (I use Ken's 3 cheese Northern Italian
- 3 T parmesan
- garlic pepper
- Salad Supreme seasoning

Direction

- Cook pasta in water well salted with kosher salt and a drizzle of olive oil, until al dente
- Rinse well with cold water to stop the cooking process and cool the pasta
- While pasta is cooking cut tomatoes and olives into large mixing bowl
- Add red pepper, onion, and kielbasa
- Add pasta when cool
- Mix together parmesan and a few shakes of garlic pepper and salad supreme
- Pour about 3/4 bottle of dressing over the pasta mixture, add parmesan mixture and mix all together well
- ((At this point, I put in fridge overnight and finish before serving.))
- About half an hour before serving, fry bacon and lay on paper towel
- Tear / chop any stems off spinach leaves
- Cube cheese
- Add bacon, spinach and cheese to salad.
- Stir and taste, I usually add a little more dressing/spices as needed as the pasta will soak up some of the dressing overnight.

---

298.   Spinach And Orzo Salad

Serving: 10 | Prep: | Cook: 10mins | Ready in:

Ingredients

- 1 (16 ounce) package uncooked orzo pasta
- 1 (10 ounce) package baby spinach leaves, finely chopped
- ½ pound crumbled feta cheese
- ½ red onion, finely chopped
- ¾ cup pine nuts
- ½ teaspoon dried basil
- ¼ teaspoon ground white pepper
- ½ cup olive oil
- ½ cup balsamic vinegar

Direction

- Bring a large pot of lightly salted water to a boil. Add orzo and cook for 8 to 10 minutes or until al dente; drain and rinse with cold water. Transfer to a large bowl and stir in spinach, feta, onion, pine nuts, basil and white pepper. Toss with olive oil and balsamic vinegar. Refrigerate and serve cold.
- Nutrition Facts
- Per Serving:
- 490.5 calories; protein 15.8g 32% DV; carbohydrates 49g 16% DV; fat 26.9g 41% DV; cholesterol 25mg 8% DV; sodium 349.2mg 14% DV.

---

299.   Spiral Macaroni Salad Recipe

Serving: 6 | Prep: | Cook: 15mins | Ready in:

Ingredients

- 8 ounce package spiral macaroni
- 1 cup cherry tomatoes halved
- 1 cup shredded cheddar cheese
- 1 small cucumber peeled and cut into chunks
- 2 tablespoons chopped green pepper
- 2 tablespoons chopped celery
- 2 tablespoons chopped green onion
- 1 tablespoon pickle relish
- 1/4 cup mayonnaise
- 1/2 teaspoon prepared mustard
- 1 pinch dill seeds
- 1 pinch celery salt
- 1 pinch celery seeds

Direction

- Cook macaroni according to package directions then drain.
- Rinse macaroni with cold water then drain.
- Combine macaroni and next 7 ingredients then toss gently.
- Combine remaining ingredients and mix well then pour over salad and toss gently.
- Cover and chill at least 1 hour before serving.

300. Spring And Summer Pasta Salad Recipe

Serving: 12 | Prep: | Cook: 12mins | Ready in:

Ingredients

- 1 package of elbow maccaroni cooked according to pkg directions
- 1 med to large cucumber (diced or chopped depending on how much you like them i dice)
- 1 med tomato diced
- Miracle Whip (put spoonfuls in one at a time and stir til you get the constistancy you like remember it soaks in the noodles as it sits, I use close to 1 cup)

Direction

- Mix all ingredients together and add salt and pepper to taste.
- Refrigerate for at least 1 hour before serving.
- ENJOY I always do

301. Springtime Pasta Salad Recipe

Serving: 8 | Prep: | Cook: 10mins | Ready in:

Ingredients

- 2 Cups spiral pasta
- 1/2 Cup sliced ripe olives
- 1 sweet red pepper
- 1 green pepper
- 1/4 Cup onion, chopped
- 1/4 Cup mayonnaise
- 1/4 Cup sour cream
- 1-1/4 tsp dill weed
- 1/2 tsp salt
- 1/2 tsp ground mustard
- 1/4 tsp pepper
- 1/4 tsp garlic salt

Direction

- Cook pasta according to package directions; drain & rinse with cold water and place in a large bowl.
- Add olives, red & green peppers & onion.
- Combine remaining ingredients; pour over salad and toss to coat.
- Cover & chill for 2 hours.

302. Stand Out Pasta Salad Recipe

Serving: 8 | Prep: | Cook: 10mins | Ready in:

Ingredients

- 1 lb tri colored rotini
- 1 C sugar
- 3/4 C cider vinegar
- 1/2 C vegetable oil
- 1 tsp salt
- 1 tsp garlic powder
- 1/2 tsp pepper
- 3-4 tblsp parsley flakes
- 1 sm onion, grated
- 1/2 green pepper, diced
- 4-5 carrots, grated

Direction

- 1. Cook pasta according to directions on box. Drain & set aside.
- 2. While pasta is cooking, grate onion & carrot and dice green pepper. Toss w/pasta.
- 3. Combine the rest of the ingredients and mix well.
- 4. Pour dressing over pasta veggie mixture and mix to coat.
- 5. For best flavor, allow to sit in the refrigerator for a few hours before serving

(tastes great fresh made, too, but the flavors meld more with time).

303. Summer Fireworks Pasta Salad For Your 4th Of July Picnic Recipe

Serving: 8 | Prep: | Cook: 12mins | Ready in:

Ingredients

- 1 - pound Radiatore, Rotini or other medium pasta shape, uncooked
- -cilantro Pesto (see recipe below)
- 3 tbsp. low-sodium chicken broth
- 1/2 - 3/4 lb. skinless, boneless chicken breast halves, cut in l-inch pieces
- 8 plum tomatoes (about 1 1/2 pounds), cut into 1-inch chunks
- 1 small red onion, slivered lengthwise
- 1/4 cup toasted pinenuts
- cilantro
- ***
- ***
- Pesto:................
- 2 cups packed cilantro leaves
- 1 cup flat-leaf parsley
- 3 garlic cloves, minced
- 3 tbsp. parmesan cheese
- 2 tbsp. toasted pinenuts or walnuts
- 1/2 cup low-sodium chicken broth
- 1 tbsp olive oil
- 1 1/2 tbsp. red wine vinegar
- salt and freshly ground black pepper to taste
- Garnish: cilantro sprigs

Direction

- Prepare pasta according to package directions. Drain and set aside in large serving bowl. Place ingredients for Cilantro Pesto in a blender or food processor, process until finely chopped.

- Heat chicken broth in non-stick skillet over medium heat.
- Add chicken and sauté 3 to 4 minutes per side, or until browned and cooked through.
- Add chicken, tomatoes, red onion and pine nuts to pasta.
- Toss with all of the Cilantro Pesto until combined.
- Garnish with cilantro sprigs and serve with blue tortilla chips.
- Serves 6 to 8

304. Summer Pasta Salad Recipe

Serving: 6 | Prep: | Cook: 15mins | Ready in:

Ingredients

- 1 Small Box of spaghetti (can use whole wheat)
- 1 green bell pepper, Chopped in Bite-Size Pieces
- 1 red bell pepper, Chopped in Bite-Size Pieces
- 1 yellow bell pepper, Chopped in Bite-Size Pieces
- 1 Small Can black olives, Halved
- 1 Cup Small Brocolli Florets
- 1 Cup snow peas
- Other Veggies as desired
- 1 Package Louis Kemp Imitation crab Meat (in chunks)
- 1/2 to 1 Full Small Bottle Italian dressing

Direction

- Cook entire box of spaghetti. Drain spaghetti, and place in a large bowl and set in the fridge to cool.
- Place vegetables into a microwavable container. Add a little bit of water to the container, cover with plastic wrap, and microwave on High for about two minutes- just enough time to lightly steam (but not completely cook) the vegetables. Drain the vegetables and let them cool.

- Break apart the crab meat into smaller chunks, slightly smaller than bite size (you can do this while the vegetables are cooking).
- Mix the spaghetti noodles, vegetables, crab meat, and 1/2 of the bottle of Italian dressing together in a very large bowl. Adjust the Italian dressing to taste.
- Refrigerate the pasta salad and let it cool completely before eating.

305.   Summer Spaghetti Salad Recipe

Serving: 12 | Prep: | Cook: 10mins | Ready in:

Ingredients

- 1 lb spaghetti
- 1 large green pepper chopped
- 1 onion chopped
- 16 ounce bottle Italian dressing
- 1 cup spaghetti sauce
- 1/4 cup red wine vinegar
- 1/2 jar of Trader Joe's salad seasonings
- 1/4 cup freshly grated parmesan cheese
- fresh basil

Direction

- Break dry spaghetti into four pieces
- Place in boiling water and cook until done
- Drain and place in large glass bowl
- Stir in the above ingredients except basil
- Cover and refrigerate overnight
- Stir again and add fresh chopped basil as garnish
- This recipe never lasts more than a day in my house. Enjoy!

306.   Summertime Ham And Pasta Salad Recipe

Serving: 6 | Prep: | Cook: | Ready in:

Ingredients

- 1 cup salad dressing
- 1/2 cup grated parmesan cheese
- 3 tablespoons milk
- 12 ounces cooked pasta shells
- 6 plum tomatoes
- 1 medium red onion
- 1 teaspoon salt
- 1 teaspoon freshly ground black pepper
- 4 slices deli ham

Direction

- Combine salad dressing, cheese and milk then mix well.
- Cut ham, tomatoes and red onion into same size pieces.
- Mix all ingredients lightly and chill 4 hours or overnight.

307.   Sundried Tomato And Spinach Bowtie Pasta Salad Recipe

Serving: 6 | Prep: | Cook: 10mins | Ready in:

Ingredients

- 1 pound pasta, bowtie type, uncooked
- 3 green onions, finely chopped
- 2 ounces sun-dried tomatoes, cut into strips
- 8 ounces spinach, trimmed and shredded
- 1/3 cup pine nuts, toasted*
- 1 tablespoon dried oregano
- 1 teaspoon salt
- 3/4 cup grated parmesan cheese, divided
- 6 tablespoons olive oil
- 3/4 teaspoon crushed red pepper

- 1 clove garlic, minced - 1 or 2 cloves
- salt and pepper

Direction

- In a large pan of boiling water, cook bowtie pasta. Drain well and rinse under cold water. Transfer drained pasta to a large salad bowl. Add finely chopped green onions, sun-dried tomatoes, shredded spinach, toasted pine nuts, oregano, salt and 1/2 cup grated Parmesan cheese.
- To make the dressing, in a small jar with a lid, combine olive oil, crushed red pepper, minced garlic, salt and pepper. Shake well. Pour dressing over salad and toss until evenly coated. Before serving, sprinkle salad with remaining 1/4 cup grated Parmesan cheese.
- *To toast, place pine nuts in a single layer on a baking sheet. Bake at 350 for approximately 10 minutes or until pine nuts are golden brown.
- NOTE: To make this gluten-free, use gluten-free bowtie pasta.

308.   Supreme Pasta Salad Recipe

Serving: 8 | Prep: | Cook: 10mins | Ready in:

Ingredients

- 1 lb. (16oz.) fusilli, rotini or shell pasta
- 1 bottle (8oz) Italian or ranch-style salad dressing (I used Italian)
- 4 tablespoons McCormick Salad Supreme seasoning
- 4 to 5 cups chopped assorted vegetables like broccoli, carrot (I shredded the carrot),red onion, cherry tomatoes, bell pepper and squash (like zucchini or yellow)

Direction

- Cook pasta according to package directions; rinse and drain.

- In a large bowl, combine pasta, salad dressing and Salad Supreme Seasoning.
- Toss in vegetables. Cover and refrigerate 4 or more hours.
- Stir before serving.

309.   Sweet And Sour Broccoli Pasta Salad Recipe

Serving: 6 | Prep: | Cook: 15mins | Ready in:

Ingredients

- Ingredients:
- 8o uncooked pasta twists
- 2 cups broccoli florets
- 2/3 cup shredded carrots
- 1 medium Red or Golden Delicious apple, cored, seeded and chopped
- 1/3 cup plain nonfat yogurt
- 1/3 cup apple juice
- 3 Tbs. cider vinegar
- 1 Tbs. light olive oil
- 1 Tbs. Dijon mustard
- 1 tsp. honey
- ½ tsp. dried thyme leaves
- lettuce leaves

Direction

- Method:
- 1) Cook pasta according to package directions, omitting salt and adding broccoli during last 2 minutes. Drain and rinse well under cold water until pasta and broccoli are cool; drain well.
- 2) Place pasta, broccoli, carrots and apple in medium bowl.
- 3) Combine yogurt, apple juice, vinegar, oil, mustard, honey and thyme in small bowl and pour over pasta mixture; toss to coat evenly.
- 4) Serve on individual dishes lined with lettuce. Garnish with apple slices, if desired.
- Calories per serving: 200

310. Sweet Dijon Pasta Salad Recipe

Serving: 4 | Prep: | Cook: 10mins | Ready in:

Ingredients

- 8 ounces tricolor rotini
- 3/4 cup plain nonfat yogurt
- 1/4 cup reduced fat mayonaise
- 2 tablespoons honey
- 1 tablespoon Dijon mustard
- 1/4 teaspoon cumin
- 1/4 teaspoon salt
- 1 can (15 oz) black beans, rinsed and drained
- 1 medium tomato, chopped
- 1/2 cup shredded carrot
- 1/4 cup chopped green onions

Direction

- Cook pasta according to package directions; drain. Rinse under cold water until cool; drain.
- Combine yogurt, mayonnaise, honey, mustard, cumin and salt in small bowl until well blended.
- Combine pasta, beans, tomato, carrot and onions in medium bowl.
- Add yogurt mixture; toss to coat. Cover and refrigerate until ready to serve.

311. Sweet Heat Fusion Pasta Salad Recipe

Serving: 8 | Prep: | Cook: 90mins | Ready in:

Ingredients

- 1lb non "noodle" style pasta(ie penne, rigatoni, etc...I used cavatelli)
- about 8oz crushed pineapple, drained(reserve 1T juice)
- 1 can Rotel tomatoes, drained

- 1 large bell pepper, or 2 small, diced
- 1 medium red onion, diced
- 1 cup mayonnaise
- 1T Chinese hot mustard
- 1t rice vinegar
- 1t fresh lemon juice
- 1/2t freshly grated ginger(or sub 1/4t ground)
- 1/2t ground cumin
- 1/2-1t red pepper flakes
- 4oz crushed macadamias or cashews
- 4-6oz crumbled goats cheese
- 1/4 cup fresh cilantro, roughly chopped
- kosher or sea salt and fresh ground black pepper

Direction

- Cook pasta per package directions and drain well, rinsing under cold water, briefly. Shake well and let drain.
- In large bowl, whisk together mayo, mustard, vinegar, lemon juice, ginger, cumin, and red pepper flakes.
- Fold in pineapple and Rotel.
- Add well drained and cooled pasta and fold to combine.
- Add cilantro, cheese, and nuts, then season with salt and pepper. Fold just to combine, once more.
- Chill until ready to serve, at least 1 hour.

312. Sweet Pasta Salad Recipe

Serving: 8 | Prep: | Cook: 10mins | Ready in:

Ingredients

- 1 pound rotini pasta
- 4 carrots, shredded
- 1 red bell pepper, chopped
- 1 onion, diced
- 1 cup distilled white vinegar
- 1 cup white sugar
- 1 (14 ounce) can sweetened condensed milk
- 2 cups mayonnaise

- 1 teaspoon salt
- 1/2 teaspoon ground black pepper

Direction

- Bring a large pot of lightly salted water to a boil.
- Add pasta and cook for 8 to 10 minutes or until al dente; drain.
- In large bowl, combine pasta, carrot, red pepper and onion.
- In medium bowl, combine vinegar, sugar, condensed milk, mayonnaise, salt and pepper.
- Toss salad with dressing and chill 4 hours in refrigerator before serving.

313.   TUNA PASTA SALAD Recipe

Serving: 1012 | Prep: | Cook: 23mins | Ready in:

Ingredients

- INGREDIENTS
- 3 cups macaroni
- 1/3 cup Italian-style salad dressing
- 1/2 cup sour cream
- 1 cup mayonnaise
- 1 onion, chopped
- 2 stalks celery, chopped
- 1/2 teaspoon garlic powder
- 1 teaspoon salt
- 1/2 teaspoon ground black pepper
- 1 (6 ounce) can tuna, drained

Direction

- DIRECTIONS
- Cook pasta in a large pot of boiling salted water until done.
- Drain.
- Marinate macaroni in Italian dressing for 2 to 3 hours or overnight.

- Mix sour cream, mayonnaise, onion, celery, garlic powder, tuna, and salt and pepper into macaroni. Chill.

314.   Taco Pasta Salad Recipe

Serving: 6 | Prep: | Cook: 20mins | Ready in:

Ingredients

- 1 pound ground beef
- 1 (1.25-ounce) package ORTEGA® taco seasoning Mix
- I only use cumin and a small amout of chili powder..
- 1 (16-ounce) package macaroni, cooked, rinsed and drained
- 1 (16-ounce) jar ORTEGA salsa - Homestyle Recipe (Mild)
- I used our HEB store brand.. I find it better.
- 2 cups shredded cheddar cheese
- I mixed with half American and chedder
- 1 cup sliced ripe olives
- Slice your own.. they taste better
- 3/4 cup sliced green onions

Direction

- Cook ground beef and seasoning according to taco seasoning package directions.
- Combine macaroni, salsa, ground beef mixture, cheese, olives and onions; mix well.
- I served with a bed of shredded lettuce and some homemade tortilla chips on side with chopped tomatoes and cilantro.
- Yummmmmmy!
- Serve warm

315.   Tangy Vegetable Pasta Salad Recipe

Serving: 6 | Prep: | Cook: 5mins | Ready in:

Ingredients

- 2-1/4 cups uncooked spiral pasta
- 2 tablespoons lemon juice
- 3 plum tomatoes, sliced
- 1/2 cup chopped green pepper
- 1/2 cup sliced radishes
- /12 cup chopped peeled cucumber
- For Dressing
- 1/3 cup picante V8 juice
- 1/4 cup orange juice
- 2 tablespoons lemon juice
- 2 tablespoons chopped green onion
- 1 tablespoon canola oil
- 1-1/2 teaspoons sugar
- 1 teaspoon grated lemon peel
- 1 teaspoon grated orange peel
- 1/2 teaspoon salt
- 1/2 teaspoon dill weed

Direction

- Cook pasta according to package directions, adding lemon juice to the water. Drain and cool.
- In a large bowl, combine the pasta, tomatoes, green pepper, radishes and cucumber. In a jar with a tight-fitting lid, combine the dressing ingredients; cover and shake well. Pour over salad; toss to coat. Cover and refrigerate until serving.

---

316.   Tarragon Dijon Pasta Salad Recipe

Serving: 0 | Prep: | Cook: |Ready in:

Ingredients

- 1lb bowtie or other whimsical shaped pasta
- 1 medium or half a gigantic sweet(Vidalia when possible) onion, diced
- 3 stalks celery, diced
- 1/4-1/2 head of cauliflower broken into small florets

- 4-5 hard boiled eggs, chopped
- 1 cup mayonnaise
- 2T Dijon
- 1T honey
- 1 lemon, juiced
- 2T fresh tarragon, minced
- 2 cloved garlic, minced
- kosher or sea salt and fresh ground pepper

Direction

- Cook pasta per package directions rinse immediately with cold water, drain and set aside.
- Combine onion, celery, cauliflower, and eggs into large bowl
- In small bowl, combine mayo, Dijon, honey, lemon juice, garlic, tarragon and salt and pepper
- Mix well
- Add drained pasta to veggies and toss to combine.
- Add dressing and stir gently until well combined.
- Refrigerate until ready to serve.

---

317.   Tarragon Macaroni Salad Recipe

Serving: 4 | Prep: | Cook: 10mins |Ready in:

Ingredients

- 1 cup sugar
- 1/4 cup flour
- 1/4 cup tarragon vinegar
- 1-1/2 cups water
- 1/4 cup mustard
- 1 cup celery chopped
- 1/2 cup carrots chopped
- 4 hard boiled eggs
- 1/2 pound cooked macaroni
- 1 teaspoon salt
- 1 teaspoon freshly ground black pepper

- 1 teaspoon celery seed
- 1/4 cup mayonnaise

Direction

- Cook sugar, flour, vinegar and water until thick then add mustard.
- In large bowl combine macaroni, carrots, celery and hard boiled eggs.
- Add cooked mixture and mayonnaise until desired consistency.
- Add salt, pepper and celery seed then chill and serve.

---

318. Tasty Tuna Macaroni Salad Recipe

Serving: 8 | Prep: | Cook: | Ready in:

Ingredients

- Tasty tuna macaroni Salad
- tuna has a tangy zip in this lively new twist on a favorite classic.
- 2 cups (7 oz.) elbow macaroni, cooked, drined
- 1 can (6 oz.) tuna, drained. flaked
- 1 cup sliced celery
- 3/4 cup Miracle Whip or Miracle Whip light Dressing
- 1/4 cup each chopped green pepper and sliced grean onions
- 2 Tbsp. chopped pimiento
- salt and black pepper
- lettuce

Direction

- Mix macaroni, tuna, celery, dressing, green pepper, onions and pimiento.
- Season to taste with salt and black pepper.
- Refrigerate.
- Serve on lettuce-lined plates.
- Makes 8 servings.

---

319. Tea Room Seafood Pasta Salad Recipe

Serving: 8 | Prep: | Cook: 8mins | Ready in:

Ingredients

- 1½ cups uncooked pasta rings or elbow or little shells or ditalini, etc - the smaller the pasta, the better
- 1/2 pound fresh crab meat (I prefer to use the refrigerated crab - or pick my own crab meat off the legs - over the shelved canned crab...it gives such a great fresh flavor that can't be matched by shelved or imitation crab meat)
- 1/2 pound fresh medium shrimp, chopped coarsely
- 4 chopped green onions, whites and some of the greens
- 1/2 cup diced celery (I prefer to peel the outer stalks of the celery first, using a potato peeler - try it sometime...the celery is tender and crispy without all the stringy-ness!)
- ¾ cup mayonnaise
- 1 teaspoon (or to taste) dried dill weed
- dash or two of Old Bay Seasoning
- juice of 1 lemon
- salt and pepper to your taste (if even needed - taste it first)

Direction

- Cook pasta per package directions; drain and allow it to cool completely.
- Mix crab, shrimp, green onions, celery, and cooled pasta.
- Mix mayonnaise with dill weed, Old Bay, and lemon juice; pour over salad mixture.
- Taste salad; season with salt and pepper, if needed.
- Keep salad well-chilled until ready to serve.
- When garden tomatoes are in season, this salad is excellent served in a scooped out tomato; or serve it on top of a bed of crisp lettuce or romaine leaves, surrounded by

sliced tomatoes and sweet onions cut into rings.

- ALTERATION: Omit the pasta from the recipe and this makes a great seafood sandwich filling, especially on lightly toasted croissants, or crusty sub-sandwich type rolls, topped with lettuce and a tomato slice.

320. Thai Shrimp Pasta Salad Recipe

Serving: 2 | Prep: | Cook: 10mins | Ready in:

Ingredients

- 2 ounces uncooked linguine or spaghetti
- 1/2 cup shredded carrot
- 1/2 pound medium to large shrimp, cooked and peeled
- 1 cup thinly sliced green leafy lettuce
- 1/4 cup fresh cilantro leaves
- 2 tbsp. chopped peanuts
- 1/4 cup lime juice
- 1 tbsp. chopped green onions
- 2 tbsp. fish sauce
- 2 1/2 tsp. sugar
- 2 tsp. vegetable oil
- 1 tsp. peeled grated ginger
- 2 garlic cloves, minced

Direction

- Bring 4 cups water to a boil in a large saucepan. Add pasta and cook 9 1/2 minutes. Add carrot; cook an additional 30 seconds.
- Drain and let cool.
- Combine pasta mixture, shrimp, lettuce, cilantro and peanuts in a large bowl; toss well.
- Combine lime juice and next 6 ingredients in a small bowl; stir well with a whisk. Pour over pasta mixture; toss gently to coat.
- Serve immediately. Serving size = 2 cups. 1 serving = 8 points.

321. The Best Bleu Cheese N Beef Pasta Salad Ever Recipe

Serving: 4 | Prep: | Cook: 15mins | Ready in:

Ingredients

- 1 tsp olive oil
- 12 oz beef tenderloin
- 8 oz radiatore pasta, cooked and cooled
- 1 cup white mushrooms, sliced
- 1/2 small red onion, thinly sliced
- 1 can artichoke hearts (13.75 oz), drained
- 1 cup frozen peas, thawed
- 1 red bell pepper, sliced into short, thin strips
- 3/4 cup Litehouse® Bleu cheese Dressing (substitute: Litehouse® Lite Bleu cheese or Litehouse® Big Bleu Dressing)
- salt and freshly ground black pepper
- Lots of sprinkled bleu cheese on top
- Sour rye bread and garlic butter.

Direction

- Heat olive oil over medium heat.
- Add steak; cook 7-9 minutes or until desired doneness, turning once. Cut beef into 1/4 inch slices.
- Using the same pan, sauté mushrooms and onions until tender, about 5 minutes.
- Mix beef, pasta, artichokes, mushrooms, peas, red pepper and toss with Litehouse® Bleu Cheese Dressing.
- Season to taste with salt and pepper.
- Serve warm or refrigerate and serve as a cold salad.

322. Theme Party Pasta Salad Recipe

Serving: 10 | Prep: | Cook: 45mins | Ready in:

Ingredients

- 6 cups (16 ounces) uncooked rotini, divided in 3 batches
- 1 1/2 teaspoons food coloring (theme color #1)
- 1 1/2 teaspoons food coloring (theme color #2)
- 1 bottle (8 ounces) Italian salad dressing
- 4 tablespoons McCormick Salad Supreme seasoning
- 5 cups assorted raw vegetables (tomatoes, carrots, cucumbers, yellow squash, or red onions)

Direction

- Bring 2 cups water to a boil.
- Add food coloring for theme color #1 and 1 cup of dry pasta. Cook according to package directions.
- Rinse under cold water to stop cooking and drain well.
- Repeat with 2 cups of fresh water, theme food coloring #2 and 1 cup pasta.
- Repeat with 8 cups of fresh water and remaining 4 cups pasta (no food coloring).
- Place pasta in large salad bowl, add dressing and seasoning, and toss gently to coat.
- Cut vegetables into bite-sized pieces. Add vegetables to pasta and mix gently.
- Cover and refrigerate at least 4 hours.

---

323. Toasted Israeli Couscous Salad With Grilled Summer Vegetables Recipe

Serving: 4 | Prep: | Cook: 1hours |Ready in:

Ingredients

- Marinade:
- 1/4 cup white balsamic vinegar
- 1/4 red wine vinegar
- 1 tablespoon Dijon mustard
- 2 cloves garlic, minced
- 1 cup olive oil
- salt and freshly ground pepper, to taste

- granulated sugar, to taste
- ~
- Grilled Veggies:
- 2 organic green zucchini, quartered lengthwise
- 2 organic yellow zucchini, quartered lengthwise
- 6 organic spears asparagus, trimmed
- 12 organic yellow and red cherry tomatoes
- 1 red bell pepper, quartered and seeded
- 1 yellow bell pepper, quartered and seeded
- ~
- Couscous:
- 1/4 cup basil chiffonade
- 1/4 cup coarsely chopped Italian parsley
- 2 tablespoons olive oil
- 1 pound Israeli couscous
- 2 cups homemade chicken or vegetable stock, heated
- hot water to cover
- ~
- Garnish:
- kalamata olives (optional)
- additonal basil leaves, hand torn

Direction

- In a small bowl, whisk together the vinegar, mustard and garlic, slowly add the olive oil and whisk until combined. Season with salt and pepper.
- Drizzle veggies with a little olive oil and season with salt and pepper
- Preheat the grill. Grill the vegetables until just cooked through.
- Cut the veggies in smaller bite size pieces if desired (I left mine whole because they look so pretty!) Pour 1/2 the marinade over the vegetables and let sit at room temperature for 15 minutes.
- Heat the olive oil over medium-high heat, add the couscous and toast until lightly golden brown. Cover the couscous with the hot stock plus hot water and bring to a boil, cook until al dente and drain well. Place in a large serving bowl, add the grilled vegetables and herbs and toss with the remaining vinaigrette. Serve at room temperature.

324.   Tomato Basil Pasta Salad Recipe

Serving: 8 | Prep: | Cook: |Ready in:

Ingredients

- 5 cups bow tie pasta
- 1/2 cup vegetable oil
- 1/4 cup balsamic vinegar
- 2 teaspoons Dijon style mustard
- 1 teaspoon salt
- 1/4 teaspoon freshly ground black pepper
- 2 cups lightly packed fresh basil leaves snipped
- 3 large tomatoes coarsely chopped
- 1/2 cup toasted pine nuts
- 1 cup shredded mozzarella cheese

Direction

- Cook pasta according to package directions.
- Drain and cool.
- In small mixing bowl whisk together oil, vinegar, mustard, salt and pepper.
- In a large mixing bowl combine pasta, basil and tomatoes.
- Pour vinaigrette over top and toss together.
- Cover and chill at least 1 hour.
- Add pine nuts and cheese just before serving.

325.   Tomato Pasta Salad Recipe

Serving: 6 | Prep: | Cook: |Ready in:

Ingredients

- 6 cups cooked large shell pasta
- 14-1/2 ounce can diced tomatoes drained
- 2-1/4 ounce sliced ripe olives drained

- 1/4 cup sliced green onions
- 1/4 cup diced yellow bell pepper
- 1/4 cup diced green bell pepper
- 1/4 cup thinly sliced carrots
- 1/2 cup Italian salad dressing
- 2 tablespoons grated parmesan cheese

Direction

- In a large serving bowl combine all ingredients except parmesan then toss to coat.
- Sprinkle with cheese right before serving.

326.   Tomato And Bacon Pasta Salad Recipe

Serving: 4 | Prep: | Cook: 20mins |Ready in:

Ingredients

- 8 oz macaroni
- ½ lb bacon
- ½ c. mayo
- ¼ c. sour cream
- 2 celery stalks diced
- ½ cucumber (de-seeded and diced)
- 1 tomato (de-seeded and diced)
- 3 hard boiled eggs diced
- 2 tbsp cider vinegar
- 2 tbsp sugar
- 1 tbsp mustard
- ¼ tsp each salt and pepper

Direction

- Cook the bacon until it is crispy, drain on paper towels
- Cook the noodles according to directions and rinse lightly with cold water.
- Whisk together the mayo, sour cream, sugar, vinegar, mustard, salt and pepper.
- Crumble the bacon.
- Add all the ingredients and stir to combine.
- Best when left overnight to let the flavors develop.

140

327.   Tomato Basil Pasta Salad Recipe

Serving: 8 | Prep: | Cook: 60mins | Ready in:

Ingredients

- 3 lg.ripe tomatoes(about 11/2lbs) coarsely chopped(31/2c.)
- 1/3 c. chopped red onion
- 1/4c extra-virgin olive oil
- 2Tbs red wine vinegar
- 1tsp. minced garlic
- 1/2tsp ea. salt and pepper
- 1/4tsp dried oregano
- 12 oz. fusilli pasta(or your favorite pasta)
- 1c fresh basil leaves,cut in thin strips

Direction

- Put tomatoes, onion, olive oil, vinegar, garlic, salt, pepper and oregano in a large bowl; toss.
- Let stand at room temperature at least 30 mins. or till tomatoes release their juices, tossing occasionally.
- Cook pasta as package directs. Drain and add to the bowl with tomatoes; lightly toss Let come to room temp. Add basil; toss Serve or refrigerate up to 1 day.

328.   Top Ramen Salad Recipe

Serving: 4 | Prep: | Cook: 20mins | Ready in:

Ingredients

- COOKS.COM RECIPE SEARCH ENGINE
- TOP RAMEN SALAD
- Printed from COOKS.COM
- 1 sm. head Napa cabbage, cut up
- 1 bunch green onions, chopped fine
- 1 pkg. chicken flavored Top Ramen, crushed
- 2 tbsp. toasted sesame seeds
- 1/2 c. toasted slivered almonds
- DRESSING:
- 2 tbsp. sugar
- 1/2 c. oil
- 3 tbsp. vinegar
- 1/2 tsp. pepper
- Seasoning packet from Top Ramen
- Combine dressing ingredients; pour over cabbage and onion. Sprinkle Top Ramen, sesame and almonds on top of dressing. Toss all well and serve.

Direction

- Toast last 3 ingredients on cookie sheet, 300 degrees for 10 minutes. Stir.
- Mix cut-up cabbage and chopped green onions in salad bowl.

329.   Tortellini And Olive Salad Recipe

Serving: 6 | Prep: | Cook: 30mins | Ready in:

Ingredients

- 1lb stuffed tortellini, cooked al dente and cooled
- 1/2-2/3 cup olives, sliced(I suggest using a mix of black, green, Kalamata, etc... specialty olives will give this salad that extra boost)
- 1 roasted red pepper, diced
- 1pt cherry tomatoes, halved
- 1/2 large or 1 small red onion, diced small
- juice from 1/2 lemon
- 1/2 cup mayonnaise
- 2 heaping T prepared pesto
- couple dashes of hot sauce
- 2t Dijon
- kosher or sea salt and fresh ground pepper

Direction

- Soak diced onion in lemon juice while preparing all the other ingredients. (You want it to soak at least 15 min or so)
- Combine drained and cooled tortellini, olives, red pepper, and tomatoes in large bowl. Toss to combine.
- In a smaller bowl, combine mayo, pesto, hot sauce, Dijon, onions WITH the lemon juice, and salt and pepper.
- Whisk well to combine.
- Add dressing to the pasta/veggies and toss gently to coat.
- Refrigerate until ready to serve.

330. Tortellini And Pepperoni Pasta Salad Recipe

Serving: 8 | Prep: | Cook: 35mins | Ready in:

Ingredients

- 1 and 1/2 pounds refrigerated tortellini*
- 5-7 ounces pepperoni slices, chopped
- 8 ounces mozzarella, chopped into 1/2 inch pieces
- 4 ounces Parmesan, chopped into 1/2 inch pieces
- 1/2 cup green onions, chopped
- 1 dry pint cherry tomatoes, halved
- 1 can medium black olives
- 1 (6 oz.) jar marinated artichoke hearts
- 1/2 cup deli-sliced pepperoncini's
- 1/4 cup balsamic vinegar, white or regular**
- 1/3 cup + 1 tablespoon olive oil
- 1 tablespoon Italian seasoning
- 2 cloves garlic cloves, smashed

Direction

- Boil the tortellini according to package instructions. (They should only boil 2-3 minutes. I added salt to the boiling water for more flavor, but it's not necessary.) Drain the tortellini and add to a large bowl. Drizzle with

a little olive oil so that they don't stick together.
- Chop the pepperoni into quarters and add to the bowl.
- Add the chopped mozzarella, chopped Parmesan, green onions, cherry tomatoes, black olives (halved if you want), artichoke hearts, and pepperoncinis to the bowl.
- Add the balsamic vinegar, olive oil, Italian seasoning, and garlic cloves to a blender and blend until smooth. Or use could add the ingredients to a bowl and use an immersion blender. Or you could mince the garlic finely and add it to a bowl, add the balsamic vinegar and Italian seasoning, then slowly drizzle the olive oil in while whisking (so that it emulsifies.)
- Drizzle the dressing over the salad and toss to combine.
- You can serve this right away, but it's even better if you refrigerate it for a few hours before serving. You can make this 24 hours in advance. Toss again before serving.
- Recipe Notes
- *You could also use a 20 ounce package and it would be fine. You might not need to use all the dressing.
- **You can use white balsamic vinegar if you don't want the tortellini to be dark.

331. Tortellini Broccoli Salad Recipe

Serving: 4 | Prep: | Cook: 1hours | Ready in:

Ingredients

- 1 7 oz pkg cheese filled tortellini (tri colored makes a pretty salad)
- 1/2 cup sliced carrot
- 2 cups broccoli flowerets
- 2 green onions, sliced
- Balsalmic Dressing:
- 1/4 c balsalmic vinegar

- 2 Tbsp olive oil
- 1 tsp dried basil, lightly crushed with heel of hand
- 1/4 tsp paprika
- 1/8 tsp salt
- 1 clove garlic, crushed

Direction

- Cook and drain tortellini, rinse well with cold water, drain.
- Prepare dressing.
- In large bowl toss vegetables and dressing.
- Add pasta and gently toss until evenly coated.
- Cover tightly and refrigerate at least 1 hour before serving.

332. Tortellini Pasta Salad Recipe

Serving: 10 | Prep: | Cook: 10mins |Ready in:

Ingredients

- 2 bags of frozen tortellini (could use 2 boxes)
- 1packet of ranch seasoning
- 1c. of mayo
- 1/2 c. of milk
- 1 can of black olives
- fresh broccoli
- fresh cauliflower
- grape tomatoes
- (could substitute with any of your favorite vegetables)
- (could also add cut pepperoni or salami for added flavor)

Direction

- 1. Bring water to a rapid boil in a large pan
- 2. Boil tortellini until it floats
- 3. Drain tortellini in a colander and run cold water on the tortellini for 2-4 minutes until chilled. Shake to remove excess water
- 4. Transfer tortellini into a large bowl

- 5. Mix packet of ranch seasoning with 1 c. up mayo and 1/2 a c. of milk. Stir well to mix all ingredients.
- (May add more milk for creamier dressing)
- (Also may make double sauce for more ranch taste)
- 6. Cut all vegetables
- 7. Mix all vegetables and ranch together with tortellini and chill for 1 hour.

333. Tortellini Salad Recipe

Serving: 4 | Prep: | Cook: 30mins |Ready in:

Ingredients

- 2 bags of frozen cheese tortellini
- fresh basil (dried basil works too, but fresh is best)
- 2 cups, chopped tomatoes
- 3 tbl. minced garlic
- 1 tsp pepper
- 1tsp salt
- 1tbl sugar
- 2tbl olive oil

Direction

- Cook tortellini according to package directions
- While pasta is cooking
- Chop the basil very fine
- Chop the tomatoes, you can chop them larger or small, (my husband prefers smaller sizes. I like the larger go figure)
- Add basil and tomatoes to a large mixing bowl
- Add salt, pepper, sugar, olive oil and garlic to bowl
- After pasta has drained at to the same bowl
- Mix well
- You can set in fridge till cool, or eat it while the pasta is still hot.
- Again my husband likes it hot, and I like it cold, so it's all up to you.

- We also change up the amount of tomatoes and salt and pepper depending on how were feeling that day.

334.   Tortellini Spinach And Sesame Salad Recipe

Serving: 0 | Prep: | Cook: 45mins | Ready in:

Ingredients

- 1 lb frozen cheese tortellini
- 1/3 cup slivered red onion
- 1 package button or bella mushrooms, thickly sliced
- 1 tspn butter
- 1 tspn sesame
- 1 tblspn toasted sesame seeds
- 1/4-1/3 cup Asian style salad dressing (I used Kraft Lite Asian toasted Sesame Dressing, but I've also heard that Newman's Own is great)
- 4 cups fresh spinach, washed, dried and torn into small pieces
- salt & pepper
- *Optional - squeeze of fresh lime juice
- *Optional (from the original - 1 bell pepper, sliced & 1 tomato, diced - I didn't have these, so I left them out.)

Direction

- Cook tortellini according to package directions.
- Meanwhile, heat butter and sesame oil in small skillet and sauté the mushrooms.
- Drain pasta, rinse quickly with cold water and transfer to large bowl.
- Stir in the onion (and pepper & tomato, if using), the mushrooms and the salad dressing and toss to coat well.
- Add 1/2 the spinach and stir into pasta mixture to wilt slightly.
- Put salad in the fridge and chill for 30 minutes.

- After salad has chilled, add the toasted sesame seeds and the remaining spinach and toss to combine.
- Taste and season as needed with salt & pepper and maybe a squeeze of lime juice.

335.   Tortellini Summer Salad Recipe

Serving: 4 | Prep: | Cook: 20mins | Ready in:

Ingredients

- 2 cups uncooked cheese tortellini, cooked as directed and cooled completely (I prefer Butoni Three cheese tortellini)
- 1 cup or more of your favorite Ceasar Dressing (I like Marie's, sold in the produce department)
- 1 yellow pepper, chopped
- 1 red pepper, chopped
- 1/2 onion, finely diced
- 1/2 cup fresh grated parmesan cheese

Direction

- Cool the pasta completely after cooking, then pour over dressing and chopped peppers; mix all together.
- Sprinkle top generously with parmesan cheese and cover bowl - refrigerate.
- Just before serving, stir in the parmesan - serve over a bed of lettuce, if desired, or serve as is.
- You can mix up the veggies any way you want for this, and you can try other cheeses, though I love parmesan with the Caesar dressing.
- Try other dressing, too:
- Greek version - to the cooked tortellini, add
- 1 cup Greek dressing
- 1 de-seeded cucumber
- 3/4 cup diced, kalamata olives
- 1/2 red onion, diced
- 20 halved cherub tomatoes
- 1 cup crumbled feta
- Italian version - to the cooked tortellini, add

- 1 cup Italian dressing
- 1 cup sliced pepperoni or genoa salami chunks
- 1/2 cup fresh grated parmesan cheese
- 1/2 cup fresh pecorino Romano cheese, and some
- 1/2 sweet onion, diced
- American version - to cooked tortellini, add
- 1 cup Ranch dressing
- 1 cup blue cheese crumbles
- 1/2 onion, diced
- 1 red pepper, diced
- Try whatever sounds good to you!! I want to try a caprese version with balsamic dressing and fresh basil and tomato chunks and mozzarella and some onion and garlic. There's so many "options" to make so many different tastes - all of them easy!!

336. Tortellini And Artichoke Pasta Salad Recipe

Serving: 4 | Prep: | Cook: 5mins | Ready in:

Ingredients

- 10 ounces tortellini, cheese-filled
- 4 marinated artichoke hearts
- 2 tablespoons red bell pepper, roasted or pimento,
- 4 tablespoons mayonnaise
- 1 tablespoon Dijon mustard
- 1 tablespoon parmesean cheese, grated
- 2 tablespoons basil, chopped
- 2 tablespoons parsley, chopped
- salt and pepper

Direction

- Cook tortellini, rinse and drain well.
- Toss with 1 tbs. of the marinated artichoke liquid to keep from sticking together.
- More may be added for flavoring of desired.
- Drain artichokes. Cut into chunks.

- Combine remaining ingredients and toss gently in a large bowl to combine.
- Refrigerate if not served immediately.

337. Tuna Pepper Pasta Salad Recipe

Serving: 4 | Prep: | Cook: | Ready in:

Ingredients

- 2 tablespoons nonfat plain yogurt
- 2 tablespoons chopped fresh basil
- 2 tablespoons water
- 1 1/2 teaspoons lemon juice
- 1 garlic clove, minced
- Freshly ground pepper (to taste)
- 2/3 cup roasted red peppers, chopped and divided
- 1/2 cup finely chopped red onion
- 4 oz chunk light tuna in water, drained
- 4 oz broccoli florets, steamed until crisp-tender and shocked
- 6 ounces whole-wheat penne, cooked and drained

Direction

- Combine yogurt, basil, water, lemon juice, garlic, salt, pepper and the remaining 1/3 cup red peppers in a blender, puree until smooth.
- In a large bowl, toss together remaining peppers, onion, tuna, broccoli and pasta.
- Add the pepper sauce and toss well to blend. Chill before serving.

338. Tuna And Egg Pasta Salad Recipe

Serving: 46 | Prep: | Cook: 15mins | Ready in:

Ingredients

- 8 oz pasta - i prefer a penne
- 1 hardboiled egg - well chopped
- 1 can tuna in water, drained
- 1 cup defrosted frozen peas (optional)
- for dressing -
- 2 tbs pickle juice
- 2 tbs dried onions
- 2 tbs yellow mustard
- 1/3 cup light sour cream
- 1/4-1/2 cup light mayonnaise
- 1 tsp chili powder
- 1 tsp dried dill
- 1 tsp hot sauce
- 1 tsp paprika
- salt and pepper to taste

Direction

- Begin with bringing water to boil to cook pasta
- Make dressing for pasta by adding the pickle juice, dried onions, yellow mustard, sour cream, 1/4 cup mayonnaise, chili powder, dill, hot sauce, and paprika to a bowl and mix well. Set aside
- When water boils add a generous amount of salt and add pasta.
- Cook until just al dente.
- Drain and toss with cold water until pasta is chilled and has stopped cooking.
- Add pasta, egg, tuna and peas (if using) to dressing and mix to combine being careful not to break pasta. Season with salt and pepper to taste. If the salad is too dry add additional mayonnaise 1 tbsp. at a time to your desired creaminess is reached.
- Refrigerate for at least 30 minutes (preferably a couple of hours). Serve chilled.

---

339.   Tuna And Feta Pasta Salad Recipe

Serving: 10 | Prep: | Cook: 20mins | Ready in:

Ingredients

- 1 12 to 16 oz. package macaroni or other small shaped pasta
- 2 6 oz cans tuna, preferably packed in water
- 3 scallions, chopped
- 1 cup chopped, seeded cucumber (I use English and leave the skin on for color)
- 2/3 cup chopped red bell pepper
- 1 cup mayonnaise, give or take
- 1 Tbsp olive oil
- 1 t. dried marjoram
- 1 clove garlic, grated
- 5 oz. crumbled tomato and basil flavored feta cheese
- 1 Tbsp chopped fresh basil
- salt & pepper to taste

Direction

- Cook pasta to al dente as per package directions; drain and rinse under cold water.
- In a large bowl, combine cooked pasta, tuna, scallions, cucumbers and red bell pepper.
- In separate bowl, whisk together mayonnaise, olive oil, marjoram and garlic. Stir into pasta mixture, adding more mayonnaise if desired. Stir in feta and fresh basil. Season with salt & pepper.

---

340.   Tuna Macaroni Salad Recipe

Serving: 12 | Prep: | Cook: 30mins | Ready in:

Ingredients

- 1 box of pasta (16 oz), I use spiral elbows or medium size shells
- 2 cans of Medium size cans of tuna, well drained
- 1 can of medium size can of tiny shrimp, well drained
- Shredded carrots
- 1 medium onion chopped finely
- salt
- pepper

- 2-3 cups of mayo, (depends on if you like dry or moist)
- 1/4 cup of Henri's Private Blend Tas-tee salad dressing (if you can find)
- 1/4 cup vinegar (I use rice vinegar)
- seafood seasonings
- shallots (dried)
- paprika
- Dried red sweet peppers (or use fresh if you like)
- parsley
- garlic powder
- dill

Direction

- Cook pasta is salted water, till al dente and drain well, Cool.
- When pasta is cooked and COOLED,
- Mix in a measuring cup, all the ingredients from salt to dill (all seasoning are to taste), and mix well
- When pasta is cold, put in bowl and add the onion & carrots, and all the drained tuna & shrimp. Pour the Mayo mix slowly, (Do not put all in just in case there's too much)
- Mix well, if you like more dressing add more.
- Adjust seasoning to taste.
- Chill before serving
- For decoration on top: sliced hard boiled eggs, olives and sliced peppers

341.   Tuna Pasta Salad Recipe

Serving: 5 | Prep: | Cook: 11mins |Ready in:

Ingredients

- 2 cups tri-colored spiral pasta, cooked and drained
- 2 cans of Light tuna in water, drained
- 1 large summer squash, diced
- 6 mini carrots, cooked and sliced
- 2 tbsp of chopped red onion
- 4 cloves garlic, chopped

- handful of chopped yellow bell pepper
- handful of chopped orange or red bell pepper
- 15 leaves of cilantro, shredded
- 1 1/2 lemons

Direction

- Mix all ingredients together, including pasta and tuna
- Squeeze juice of 1 1/2 lemons
- Sprinkle Cilantro on top of mixture
- Mix together
- Serve
- Enjoy :)

342.   Tuna Seashell Pasta Salad Recipe

Serving: 6 | Prep: | Cook: 15mins |Ready in:

Ingredients

- 1 pkg. (12 oz.) Seashell macaroni
- 1 pkg. (8 oz.) frozen peas, thawed and drained
- 2 cans (6 1/2 oz.) albacore tuna, drained and flaked
- 1 c. cheddar cheese, diced
- 2 stalks celery, diced
- 1 med. green pepper, diced
- 1 med orange pepper, diced
- 1 small white onion, chopped
- 1 small jar sliced pimentos, drained (optional)
- 1/2 c. sweet pickles, chopped
- 1 c. Hellman's mayonaise
- 1/2 tsp dry mustard
- 1 tsp dill weed
- salt & pepper to taste
- romaine lettuce

Direction

- Cook macaroni as directed. (No salt.)
- Rinse in cold water.
- Mix your dressing, using the mayo, sweet pickles, dry mustard and dill weed.

- Combine the pasta, tuna and vegetables.
- Pour dressing over salad, mix gently.
- Chill for about two hours.
- Fill long romaine lettuce leaves with pasta (looks like a boat)
- Salt and pepper to guests taste.

343. Turkey Club Pasta Salad With Lemon Basil Dressing Recipe

Serving: 4 | Prep: | Cook: 10mins | Ready in:

Ingredients

- 1 package small pasta shells
- 6 slices bacon crisply cooked
- 1-1/2 cups fully cooked smoked turkey cut in strips
- 1 cup shredded swiss cheese
- 1 large tomato chopped
- Dressing:
- 3/4 cup mayonnaise
- 2 tablespoons chopped fresh basil
- 1 teaspoon grated lemon peel
- 1 teaspoon lemon juice

Direction

- Mix all dressing ingredients in a large bowl then set aside.
- Cook and drain pasta as directed on package then rinse with cold water and drain.
- Crumble bacon reserving 2 tablespoons for topping
- Mix pasta, dressing, bacon and remaining ingredients then cover and refrigerate 2 hours.
- Sprinkle with reserved bacon.

344. Turkey Dried Cherry Pasta Salad Recipe

Serving: 8 | Prep: | Cook: 10mins | Ready in:

Ingredients

- 1 lb. rotini pasta cooked and chilled
- 2 Cups diced cooked turkey
- 1 Cup dried cherries
- 1 medium sweet onion diced
- 4 stalks celery diced
- 1 Cup whole roasted almonds
- Dressing:
- 1/4 Cup powdered sugar
- 2 T. champagne vinegar
- 2 Cups good mayonaisse
- 2 T. cold water
- 2 T. poppyseeds
- 2 t. kosher salt
- 1/2 t. black pepper

Direction

- Put salad ingredients in a bowl. (Really?)
- Whisk together dressing ingredients in a different bowl. (Wow)
- Fold dressing into salad.

345. Twisted Pasta And Chicken Salad Recipe

Serving: 6 | Prep: | Cook: 20mins | Ready in:

Ingredients

- Twisted pasta Salad
- 3 cups of chicken, cooked and chopped
- 1 lb tri color rotini
- 1/2 cup Italian salad dressing (your choice, I used Good seasons)
- 1 cup mayonnaise (not Miracle Whip)
- 6 Tbs lemon juice
- 2 Tbs yellow mustard
- 1 medium onion, chopped

- 3/4 cup black olives, sliced
- 1 cup chopped celery

Direction

- Cook macaroni; drain but do not rinse.
- Add Italian dressing while still hot.
- Let cool.
- Blend mayonnaise, lemon juice and mustard; pour over pasta.
- Add chicken, olives and celery.
- Mix well and refrigerate for several hours to blend flavors.
- Serves 6 to 8

---

346. Unique Macaroni Salad Recipe

Serving: 25 | Prep: | Cook: 30mins | Ready in:

Ingredients

- 1 pound shell macaroni cooked and drained well
- 2 cans pineapple tidbits (drained)
- 1 pounds ham - diced
- 1 large can peas, drained
- 1 large onion chopped FINE
- 4 cups celery -choppped FINE
- 1 dozen hard boiled eggs-peeled and chopped
- 1 small can/jar pimentos-chopped fine
- 5 oz cashew nuts
- Dressing:
- 1 qt. salad dressing (Miracle Whip)
- 3 tsp. light mustard
- 3 tsp. sugar
- salt to taste

Direction

- Combine all ingredients.
- Then add dressing.
- Stir gently.

---

347. Vegan Italian Pasta Salad Recipe

Serving: 4 | Prep: | Cook: 8mins | Ready in:

Ingredients

- 8 oz (uncooked) whole wheat spiral pasta
- 1 1/2 tbsp balsamic vinegar
- 1 tbsp vegetable broth or pasta cooking water
- 1/2 tsp dried oregano
- 1 cup cherry tomatoes, halved
- 1/2 cup basil, fresh, chopped
- 1/2 cup fresh baby spinach leaves, washed
- 1/4 tsp table salt, or to taste
- 1/4 tsp black pepper

Direction

- Cook pasta about 8 minutes, until al dente.
- Drain and transfer to a large bowl.
- Add vinegar, broth and oregano; toss to coat.
- Fold in tomatoes, basil and spinach.
- Season to taste with salt and pepper.
- Serve room temperature, or chilled if desired.

---

348. Vegetable Pasta Salad Recipe

Serving: 8 | Prep: | Cook: 10mins | Ready in:

Ingredients

- 1 cup broccoli chopped fine
- 1 cup carrot thinly sliced
- 1/2 cup green pepper chopped fine
- 1/4 cup white onion chopped very fine
- 1/2 cup peas
- 1/3 cup green olives with pimento chopped fine
- 1 small box macaroni cooked and still warm
- 1 cup mayonnaise
- 1/2 teaspoon marjoram leaves

- 1/2 teaspoon thyme leaves
- 1 teaspoon rosemary leaves crushed
- 1/2 teaspoon salt
- 1 teaspoon freshly ground black pepper
- Chop vegetables.
- cook pasta el dente then drain.

Direction

- Mix all ingredients together promptly then chill before serving.

---

349.   Vinagrette Veggie Pasta Salad Recipe

Serving: 68 | Prep: | Cook: 35mins | Ready in:

Ingredients

- 1 lb elbow macaroni
- 1 green zuchini, cut in 1/4inch half moons
- 1lb crimini mushrooms, quartered
- 1 small jar marinated artichoke hearts, quartered
- 2 tlbs olive oil (for sauteing vegetables)
- 3 green onions finely sliced
- 1/2 cup red wine vinegar
- 3/4c extra virgin olive oil
- 2tlbs dried italian herbs
- 2 cloves garlic - finely minced
- 1/2 lemon
- 1/4 cup choped fresh italian flat leaf parsley
- salt and pepper to taste

Direction

- Boil water and add a good amount of salt to cook macaroni noodles
- While noodles cook, sauté veggies.
- Add 2 tbsp. olive oil to a hot pan and add zucchini. Sauté until cooked through, but still crunchy
- Remove zucchini and place in a separate bowl.
- Add mushrooms to pan and sauté until cooked through and slightly golden

- Remove from pan and add to bowl with zucchini
- Remove artichoke hearts from marinade and add to veggie mix
- Add green onions to the top and set aside
- Drain noodles when al dente
- Rinse with cool water and set to the side
- Make vinaigrette by mixing vinegar, olive oil, herbs, garlic and lemon juice, whisk together
- Toss all ingredients together and top with vinaigrette. Mix in parsley and season to taste with salt and pepper.
- Allow about an hour or two in the refrigerator for the flavors to blend.
- Serve and enjoy!

---

350.   Virginias Pasta Salad Recipe

Serving: 8 | Prep: | Cook: | Ready in:

Ingredients

- - 2 (7 oz) pkgs shell pasta
- - 4 tblspns vinegar
- - 1 cup edamame (soy beans)
- - 2 cups diced American cheese
- - 1 cup chopped green bell pepper
- - 1/2 cup diced celery
- - 4 tblspns pimento
- - 3-4 tblspns minced onion
- - 1 1/3 cup Mayo
- - Dash of celery salt and salt and pepper

Direction

- Cook Shell pasta and rinse in cold water. Add vinegar and let sit for 10 minutes.
- Dice Cheese, Bell Pepper, Celery and mince Onion.
- In a serving bowl add all ingredients to pasta and mix until consistent.
- Throw in the fridge for about 20 minutes and enjoy!

351. WW Greek Pasta Salad Recipe

Serving: 8 | Prep: | Cook: |Ready in:

Ingredients

- Salad:
- 12 ozs (375 g) bow-tie pasta
- 2 2/4 cups (675 ml) diced tomatoes
- 1 cup (250 ml) diced cucumbers
- 1 cup (250 ml) diced sweet green peppers
- 3/4 cup (175 ml) sliced red onions
- 3 1/2 ozs (90 g) crumbled feta cheese
- 1/3 cup (75 ml) sliced black olives
- 1/2 cup (125 ml) chopped fresh oregano (or 1 tbsp (15 ml) dried)
- Dressing:
- 1/4 cup (50 ml) olive oil
- 3 tbsp (45 ml) lemon juice
- 2 tbsp (25 ml) water
- 2 tbsp (25 ml) balsamic vinegar
- 2 tsp (10 ml) crushed garlic

Direction

- Cook pasta according to package instructions or until firm to the bite. Rinse in cold water. Drain and place in a serving bowl.
- Add tomatoes, cucumbers, green peppers, onions, feta cheese, olives and oregano.
- Make the dressing: In a small bowl, combine oil, lemon juice, water, vinegar and garlic until mixed. Pour over pasta and toss.

352. Warm Pasta Salad Recipe

Serving: 6 | Prep: | Cook: 1mins |Ready in:

Ingredients

- 1-2 lbs. chicken breasts
- 1 stick butter
- 3 cups broccoli florets
- 2 cups baby carrots
- 2 cups cauliflower
- 1/2 cup chopped onion
- 1/2 cup chopped green scallions
- 1 lb. pasta, penne preferred or corkscrew
- 1/2 cup milk
- 1 cup grated parmesan/romano cheese
- Fresh or dried herbs- 1 tablespoon each- parsley,basil, oregano,garlic/pepper-more if desired to taste
- salt and pepper to taste

Direction

- Sauté chicken breasts and onions (both) in 2 tablespoons butter. When cooked and cooled, cut into cubes and set aside
- Steam broccoli, carrots and cauliflower until crisp tender, drain and set aside
- Boil pasta al dente. Drain and set aside.
- In a large pan, melt rest of butter stick with milk. Add pasta, cubed chicken breasts, all vegetables and herbs. Stir well but gently. Add salt and pepper then add the parmesan/Romano cheese and gently stir again. Sprinkle with parsley to garnish.

353. Warm Pasta Salad With Grilled Tomatoes Zucchini Pecorino Recipe

Serving: 12 | Prep: | Cook: 30mins |Ready in:

Ingredients

- 1 1/2 lb. ripe plum tomatoes (about 8), cored and halved lengthwise
- 1 1/4 lb. small zucchini (about 4), trimmed and halved lengthwise
- 5 Tbs. extra-virgin olive oil
- 4 tsp. chopped fresh thyme
- 2 tsp. kosher salt; more as needed

- 1 tsp. freshly ground black pepper; more as needed
- 6 oz. Pecorino Romano, shaved with a vegetable peeler (about 2 cups)
- 1 lb. dried penne
- 1/4 cup thinly sliced fresh chives
- 2 tsp. balsamic vinegar

Direction

- Prepare a medium fire on a gas grill or a medium-hot charcoal fire.
- In a large bowl, toss the tomatoes and zucchini with 2 Tbs. of the oil, 2 tsp. of the thyme, and the salt and pepper.
- Set the vegetables cut side down on the grill and cook without moving them until they have good grill marks, 5 to 7 minutes.
- Flip and cook until browned and tender, 6 to 8 more minutes.
- Transfer to a cutting board and let cool for a couple of minutes.
- Coarsely chop, return them to the same large bowl along with 1 1/2 cups of the pecorino, and toss.
- Let sit for up to a couple of hours at room temperature.
- Bring a large pot of well-salted water to a boil over high heat.
- Add the pasta and cook, stirring often, until just al dente, about 11 minutes.
- Drain well and toss with the tomato mixture, 3 Tbs. of the chives, the remaining 3 Tbs. olive oil and the balsamic vinegar.
- Season generously with salt and pepper to taste and transfer to a serving bowl.
- Sprinkle with the remaining 1 Tbs. chives, 2 tsp. thyme, and 1/2 cup pecorino, and serve.
- Make ahead: You can grill the tomatoes and zucchini a couple of hours before serving. Hold them in a large bowl at room temperature. Cook the pasta just before guests arrive and toss it with the vegetables.

354. Warm Penne Pasta Salad Recipe

Serving: 8 | Prep: | Cook: 30mins | Ready in:

Ingredients

- * salt
- * 1 pound penne pasta
- * 4 tablespoons butter
- * 2 cloves garlic, finely chopped
- * 1 small onion or 1 large shallot, finely chopped
- * 2 cups peas
- * salt and pepper
- * 1 1/2 cups fresh ricotta cheese
- * 4 tablespoons thyme, finely chopped
- * 1/2 cup grated parmigiano-reggiano cheese, a couple of handfuls

Direction

- Bring a pot of water to a boil, salt it and cook pasta to al dente.
- * Heads up: reserve 1 cup of starchy cooking liquid before draining.
- Meanwhile, over medium heat in medium skillet, melt butter, add garlic and onions and sauté gently for 7-8 minutes.
- Add peas and heat though.
- Drain pasta and add it back to the pot with reserved water, ricotta, parsley, parmesan and onion-pea mixture.
- Toss 2 minutes to coat and combine flavors.

355. Wasabi Chicken Pasta Salad Recipe

Serving: 6 | Prep: | Cook: 8mins | Ready in:

Ingredients

- 2 cups Cooked chicken breast, diced (if starting from scratch, roast the chicken breast with a little soy sauce for a nuttier flavour)

- 2 cups cooked pasta (rotini or penne works best)
- 1 green bell pepper, diced
- 2 Stalks of celery, diced
- 2 green onions, minced
- 1/2 small onion, minced
- 1 small cucumber, diced
- 2 heads of romaine lettuce or butter lettuce, washed, dried and torn.
- For the dressing:
- 1 cup mayonnaise
- 2 tbsp lemon juice
- 1 tbsp red wine vinegar (or rice wine vinegar, if you have it)
- 1 tbsp soy sauce
- 1/2 tsp wasabi powder or paste (more if you like it spicy)
- 1 clove garlic
- salt, pepper and a little sugar to taste

Direction

- In a bowl, assemble all ingredients except the lettuce. It's not a bad thing if the pasta is still warm from cooking - it will "suck up" the dressing better.
- For making the dressing, put all dressing ingredients in a blender, making sure that the garlic becomes finely minced. Taste and add sugar or salt if needed. You're after a slightly sweet and sour zing.
- Add the dressing to the bowl full of ingredients and toss until all elements are thoroughly coated. Chill in fridge for at least 4 hours.
- Serve on a bed of lettuce.

356. Windys Tuna Macaroni Salad Recipe

Serving: 8 | Prep: | Cook: 10mins | Ready in:

Ingredients

- 2 cups uncooked macaroni

- 4 hard-boiled eggs, chopped
- 1 (12-oz) can tuna, well drained
- 1 medium onion, chopped
- 2 stalks celery, chopped
- 1 small can sliced black olives, drain and discard liquid
- 1-1/2 cups Miracle Whip
- salt, to taste
- black pepper, to taste

Direction

- Cook macaroni per package directions. Drain well in a colander (do NOT rinse) and spread out on a jelly roll pan to cool.
- In a large mixing bowl, combine boiled eggs, tuna, onion, celery, black olives, salad dressing, salt and pepper. Fold in macaroni, mixing well.
- Cover and refrigerate for several hours to blend flavors.
- Serve well chilled.

357. Yam Woon Sen Thai Glass Noodle Salad Recipe

Serving: 0 | Prep: | Cook: 25mins | Ready in:

Ingredients

- 2 tbsp vegetable oil
- 2 cloves garlic, minced
- 1/8 pound of shrimp, minced (substitute w/ soy bean protein and mushrooms for vegetarian option)
- 1/8 pound of chicken, minced (substitute w/ soy bean protein and mushrooms for vegetarian option)
- 1 tbsp soy sauce or fish sauce
- 1/4 cup water
- 2 cups of glass noodles, boiled and drained
- Handful cilantro, chopped
- 2 shallots, sliced
- 2 stalks of lemongrass (white part only), finely sliced

- Handful spring onions
- 3 tbsp roasted peanuts
- Pinch of salt
- Dressing
- Pinch of salt
- 2 tbsp chopped Thai chilies
- 1/4 tablespoon palm sugar
- 4 tbsp lime juice
- 3 tbsp fish sauce (or soy sauce and fermented soy bean paste for vegetarian option)

Direction

- Heat oil in a medium sauté pan, add garlic, and fry until fragrant.
- Add minced chicken, fish sauce and shrimp and stir occasionally until cooked, about 2 minutes, to the same oil.
- Add water and soy sauce to taste.
- Remove from heat.
- Mix the rest of the ingredients to the cooked chicken in a mixing bowl.
- Make dressing by pounding all the ingredients in pestle and mortar or put them in a food chopper/processor. Pour dressing on top of the chicken and noodles mixture and mix well.

358. Zesty Pasta Salad Recipe

Serving: 8 | Prep: | Cook: 10mins | Ready in:

Ingredients

- One 16 oz pkg angel hair pasta, cooked, drained, and cooled
- One 4 oz jar sliced pimientos, drained
- 8 green onions, chopped
- One 2.25 oz can, or 1/4 cup, sliced black olives, drained
- 3/4 cup vegetable oil
- 3 tablespoons steak seasoning salt (example: McCormick's Grill Mates Montreal steak seasoning)
- 3 tablespoons mayonaise
- 4 tablespoons fresh lemon juice

- Pepper
- Dash of hot sauce (example Tobasco)

Direction

- In a large bowl, combine the pasta, pimientos, onions and olives. In a small bowl whisk the oil, steak seasoning salt, mayonnaise, lemon juice, pepper to taste and Tabasco sauce until well blended. Pour over pasta.

359. Cold Pasta Salad Recipe

Serving: 46 | Prep: | Cook: 10mins | Ready in:

Ingredients

- angel hair pasta 1 lb
- cherry tomatoes
- large pitted black olives 1 can
- wishbone Italian dressing 1 16oz bottle
- McCormick salad supreme seasoning
- optional
- fresh mozzarella cheese

Direction

- Cook pasta
- Cut cherry tomatoes in half
- Slice black olives
- Cut cheese in to 1in cubes
- *when pasta is ready run it under cold water place in to a bowl
- *add the tomatoes and black olives and cheese if u desire it
- *pour some of the dressing and sprinkle some of the salad supreme
- *mix it together with hands then repeat this process a few times
- * You should use 3/4 of the Italian dressing and about a 1/4 of the salad supreme
- *place in fridge till cold
- *you may have to add a little more Italian dressing when serving

360. My Mamas Parsely Ham Pasta Salad Recipe

Serving: 68 | Prep: | Cook: 15mins | Ready in:

Ingredients

- 2 cups un cooked elbow macaroni
- 2 cups {12 oz.} ham   cut in strips
- 1 cup sliced celery
- 1/2 cup sliced green onion
- 1 cup mayoniase
- 1 cup packed fresh parsley {Finelyt chopped
- 1/4 cup grated parmeasen cheese
- 1/4 white wine vinegar
- 1 clove garlic minced

Direction

- Cook macaroni according to directions
- In a large bowl, combine ham, macaroni, celery, and green onions. In a small bowl combine, mayonnaise, parsley, cheese, vinegar, garlic, toss with pasta, cover and refrigerate 1-2 hours.

361. Pasta Salad Recipe

Serving: 5 | Prep: | Cook: 15mins | Ready in:

Ingredients

- 1 lb rotina pasta
- 2 large tomatoes
- 1- 2 green bell peppers
- 1 cup of red onion
- 1/2 lb. feta cheese
- 1/2 cup or more of black olives
- dressing...
- 1/2 cup olive oil
- 4 tbs. fresh lemon juice
- 4 tbs. red wine vinegar
- 2 tsp. oregano

- 4 tbs. dill weed
- 1 tbs. súgar
- salt and pepper

Direction

- Cook pasta, drain well and cool.
- Cut up the onions, pepper, olives in small pcs. Add to pasta
- Crumble cheese and add to cooled pasta
- Mix up dressing ingredients well and pour over all
- Stir well, cover and chill for 1 hr. or so...

362. Pasta Salad With Pesto And Fried Mushrooms Recipe

Serving: 2 | Prep: | Cook: 20mins | Ready in:

Ingredients

- 250g fusilli
- 2-3 tablespoons of basil-pesto
- 1 shallot, finely diced
- 4 strips of streaky bacon, cut in small cubes or strips
- 150g cremini mushrooms, sliced
- a hand full of fresh tyme
- freshly ground salt and pepper
- a hand full of lightly roasted pine nuts

Direction

- Boil some salted water in a pan and cook the fusilli until al dente.
- Heat some olive oil in a frying pan, cook the shallots until just turning soft, add crimini mushrooms and cook until soft. Then add the bacon and fry until lightly browned and add thyme. Season with salt and pepper and mix well.
- Drain pasta, put in a bowl and mix with the pesto while pasta is still warm. Then add mushroom mixture, mix well and sprinkle with the pine nuts.

- Tuck in!

363.   Pasta Salad With Watermelon And Goats Cheese Recipe

Serving: 4 | Prep: | Cook: 10mins | Ready in:

Ingredients

- puntalette, cooked al dente & cooled
- cucumber, peeled & cut in tiny cubes
- water melon, cut in tiny cubes
- dried tomatoes, finely diced
- spring onions, finely diced
- olives, finely diced
- basil, finely diced
- some fresh goats cheese, torn in small pieces
- sauce:
- 250ml olive oil
- 125ml red wine vineggar
- 1 tablespoon runny honey
- juice of half a lemon

Direction

- Mix everything from cucumber to goat's cheese in a large bowl.
- Mix all ingredients for the sauce and pour a couple of tablespoons over the salad. Rest of sauce keeps in the fridge for about a week.

364.   Shrimp Pasta Salad Recipe

Serving: 8 | Prep: | Cook: 20mins | Ready in:

Ingredients

- 1 lb macaroni noodles
- 1/4 lb -1/2 lb xtra large shrimp
- 1 stalk celery, finely diced

- 1 -2 green onions finely chopped
- 1/4 c light mayo
- 2 t-3 lbs light ranch dressing
- 1/2 tlbs dill
- salt and pepper to taste

Direction

- Bring water to a boil
- Heavily salt when boiling
- Cook shrimp in water
- When fully cooked, remove from water and rinse with cold water
- Cook macaroni
- While macaroni cooks -
- Peel shrimp and chop in to pieces (I cut each shrimp in thirds)
- Mix mayo, dressing, celery, onion and seasonings in to dressing
- Drain and rinse macaroni noodles in cold water
- Toss macaroni with shrimp and dressing
- Add extra salt and pepper to taste
- Chill in refrigerator
- Enjoy

365.   Spaghetti Salad Recipe

Serving: 10 | Prep: | Cook: 20mins | Ready in:

Ingredients

- 1 Lb cooked spaghetti
- 1 jar Mc Cormick Salad Supreme seasoning
- 1 large green pepper, diced
- 1 large tomato, diced
- 1 bottle Italian dressing

Direction

- Cook spaghetti until done, drain
- Mix salad supreme, pepper, and the tomato with the hot pasta
- Pour salad dressing over spaghetti mixture and mix well

- Chill in refrigerator for a day before serving
- Before setting out, I put cherry tomatoes around the inside of the bowl and some curly parsley and a cherry tomato in the middle to make it look nice.

Index

Conclusion

Thank you again for downloading this book!

I hope you enjoyed reading about my book!

If you enjoyed this book, please take the time to share your thoughts and post a review on Amazon. It'd be greatly appreciated!

Write me an honest review about the book – I truly value your opinion and thoughts and I will incorporate them into my next book, which is already underway.

Thank you!

If you have any questions, **feel free to contact at:** *author@fetarecipes.com*

Lisa Ford

fetarecipes.com

Made in United States
Cleveland, OH
05 July 2025

18279752R00090